VAQUEEROS, CALACAS, AND HOLLYWOOD

CONTEMPORARY CHICANO PLAYS

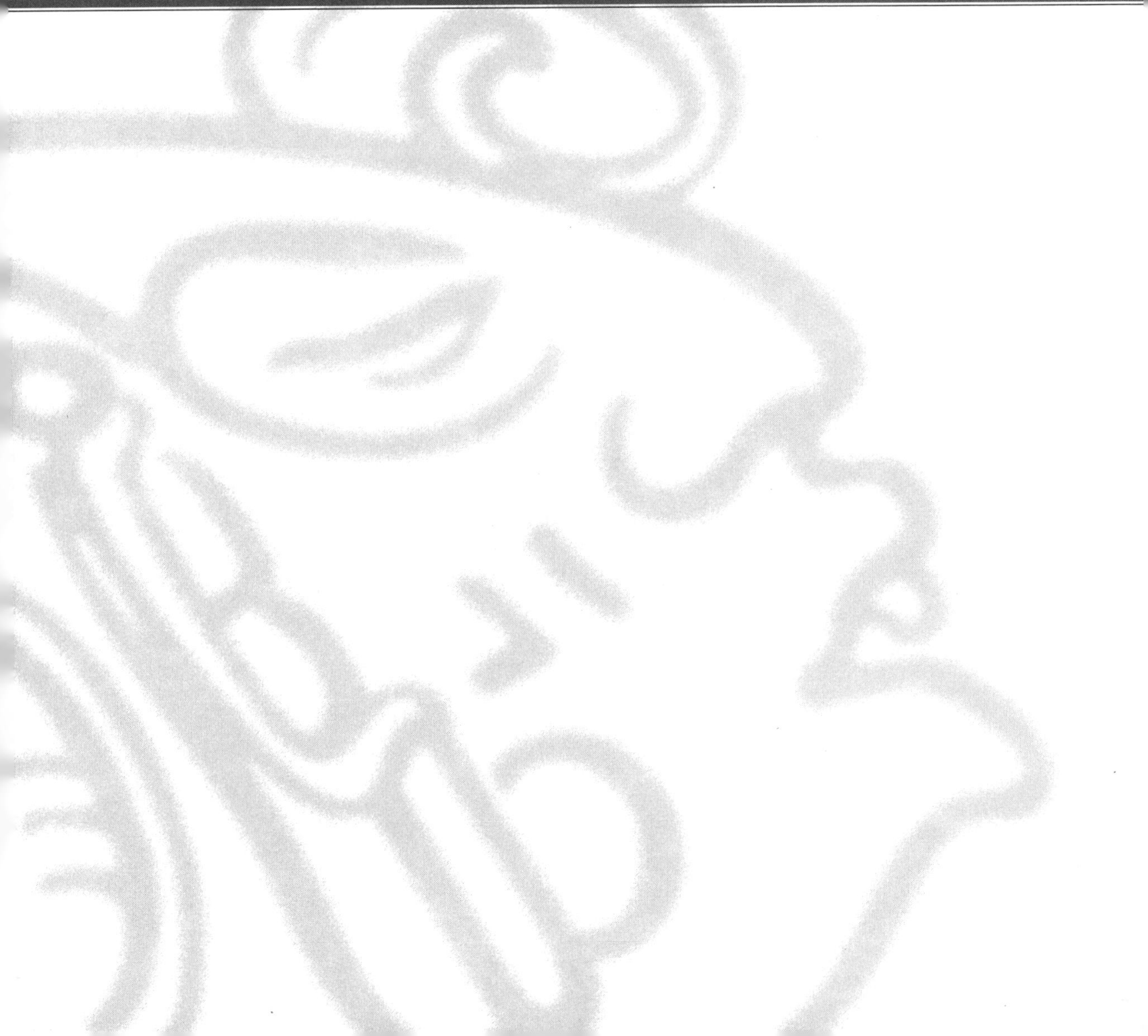

Bilingual Press/Editorial Bilingüe

Publisher
Gary Francisco Keller

Executive Editor
Karen S. Van Hooft

Associate Editors
Adriana M. Brady
Brian Ellis Cassity
Amy K. Phillips
Linda K. St. George

Address
Bilingual Press
Hispanic Research Center
Arizona State University
PO Box 875303
Tempe, Arizona 85287-5303
(480) 965-3867

VAQUEROS, CALACAS, AND HOLLYWOOD

CONTEMPORARY CHICANO PLAYS

edited by
Carlos-Manuel

Bilingual Press/Editorial Bilingüe
TEMPE, ARIZONA

Library of Congress Cataloging-in-Publication Data

Vaqueeros, calacas, and Hollywood : contemporary Chicano plays / Carlos Manuel editor.
    p. cm.
  In English and Spanish.
  ISBN 978-1-931010-70-2 (pbk. : alk. paper)
  1. Mexican Americans—Drama. 2. American drama—Mexican American authors. 3. American drama—20th century. I. Manuel, Carlos.
  PS628.M4V37 2010
  812'.5408035296872073—dc22

            2010018027

who has always been there for me

CONTENTS

ACKNOWLEDGMENTS

would like to thank my familia, Mamá Margarita; Tía Gela; my hermanos Francisco, Arturo, and Martín; my hermanas Blanca, Lourdes, and Maco; and of course, my nephews and nieces. They all knew that when Tío Carlos was in his office, he was writing and needed to be left alone.

I thank Dr. Jorge Huerta and playwright Guillermo Reyes, whose enthusiasm and love for U.S. Latino-Chicano theater inspired me to continue on this path of self-discovery, self-affirmation, and self-worth. They both have become mentors, colleagues, and friends.

I'm also grateful to the playwrights in this anthology, who believed in this project and patiently waited for it to flourish.

Last, I thank la Raza for keeping with the fight and for sharing their experiences so we playwrights can artfully show them on the stage.

INTRODUCTION

After a couple of years of teaching U.S. Latino and Chicano theater, searching for contemporary plays, and exchanging copies of original works with Chicana/o and Latina/o playwrights and colleagues, I decided it was time to create a collection of plays that would express the views of the contemporary Chicana/o-Latina/o community.

For several years many college professors, including myself, have made good use of Dr. Jorge Huerta's Chicano play anthology, *Necessary Theatre.* But the anthology, which is indisputably excellent, is a collection of older plays that express and dramatize situations from the past. After using this anthology for several years in my classes, I realized students yearned for more current material. I decided it was time to create an anthology of original, contemporary works, plays would appeal to a younger audience.

The search for original works was easy, and the response was overwhelming; however, the selection process was arduous. My criteria were fairly straightforward: the plays were to be previously unpublished (although by press time, one of them would be), and they needed to express both the Chicana/o and the Latina/o experiences. With that in mind, I decided to include plays that were not only rich in symbolism and content but that were also captivating, challenging, fun to read, and varied in subject matter. My ultimate goal was to provide an overview of what it means to be Chicana/Chicano or Latina/Latino or both in the United States of America.

At the end of my search, four plays were chosen, each because of its unique approach and because each playwright had a distinctive voice for expressing important matters, thus giving different views on similar subjects.

Barrio Hollywood, written by Elaine Romero, uses boxing as a theme to create the characters' stories. But while boxing is a theme, it never becomes the central to the story. Reflecting magical realism, *Barrio Hollywood* uses distinct cultural symbolism to explore interracial dating and family loyalty. A well-placed plot twist leaves the reader trying to come to her or his own conclusions.

Silviana Wood's *"Yo, Casimiro Flores"* is rich with symbolic, allegorical, and cultural meaning from its title to the characters' names, activities, and situations. This trilingual (Spanish, English, and Yaqui*) play mixes rituals, languages, and cultural traditions to craft an intellectual and historical dramatic work that sheds light on what being an immigrant, as well as a Chicano, means in today's society.

We Lost It at the Movies (With a Special Appearance by Rock Hudson) by Guillermo Reyes offers us the story of a Chilean mother and her son as they struggle to make it in the land of the free. Reyes presents an immigrant story that is colored by the mother's idealization of a Hollywood movie star, revealing the characters' dreams and the willpower it takes to make those dreams come true. Funny and dramatic, *We Lost It at the Movies* is not only moving, but it is also an examination of the characters' motives.

Last we have *Vaqueeros*, an ethnodrama based on interviews. The play inspires audience members to recognize people in their own lives who resemble the characters on stage. *Vaqueeros* is an important work because it exposes a taboo seldom explored in Chicana/o-Latina/o works: hidden sexual practices among Chicano/Latino men and their fear of being discovered. The play speaks about the consequences of such practices and the responsibilities that come with such behavior. It explores homophobia, infidelity, betrayal, and HIV/AIDS, among other issues.

The plays presented in this anthology were written by two women and two men. Three of the playwrights are from Arizona; the fourth is from California, but his play is about people from Arizona. Despite this coincidence, the plays reflect common themes with regard to Chicana/o and Latina/o experience: the border, immigration, sexuality, and culture clashes.

The playwrights' views on the Chicana/o and Latina/o experience differ from one play to the next, as well as from one experience to another. Yet, the four plays are connected in more than one way. I hope you will enjoy reading these plays as much as I have enjoyed putting them together and that the experience will enhance your knowledge about our raza, our familia, and our lives.

Carlos-Manuel
C/S

---

*The Yaqui prayers and other words included in the dialog were transcribed from spoken language and were intended to assist the actors with pronunciation of their lines. The publisher and playwright make no claim to be reproducing the words as they would be written using Yaqui orthography.

BARRIO HOLLYWOOD

ELAINE ROMERO

For Brad

About the Play

hen I first encountered *Barrio Hollywood*, I became very involved in its reading. Many recent Hollywood movies, as well as television series and specials, depict boxing as a main ingredient in Chicano family life. And even though I have watched such movies and television programs, I still don't understand why Hollywood and TV producers use boxing as the main element to represent the lives of Chicano families. The truth is that it has been done several times, most often unsuccessfully.

Set in Mexico and Arizona, *Barrio Hollywood* is the story of a mother and her two grown children. The older child, a son, is a successful boxer. When tragedy occurs, an outsider becomes "part of the family," and the lives of all involved are severely transformed. But unlike the cliché movies and TV series that use boxing as the driving force for a story, this play depicts boxing as a symbol of strength and survival and as a means to bring the characters together. At first, boxing seems to be the impetus that will propel the characters on their own journeys, but, surprisingly enough, it becomes secondary, a shadow in the background, and a symbolic image that is used throughout the play. Through unexpected twists and events, the playwright creates a mystery that formulates questions of morality, duty, loyalty, and love. By the end, the reader is left with a multifaceted understanding of the lives of each character and pondering one main question: "What would I do if I were in that situation?"

Elaine Romero's *Barrio Hollywood* was developed at the San Diego Repertory Theatre through the National Endowment for the Arts/Theatre Communications Group Theatre Residency Program for Playwrights, granted as part of the Calafia Initiative from 1997 to 1999. In 1998 the play was formally read several times: at Colorado University as part of the World Affairs Conference under the direction of Leigh Kennicott; at Brava! for Women in the Arts with Karen Amano as dramaturg; and at Damesrocket Theatre in Tucson, Arizona, under the direction of Caroline Reed, where the play was named "Best New Work" by the *Tucson Weekly*. In 1999 the San Diego Repertory Theatre hosted a workshop on the play, with William A. Virchis directing and Nakissa Etemad as dramaturg. *Barrio Hollywood* had its professional world premiere at New Theatre, Coral Gables, Florida (Rafael de Acha, artistic director; Eileen Suárez, managing director), on October 14, 2004. Finally, the play was featured with a stage reading in the Phoenix Theatre's New Works Festival, under the direction of Arizona Theatre Company's associate director, Samantha K. Wyer.

For additional cast and production information, see Appendix A.

About the Author

 laine Romero is a prolific, award-winning playwright who holds an MFA in playwriting from UC Davis. Her plays have been performed not only throughout the United States, but also in Toronto, Sydney, and Panama. These works, including *Barrio Hollywood, Wetback, Mother of Exiles, Ponzi, A Work of Art, Walk into the Sea, Secret Things, ¡Curanderas! Serpents of the Clouds,* and *Graveyard of Empires,* have been developed and produced at such prestigious venues as the Kennedy Center for the Performing Arts, Alley Theatre, Actors Theatre of Louisville, New Theatre, Kitchen Dog Theater, Chicago Dramatists, Arizona Theatre Company, Arkansas Repertory Theatre, and Borderlands Theater, among many others. The Goodman Theatre's Playwrights' Unit launched Romero's *A Work of Art* in a co-production with Chicago Dramatists and the Goodman Theatre. Orlando Shakespeare Theatre commissioned a Spanish translation of *Barrio Hollywood,* which premiered at Aurora Theatre in Lawrenceville, Georgia. Other organizations that have commissioned her work include the Goodman Theatre, the National New Play Network (NNPN), the Kennedy Center for the Performing Arts, Cornell University, ZACH Theater, and the Magic Theatre/Alfred P. Sloan Foundation Science & Technology Initiative (for *Walk into the Sea,* which was written at the Sundance Institute Playwrights Retreat at the Ucross Foundation in Wyoming).

A past guest artist at South Coast Repertory, the Mark Taper Forum, and the Denver Center Theatre Company, Romero serves as playwright-in-residence at the Arizona Theatre Company, judging its National Latino Playwrights Award. She has participated in NBC's Writers on the Verge Program and the CBS Diversity Institute's Writer's Mentorship Program, and she has been in residence at the Hermitage Artist Retreat, ENVISION Retreat, Voices at the River, and the Orchard Project.

In 2012-2013 she was the Djerassi Fellow in Playwriting at the University of Wisconsin-Madison. Other awards and recognitions include the Edgerton Fund for New American Play Award, the Theatre Communications Group/Pew National Theatre Artist in Residence grant, the National Endowment for the Arts (NEA) Theatre Residency Program for Playwrights grant, Arizona Commission on the Arts playwriting and project fellowships, the Blue Ink Playwriting Award, the Sprenger-Lang New History Play Prize, the Tennessee Williams One-Act Play Award, and the Chicano/Latino Literary Award.

Romero has taught at the University of Arizona, Northwestern University, the University of Wisconsin-Madison, and Linfield College, and she has served as a judge for the Theatre Communications Group, the NEA, and the Kennedy Center.

Her many plays have been published by Vintage Books, Samuel French, the University of Arizona Press, the University of Iowa Press, Smith & Kraus, Playscripts Inc., Heinemann, Simon & Schuster, and Bedford/St. Martin's Press.

Currently Elaine Romero is a resident playwright at Chicago Dramatists and lives in Chicago.

CHARACTERS

ALEX MORENO:	A twenty-four-year-old Latino boxer
GRACIELA MORENO:	Alex's older sister. A twenty-nine-year-old ballet folklórico dancer *(When her lines are in ALL CAPS, she raises her voice. There is no build to these moments.)*
AMÁ:	The pretty forty-eight-year-old mother of Alex and Graciela. Sometimes a little girl who never grew up. Has a difficult time facing things.
MICHAEL:	A white man in his early thirties. Beautiful, but he doesn't know it. Self-deprecating. He is a medical resident.

TIME AND PLACE

1999; Kino Bay, Sonora, Mexico, and Barrio Hollywood, Tucson, Arizona

SET

A flexible space upon which the play takes place. Scenes should move fluidly. Realistic set pieces should be kept to a minimum.

Top right: Graciela (Beatriz Montañez)
Upper right: Graciela (Beatriz Montañez) and Amá (Marta Velasco)
Lower right: Graciela (Beatriz Montañez)
Bottom right: Michael (John Baldwin) and Graciela (Beatriz Montañez)

Photo credits: Eileen Suárez (New Theatre, Coral Gables, FL. Rafael de Acha, director)

SCENE 1

Cinco de Mayo. Lights come up on ALEX MORENO *on one side of the stage in a Mexican boxing ring, indicated by a Mexican flag, and* GRA-CIELA MORENO *at Kennedy Park prepping for her dance. She wears a white dress with red trim.*

She lights the candle on her headdress. ALEX *warms up for his fight with his back to the audience. They start performing simultaneously.* GRACIELA *performs the folklórico dance, La Bruja.* GRACIELA'S *dance and* ALEX'S *fighting are both slow and rhythmic. Their performances continue until* ALEX *takes a blow to the left side of his head. He falls, but slowly gets up. He slugs some more until he gets knocked unconscious.* GRACIELA *looks over at him, seeing across the limitations of physical space.*

Soft blue light as GRACIELA *holds her unconscious brother in her arms. The candle on her headdress is still lit. A distinct echo of* ALEX'S *little-boy laugh against pitch black.*

SCENE 2

Later that day. White lights up to an institutional bright. The hospital. The light accentuates a brick/partial lime green wall—la migra green. AMÁ *lays a pretty handkerchief on the desk/table. She whips a small votive candle in blue glass out of her purse. She lights it with a cigarette lighter. She fans herself with the smoke. She takes out a shaker of salt, shakes a handful of salt into her left hand and throws it over her right shoulder. She twirls three times. She claps her hands together. She puts them together in a prayerful position. She looks in both directions. Assured that the coast is clear, she pulls her rosary out of her bra and begins running the beads through her fingers. Whatever her movements are, she is clearly partaking in an idiosyncratic, eccentric ritual.*

AMÁ: I'll say a rosary every day. I'll go to mass every morning at five o'clock. I'll go to confession twice a week. Make it three. I'll fast every Friday, and not only during lent. For just this one thing, God. I don't ask for much. You know, I never do. I'm happy with what you give me. Muy contenta with your plan. Tu camino loco. (*She laughs.*) We know. (*A disturbing vision undercuts her laughter.* ALEX *appears behind the scrim. The boxing bell rings, not once, not twice, but three times. Each time corresponds to a blow* ALEX *takes to his head. It is as if* AMÁ *is stuck in that moment. She grabs her head.*) But that picture in my mind, en mi mente. Mi hijo. Flat like that. You can change that picture. I know you can. Alex will be fine and will kiss me on the cheek. (*Points to her cheek.*) Right here. Right, God? (*Beat.*) Fifteen years with my husband. And fifteen without him. Years where he just drifted off. We waved good-bye to him from the front porch, me and mis hijos, but he did not turn around to say good-bye. My husband, Ernesto, the only husband I'll ever have. Oh, I am faithful to him. Like I promised. Even though he is not faithful to me. Yeah. We gotta a deal, You and me.

AMÁ gives God a knowing grin. MICHAEL enters.

MICHAEL: Mrs. Moreno?

AMÁ: Yes?

MICHAEL: We've been checking your son.

AMÁ: Yes?

MICHAEL: The doctors are looking him over right now. (*MICHAEL references ALEX's chart. He seems awkward in his role as physician.*) Currently, his condition is—indeterminable.

AMÁ: I don't know what you mean.

MICHAEL: (*Not sure how to simplify.*) Um . . .

AMÁ: (*Gesturing.*) Find a little word. A tiny word.

MICHAEL: I—

AMÁ: I want to know what's happening with my son!

GRACIELA: (*Offstage.*) (*Responding to nurse.*) Guadalupe Moreno. My mother.

GRACIELA walks in stunned, white, scared. She wears her dance costume. MICHAEL immediately takes notice.

MICHAEL: (*To GRACIELA.*) Hello, Miss.

AMÁ: My daughter.

GRACIELA: I—I—I—

MICHAEL: Just take a couple deep breaths.

GRACIELA: I—saw him.

AMÁ: Mija, could you explain what the doctor means? I don't know what he means.

GRACIELA grabs MICHAEL's hand.

GRACIELA: Hallway—bed. Door. They wouldn't let me in.

MICHAEL gently removes GRACIELA's hand. She sinks into a chair.

AMÁ: Mija, mija, mija.

GRACIELA: He—he—he—

AMÁ: Shhh.

GRACIELA: (*To AMÁ.*) He—can't—talk.

GRACIELA breaks out crying. MICHAEL hands GRACIELA a tissue. She blows her nose.

MICHAEL: There's no evidence of that.

AMÁ: Of course he can talk. He's been talking since he was eighteen months old. You should know, you taught him yourself. (*Imitating her.*) Cookie, taco, refrigerator. (*To MICHAEL.*) His third word—refrigerator—she taught him that.

GRACIELA: I screamed, "Alex. Alex!" But he doesn't hear. Me. (*Pointing at herself.*) Me.

MICHAEL: You need to believe he can hear you. It's very important you believe he can get better. Do you?

GRACIELA: I—

MICHAEL: Do you believe?

GRACIELA: I—

AMÁ: (*Innocently.*) I believe.

GRACIELA: He can't say his name.

MICHAEL: It's really early to jump to those kinds of conclusions.

GRACIELA: He didn't answer . . . today. He didn't say, "Yes, Gracie. I can hear you. I'm still here." (*To MICHAEL; piercing.*) Is he still there?

MICHAEL: (*Taken aback; beat.*) I—we don't know. (*Quickly.*) When the swelling goes down, we'll be in a much better position to answer your questions.

GRACIELA: What swelling?

MICHAEL: In the brain. (*Quickly.*) Now, don't worry. Brain swelling happens all the time with athletes.

GRACIELA: (*Overlapping with MICHAEL.*) God.

AMÁ: Shh. We're at the hospital.

GRACIELA: (*Pointing.*) Your son's dying in there.

MICHAEL: He's not . . . dying. He's stabilized.

GRACIELA: (*Numb.*) *You* saved him?

MICHAEL: (*Proudly.*) I was on the emergency room staff when they flew him in. I guess you can say that.

GRACIELA: (*Rocking; still numb.*) I heard it on the radio. They play the radio between sets at the park. They were playing a new song called "Cheech's Chones" for Cinco de Mayo and everybody was laughing.

AMÁ: (*Singing.*) "He don't wear no chones. Naa."

MICHAEL: And chones are?

AMÁ: Underwears.

GRACIELA: And then they made this announcement, about Alex Moreno, the state welterweight champion—how he was illegally boxing in Mexico and he got caught. 'Cause God doesn't let you cheat! (*Calmer.*) It was a news flash. (*Upset.*) About my brother. And everything they said, doctor, did not give me the impression—THAT HE WAS OK!

MICHAEL: "OK" would be too strong a word.

GRACIELA: "OK" would be a lie.

MICHAEL: It would be.

GRACIELA: He got fucked.

MICHAEL: (*Under his breath.*) It appears he did.

GRACIELA: (*Finally, the truth.*) Thank you.

AMÁ: (*Distracting herself.*) Doctor, you don't wear no chones neither, do you?

MICHAEL: I— (*Blushing.*)

GRACIELA: When will we know?

MICHAEL: About my underwear?

GRACIELA: About Alex.

MICHAEL: I'm not sure. There may be complications.

AMÁ: You have to let me visit. I always can cheer him up. He says, "Amá, you make me laugh sooo hard I cry." (*Reality seems to be dawning on her.*) I want to see my little boy.

MICHAEL: (*To AMÁ.*) You can see him as soon as it's safe, Ma'am.

GRACIELA: After the swelling goes down?

MICHAEL: Then.

AMÁ: I'm not leaving here until I see my son. Go get him, Graciela. Wheel him in.

GRACIELA: We can't, Amá.

AMÁ: Why not?

MICHAEL: It's best not to move him.

AMÁ: Bring him in here. Or I'm going there.

> *She gets up.*

MICHAEL: Mrs. Moreno. Your son is in critical condition.

AMÁ: (*To GRACIELA*) Why can't you do what I say? Wheel him in. (*Demanding like a child.*) Why not? Why not?

GRACIELA: They don't know what's wrong with him.

AMÁ: What?

GRACIELA: It could be really bad. That's what they said on the radio. Wheelchair. Crippled. FUCKED UP.

AMÁ: You don't need to yell.

GRACIELA grabs MICHAEL by the collar.

GRACIELA: I want to know what's wrong with my brother and I want to know now!

MICHAEL: We have no information.

GRACIELA: Well, maybe if you got your ass in there and started taking some tests, YOU WOULD.

AMÁ: Mija. Don't lose control. (*To MICHAEL.*) You don't know what happens when she loses control.

GRACIELA: I GO CRAZY!

GRACIELA tightens her grip on MICHAEL's collar.

MICHAEL: (*Constricted breathing.*) Stop.

GRACIELA releases his collar.

AMÁ: She gets a little upset. (*Loud whisper; to MICHAEL.*) It's that alcoholism. From her father.

GRACIELA: I'm not an alcoholic!

AMÁ: She's not an alcoholic.

GRACIELA: I'm not an alcoholic. Geez!

AMÁ pulls GRACIELA into herself. Resting GRACIELA's head on her shoulder, she pats GRACIELA's head.

AMÁ: We're gonna get over this. We've been through worse. Like when your father left.

GRACIELA: (*Matter-of-factly.*) My father left.

AMÁ: So sad. The kids cried for two years, ¿que no? (*Matter-of-factly.*) I'd run out of candles on my *altar*. That's why he left. Oh, he didn't know that was the reason, but that was why.

GRACIELA: So sad.

AMÁ: You got to keep those candles burning or Nuestra Señora won't look down.

MICHAEL: I'm sure after we've had a chance to examine him we'll realize that everything is fine.

GRACIELA: (*Still a bit dazed.*) I like that song, do you?

AMÁ: You should hear her sing, doctor. She played María in *The Sound of Music* at Catholic school. Well, she was the understudy. And the other María got laryngitis. (*Singing with a laryngitic voice.*) Y cantó así. (*Normal.*) And they sent Graciela up. And she sang like an angel. Better than that Anglo girl.

GRACIELA: Amá.

AMÁ: You did. And everybody said, "Why didn't they give Graciela that part in the first place?" And the nuns, and I don't ever forget this, because we gave las monjitas mucho dinero. They said they just couldn't see a little Mexican girl playing María. Her name was María. (*Louder.*) She was a Mexican girl. Son pendejas. And they never taught you nothing, except que el inglés was mejor que el Spanich.

GRACIELA: (*Beat.*) We'll sing that song for him. We'll bring him back to the world with something he loves.

AMÁ: Something he loves.

GRACIELA: Boxing. He loves her like a lover, he told me. He has no woman except her.

AMÁ: He has us. He doesn't need a woman.

GRACIELA: (*Quoting ALEX.*) "Boxing is in my blood. It's what keeps me alive, Little Sis."

GRACIELA chokes up.

MICHAEL: Everything's going to be fine. Candles or no candles.

GRACIELA looks up at him.

GRACIELA: I believe in you.

GRACIELA's and MICHAEL's eyes meet. She entrusts herself to him.

AMÁ: The candles are very important. The fire catches La Virgencita's attention. Como una estrella. The light guides her to see into your house—then your heart. That's why I always keep my candles burning. Don't I, mija?

GRACIELA: Oh she's a nut about it. The house glows like a church.

GRACIELA smiles at the doctor, but AMÁ seems to be realizing something important.

AMÁ: Mija, you stole my candle today. (*GRACIELA seems taken aback.*) Para tu danza. You took la protección!

GRACIELA: That's crazy!

AMÁ: You did. (*Beat.*) Doctor, I must see my son.

MICHAEL: You can see him through the glass.

GRACIELA: Amá, the Virgin wouldn't punish you like that.

AMÁ: It's an emergency. ¡Híjole!

GRACIELA: Amá, don't overreact.

AMÁ: I want to see him in his room. Right now!

MICHAEL: Three minutes.

AMÁ: Five.

MICHAEL: This is not a negotiation. I'm breaking the rules.

AMÁ quickly applies her lipstick, upset.

AMÁ: Estoy lista.

MICHAEL: Excuse me.

AMÁ: (*Harried.*) I'm ready.

MICHAEL: Cinco minutos. Nomás. (*GRACIELA looks surprised at the Spanish.*) Head nurse taught me that. It's tough to get you guys to leave your family members alone.

GRACIELA: Well, we don't just give up on each other.

AMÁ stands up, grabs the doctor by the hand.

AMÁ: (*To GRACIELA.*) This is your fault.

GRACIELA: They're just candles!

As AMÁ drags MICHAEL out the door, he looks back.

MICHAEL: You just wait right there. Make yourself at home.

GRACIELA: OK.

MICHAEL: (*As they leave.*) The swelling makes it look much worse than it is.

GRACIELA drops her head in her hands, wringing her hair. She looks up. Her song is more along the lines of a show tune than a traditional Mexican song.

GRACIELA: (*Singing.*) Everything is fine. Everything is fine. (*Launching into the tune loudly.*) EVERYTHING IS FINE (*softer*) if only I'd believe it. (*Belting it out.*) EVERYTHING, EVERYTHING (*spoken*) is fine.

GRACIELA turns her head in both directions to look for listeners. Blackout.

SCENE 3

Out of time. The stage is black. AMÁ lights a long match. It burns as a light comes up on her. She lays a blue star-studded cloth on the floor. Wrapped in the cloth are a round box of long wooden matches, a Virgin of Guadalupe religious candle, and a shaker of salt. She lights the candle, fanning herself with the smoke. She shakes a handful of the salt into her left hand and throws it over her right shoulder. She twirls three times. She claps her hands together. She puts them together in a prayerful position. When she looks up from the prayer, ALEX and GRACIELA appear in separate light on either side of her.

> *Each person partakes in his/her own sacred movement, boxing and
> dancing, respectively. There is something very dancelike about* ALEX's
> *boxing and something very boxinglike about* GRACIELA's *dancing.*
>
> *A game ensues: the three begin to move into each other's spaces,
> taking on each other's movement whether it be praying, boxing, or
> dancing. The frenzy ends when all fall to the ground as in a children's
> game.* ALEX's *little-boy laugh echoes in voice-over, ending abruptly.*

GRACIELA: You vanished. Like breath. I want to feel you again inside my lungs, like the steam of the peppermint tea Amá used to give us when we were sick. Because I am sick. So tired. So much older than me. I look in the mirror and watch myself turn thirty. That's when you finally, after all those years, become a real woman.

SCENE 4

> *Two months after Cinco de Mayo. Lights up on Moreno home.* AMÁ
> *and* MICHAEL *sit at the kitchen table.* ALEX *lies flat on a hospital bed
> with wheels. An intravenous feeding tube is hooked up to his arm.*

MICHAEL: They have full-time nurses who really know what they're doing.

AMÁ: But will they give him love?

MICHAEL: They read to the patients and everything.

AMÁ: What do they read?

MICHAEL: (*Stumped.*) I'm not sure.

AMÁ: I don't want them reading him some gabacho story that he doesn't understand.

MICHAEL: I'm sure they'll read him what he likes.

AMÁ: If he can't talk, how will they know what he likes? (*Disgusted.*) Nursing homes.

(MICHAEL *has no response.* GRACIELA *walks in, immediately checks on* ALEX, *adjusting a pillow to make him more comfortable.*) Here's the girl.

MICHAEL: Hi.

GRACIELA: (*Shyly.*) Hi. (*This is obviously more than a house call. There seems to be some attraction here.*) Are you sure it's OK—you coming over here to visit?

MICHAEL: Alex isn't my patient anymore. I waited two whole months to even ask you out.

GRACIELA: I'm glad you did.

MICHAEL: You're glad I waited?

GRACIELA: No, called. (*Beat.*) I loved that place you took me on Tuesday night.

MICHAEL: Club Congress?

GRACIELA: The girl in the cage. Really wild! I'd never have the guts to dance half-naked and crazy like that. And she was a homegirl.

MICHAEL: (*Embarrassed.*) I didn't know they'd have people doing that there. (*Quickly.*) I loved *your* dance performance. Thanks for inviting me.

GRACIELA: Well, when you called to follow up on Alex, I was really touched.

MICHAEL: I liked the way you had your hair up.

GRACIELA: Oh, that wasn't my hair.

MICHAEL: It wasn't? (*Disappointed.*) Oh, I thought—(*it was*).

GRACIELA: I used to have hair like that. (*Wanting to please.*) I could grow it out again.

MICHAEL: It was really pretty on you, even if it was fake.

GRACIELA: Thanks.

> MICHAEL *touches* GRACIELA's *hand, intertwines his pinkie with hers. They just stare at each other. They clearly want to kiss.* AMÁ *has to split up this mutual admiration party. She clears her throat.*

AMÁ: She changes the IV. She knows how to do it. Those mechanical things confuse me. I've broken everything Alex bought me.

GRACIELA: (*Explaining.*) She broke the garbage disposal in three days. On avocado pits.

AMÁ: (*A loud whisper.*) I was making guacamole.

MICHAEL: (*Suddenly serious; to* GRACIELA.) So, he's been the same since he left the hospital?

GRACIELA: If you want to take a look—(*at him*).

AMÁ: She's the one to ask. She watches him all day long. She won't even look up at the television.

GRACIELA: (*Embarrassed.*) Amá.

MICHAEL: It's beautiful. You care.

GRACIELA: Well, I know my brother. Like when he boxed, he could beat the biggest guy in the world as long as there were people cheering for him.

AMÁ: (*To* ALEX.) Go, Alex!

GRACIELA: (*Back to his question.*) His eyes.

MICHAEL: What about the eyes?

GRACIELA: They open and shut. Once in the morning. When I lift the blinds and the sun gets in his face. And again after dinner.

MICHAEL: That's great.

GRACIELA: Me and Amá have been trying to figure out what it all means.

AMÁ: I told her—it's a sign from God. When Alex wakes up, he'll walk over and give me a kiss right here. Won't you, mijo? (*AMÁ waves at ALEX.*) ¡Hola!

Graciela: And his toes. I saw him wiggle his toes a few times. That counts, doesn't it?

MICHAEL: Wonderful.

GRACIELA: I knew these were good signs.

AMÁ: I started lighting La Virgen's candles again to make up for that other time. On Cinco de Mayo.

GRACIELA: He gets better every day.

AMÁ: Give La Virgen time. Con tiempo, ella siempre perdona. With time, she always forgives.

MICHAEL: I'll have to talk to the neurologist about these signs, but I find any movement at all very, very encouraging.

GRACIELA: Encouraging. (*To AMÁ.*) Did you hear that?

AMÁ points at the casserole dish in the middle of the table.

AMÁ: Have some enchiladas. Graciela made them. It's her specialty. Actually, it's the only thing she knows how to make.

GRACIELA: (*With a smile.*) That's not true.

AMÁ: She uses a little *mole.* You won't taste them like that out of the freezer section.

MICHAEL: (*To AMÁ.*) You first.

AMÁ: No. I'm just having a little salad.

AMÁ reaches for a small bowl of salad, crosses herself, and begins eating.

MICHAEL: You're not eating Graciela's enchiladas?

GRACIELA: Will you tell her that *woman* cannot live on lettuce alone?

AMÁ: I'm the only woman out of all of my sisters that doesn't have the *diabetes.* And you know why?

MICHAEL: You didn't inherit it.

AMÁ: No, you know really why?

MICHAEL: That's really why.

AMÁ: Because I watch my diet very carefully. What goes in and what goes out.

MICHAEL laughs.

GRACIELA: (*Looking at ALEX.*) When Alex is thirsty, I give him ice cubes. That's the highlight of his day. Sheer oral pleasure.

GRACIELA catches herself—she's embarrassed.

AMÁ: She takes good care of him. I tell her she should go to school to become a nurse.

MICHAEL: Are you going to become a nurse?

GRACIELA: The dance school is my dream. Passing down the dance the way it was done by our ancestors. In little villages all over México. And never forgetting that it's all supposed to be fun. I'd forgotten that. But after Alex got hurt, I could hear him talking to me in my head. Like he was dead.

MICHAEL: You mean alive.

GRACIELA: I mean dead.

AMÁ: The dead talk to us, you know.

GRACIELA: And he told me, "Gracie, you need to have more fun." (*Pained.*) Because he loves me. And he wants me to be happy. He used to fill up this place with his laughing.

AMÁ: I think she should become a nurse. It's a good job.

MICHAEL: It's a solid job. You can work wherever you want.

GRACIELA: Like where?

MICHAEL: I don't know—New York, Miami, Michigan—

GRACIELA: Why the hell would I want to go to Michigan?

MICHAEL: I'm from Michigan.

GRACIELA: Oh, I see how this works. You know I just threw out that I'd consider nursing to make her happy and now she won't forget about it.

AMÁ: (*Hurt.*) Mija.

GRACIELA: Nurses, doctors, lawyers. Amá, we're from the most beat up street in Barrio Hollywood. We don't have the money to become those kinds of things.

AMÁ: Alex has a little money saved. I'm sure he'd want you to follow your dream.

GRACIELA: (*Firmly.*) My dream is to own a dance studio. (*Softens.*) I like being a dance teacher. It makes me happy.

GRACIELA *walks over to* ALEX's *bed by the window and moves him.*

MICHAEL: What are you doing with him?

GRACIELA: Giving him a different view.

AMÁ: He likes to watch the neighbors.

MICHAEL: Those vatos on their porch across the street smoking pot?

GRACIELA: It's part of his massage.

AMÁ: We give him a massage every night.

GRACIELA *walks over to* ALEX, *focuses on him, starts massaging his arms.* AMÁ *massages* ALEX's *feet.*

GRACIELA: It makes him feel more alive.

AMÁ: Because he is alive.

GRACIELA: (*Sarcastically.*) That's why he hasn't said a goddamn word in two months.

AMÁ: She gets a little upset.

GRACIELA: (*Getting upset.*) I do not get upset.

MICHAEL: Even for a few days, one of those homes might be nice.

AMÁ: Maybe he's right.

GRACIELA: We're not putting him in a home.

AMÁ: Listen to the *doctor*.

GRACIELA: He's a medical student.

MICHAEL: Resident.

AMÁ: It might be best.

GRACIELA: Alex is fine. He's got it made. He gets his massage every night at 6:30. Eats through that thing in his arm. He's just taking a time out. A breath. (*GRACIELA takes a deep breath in and out. AMÁ and MICHAEL are transfixed by the breath as if ALEX's fate is hanging on it. GRACIELA lines up a row of religious candles on both sides of ALEX, lighting them one by one. There are two levels of window sills, so some of them are on each side of ALEX's head. MICHAEL looks like he wants to ask a question. AMÁ stops him. It is a spiritual moment that should not be interrupted. GRACIELA puts her hands together, nods in prayer and returns to the dinner table.*) (*To MICHAEL.*) I'm sorry. I just want him to get well.

MICHAEL: (*Understanding.*) I know.

GRACIELA: Maybe you could take a look at him—

AMÁ: After dinner.

GRACIELA: (*Continuing.*) I know you're qualified. You saved him and everything.

MICHAEL: (*Not sure if he's been saved.*) We did.

GRACIELA: It was the right thing to do.

AMÁ: Do you like the enchiladas?

MICHAEL: Yes. Delicious.

AMÁ: Why don't we feed some to Alex? He loves Graciela's enchiladas. (*GRACIELA and MICHAEL look at each other uncomfortably. ALEX is not conscious enough to eat. AMÁ starts to put a fork full of food up to ALEX's lips.*) Eat up, mijo.

A magical moment as a red light comes up on ALEX. ALEX opens his mouth, licks the enchilada, smacks his lips, shuts his mouth.

GRACIELA: He moved! (*GRACIELA and MICHAEL rush over. GRACIELA takes over the fork, starts trying to feed ALEX the enchilada. AMÁ hangs onto ALEX's feet, trying to wake him up. ALEX lets out a huge burp. End of movement. They all try to wake ALEX but to no avail. He's out again. The red light fades.*) I believe. I believe.

AMÁ: Alex. Alex.

They all stare at ALEX, transfixed by what has just happened. ALEX doesn't stir. Lights dim slightly on the tableau for a moment. Then, MICHAEL begins to check ALEX's vital signs. MICHAEL slows down. There is no further movement from ALEX. AMÁ seems the most distraught.

GRACIELA: It's OK, Amá.

MICHAEL: (*Beat.*) Do you think we all imagined it? (*Beat.*) That really was an amazing amount of movement for—

GRACIELA: For what?

MICHAEL: (*Knows he's saying the wrong thing.*) A comatose patient.

GRACIELA: (*Disappointed.*) Oh.

AMÁ: Did you see him, mija? He wanted to eat dinner with us.

GRACIELA: He eats dinner with us every night, ¿verdad?

AMÁ: The other night I went into his room and he was sleeping on his side. Like a baby. And I touched his forehead right there, and he smiled at me.

MICHAEL starts to interrupt. GRACIELA stops him.

GRACIELA: It's Friday night, Amá. Poker night.

AMÁ: Why don't you two go out? Have another real date.

GRACIELA: No. You go out. Have your poker night.

AMÁ: Really?

GRACIELA: Yes, really. You deserve a break.

AMÁ: Are you sure?

GRACIELA: I'm certain. It's only one night, and we have a real doctor here to take care of Alex.

AMÁ: Well, you know I did very well last week.

GRACIELA: I'm sure you did. Now, go win.

AMÁ: (*Clearly cheered up.*) Oh, thank you, mija. (*AMÁ looks at the dishes.*) Oh, the dishes.

GRACIELA: I'll get them. (*AMÁ smiles and leaves.*) She sees what she wants to see. Alex on his side. Smiles. Tears. It's all part of the movie in her head.

MICHAEL: Let her have her hope.

GRACIELA: It's senseless hope, isn't it?

MICHAEL: Hey, don't give up.

GRACIELA: Why not?

MICHAEL: Hope matters.

GRACIELA: She sometimes stops being an adult when it gets hard. She makes popcorn and goes into Alex's room and flips on the TV. Boxing. "It'll cheer him up, mija."

MICHAEL: I've seen things. People recover who were supposed to be dead. Real miracles. When I was in that trauma unit that night, I didn't think we were going to save him.

GRACIELA: But you did. (*MICHAEL touches GRACIELA's hand, comforting her.*) You make me strong.

MICHAEL: You make me strong, too.

GRACIELA: Why do you need to be strong?

MICHAEL: (*Embarrassed.*) I don't know. It sounded good?

GRACIELA: You're funny.

MICHAEL: (*Beat.*) I can get an appointment to talk to the neurologist next week.

GRACIELA: I'd appreciate that.

MICHAEL: It's gonna be OK.

GRACIELA: Yeah.

MICHAEL strokes her face. GRACIELA receives it.

MICHAEL: You're amazing—the way you love him.

GRACIELA: It's just—normal.

MICHAEL: Maybe to you it is, but not to the rest of the world. (*GRACIELA smiles at him. MICHAEL strokes her face, moves in and French kisses her. She enjoys it for a second and then pulls away. It is more of an awkward than a romantic moment.*) It's me. I'm hopeless with my tongue.

GRACIELA: It wasn't that.

MICHAEL: I was trying not to use my teeth.

GRACIELA: It's not that either. (*Long beat.*) It's just I've never dated anyone like you before.

MICHAEL: What do you mean?

GRACIELA: Well, you're a doctor. Which means you have a job.

MICHAEL: Yeah.

GRACIELA: And you're tall.

MICHAEL: Yeah.

GRACIELA: (*Blurting it out.*) And I've never dated an Anglo before.

MICHAEL: (*Disappointed.*) Oh.

GRACIELA: It's OK. I've just never done it. It's not like I'm a racist. I'm open-minded.

MICHAEL: OK, I believe you.

GRACIELA: I feel stupid for even bringing it up.

MICHAEL: No, it's worth bringing up.

GRACIELA: (Beat.) You're very cute.

MICHAEL: Thanks.

> GRACIELA *crosses to* ALEX, *tucks in his sheet.*

GRACIELA: I'll just put him to bed.

MICHAEL: Graciela.

> GRACIELA *turns.*

GRACIELA: Yeah.

MICHAEL: I like that we're different.

GRACIELA: You do?

MICHAEL: I don't know the rules here. I don't even know how to be polite.

GRACIELA: (*Happy.*) Good. (GRACIELA *wheels* ALEX *off.* MICHAEL *picks up the plates and puts the leftover food onto one plate. He does the job with great care.* GRACIELA *moves back into the room unnoticed. She watches him. Startling him.*) You do dishes.

MICHAEL: And I cook.

GRACIELA: Mexican food?

MICHAEL: My mother's meat loaf, but I can learn.

GRACIELA: Family secret?

MICHAEL: Betty Crocker.

GRACIELA: Tell me another—

MICHAEL: What?

GRACIELA: Secret.

MICHAEL: About my family?

GRACIELA: About you.

MICHAEL: (*Beat.*) When I went to that dance, and you were wearing your dance costume with all the colorful skirts, I thought you were the most beautiful woman I'd ever seen.

GRACIELA: Naa.

MICHAEL: You were. And when you danced, with your face really serious like that, I thought, "I know how to make that woman smile."

GRACIELA: (*Challenging him.*) Yeah?

> MICHAEL *moves and kisses her tenderly and less aggressively.* GRACIELA *smiles. Lights fade.*

SCENE 5

A week later. Lights come up on GRACIELA*'s front porch. Music blasts from a boom box.* MICHAEL *and* GRACIELA *dance together.* MICHAEL *stops. He talks to her over the music.* GRACIELA*'s backpack sits on the porch.*

MICHAEL: I don't know how to do it now that you said I dance funny.

GRACIELA: I didn't mean anything by it. You've just got different . . . rhythm.

MICHAEL stops dancing.

MICHAEL: Now, that's a way to get me to cut loose and dance. Gee, I think I'll just move here and explore my different rhythm, like a catatonic on heavy meds.

GRACIELA laughs.

GRACIELA: It's beautiful . . . in its own way. Like an irregular heartbeat. I'm behind you, Michael. Behind your aspirations to become a dancer.

MICHAEL: A true teacher at heart.

GRACIELA: Yes.

MICHAEL: So, don't laugh at me anymore. Teachers aren't supposed to laugh.

GRACIELA: (*She gestures.*) OK, no more laughing. Dance teacher's honor. (*They start gazing at each other.*) You're growing on me—like a fungus. (*She laughs. Suddenly serious.*) You're growing on me. (*Beat.*) I'm not very good at all this, having boyfriends and stuff.

MICHAEL: Oh, and I'm some Mr. Smooth Guy. I'll tell you a little secret. All those years in college and medical school—you can call it a romantic dry spell. I don't think I even went to coffee with anyone in eight years.

GRACIELA: Yikes.

MICHAEL: So you, my darling, are the expert here.

GRACIELA: Wow, I thought—

MICHAEL: Embarrassing, but true.

GRACIELA: I feel guilty—about Alex.

MICHAEL: Hey, I don't like the way we met, either. But the fact we met, that's what matters. And if we didn't meet . . .

GRACIELA: Yes.

MICHAEL: We wouldn't know each other.

GRACIELA: Yes.

MICHAEL: And that would be tragic because some people you're just supposed to meet. You're supposed to touch their lives and let them touch yours.

GRACIELA: And I'm a person like that?

MICHAEL: You are that.

GRACIELA: That's very sweet.

MICHAEL: Oh, don't call me sweet. That makes me feel like a real loser.

GRACIELA: You are not a loser. You saved my brother.

MICHAEL: (*Ambivalent.*) I did.

GRACIELA: So, you're not a loser. We have Alex because of you.

MICHAEL: Yeah.

GRACIELA: What is it?

MICHAEL: You have Alex.

GRACIELA: Because of you.

MICHAEL: Do you really have Alex?

GRACIELA: He's right inside, silly. Hey, I almost forgot. You absolutely must try on the belt. No self-respecting male folklórico dancer would dare dance without the proper accoutrements. (GRACIELA *reaches into her backpack to pull out the belt. She can't find it. She starts rummaging through the backpack.*) Where is the darn thing?

MICHAEL *grabs the backpack. She starts to grab back and a book falls out.*

MICHAEL: (*Reading the title.*) Boxing and Medicine: Head Trauma and the Pugilistic Patient.

GRACIELA: (*Backing off.*) I . . . (*She takes the book back.*) The librarian ordered it for me from some medical school. They're so good at helping. Give to your public library. I just thought if there was something I could learn, I ought to learn it. I just—just forget it.

MICHAEL: No.

GRACIELA: I mean this doing nothing thing. I just can't do the doing-nothing thing. Is there someone out there who we can talk to?

MICHAEL: I don't know. That neurologist ended up canceling our appointment and then he left the country.

GRACIELA: Will you try somebody else?

MICHAEL: Can I have this?

GRACIELA: I didn't understand the medical jargon anyway. If you could make some calls—ask some questions—

MICHAEL: I'll call the editor of this book.

GRACIELA: Thanks. (*Beat.*) Shall we try the belt? (GRACIELA *wraps a ballet folklórico belt around* MICHAEL'S *waist.*) Much better. Almost perfect.

MICHAEL: What would it take for me to be perfect?

GRACIELA: You are perfect. Shut up.

MICHAEL: I don't believe you.

GRACIELA: Believe me. You're perfect.

GRACIELA rises to her toes to kiss him.

MICHAEL: Wow.

GRACIELA: What?

MICHAEL: Did you feel the spark between our lips?

GRACIELA: (*Giggles.*) You shock me.

MICHAEL: I shock you.

GRACIELA: We shock each other.

MICHAEL just holds her and holds her from behind.

MICHAEL: I'm so glad I know you.

GRACIELA: But do you really know me? That is the question.

MICHAEL: Getting to know you.

GRACIELA: And if you really knew me would you still want me?

MICHAEL: I can't think of anything more amazing than truly knowing you. All the crevices and uncharted places.

GRACIELA: Now shut up and dance. (*MICHAEL takes a couple of decent folklórico steps. He stops, awaiting her approval.*) What do you want?

MICHAEL: Credit. They were pretty damn good.

GRACIELA: Pretty is not perfection. Keep working. You'll have to establish a regular rehearsal schedule in order to eradicate your deficiencies in dancing.

MICHAEL: Tomorrow. Same place? Same time?

GRACIELA: And wear something with belt loops. (*MICHAEL laughs. Suddenly more serious.*) I can count on you—to make those calls?

MICHAEL: Yes, of course.

GRACIELA: I just want to know that we've done everything we could.

MICHAEL: Of course.

GRACIELA: I miss Alex.

MICHAEL: If we could start at a different place, I'd give you that.

GRACIELA: Maybe it's the place that allowed us to start. Maybe some places open up spaces for an extraordinary phenomenon like you and me.

MICHAEL: You are—extraordinary.

GRACIELA: You.

MICHAEL: What?

GRACIELA: Extraordinary. Beyond adjectives. Beyond comprehension.

MICHAEL: Me? Beyond comprehension?

GRACIELA: Like a big fat book with lots of stories intertwined. Complicated and thorough. Something that can be delved into like the sea.

MICHAEL: That's quite a compliment.

GRACIELA: Find us the right brain doctor and I'll have more.

MICHAEL: Agreed.

GRACIELA: I'll shower you with praise.

MICHAEL: You'll shower with me?

GRACIELA: In your dreams.

MICHAEL: I have an active imagination.

GRACIELA: Save it for later.

MICHAEL: When's later?

GRACIELA: For when Alex gets well and I can leave this house.

MICHAEL: Well, uh—

GRACIELA: I say a rosary for him every night. Two, actually.

MICHAEL: I've got to get going.

GRACIELA: Michael. Don't you believe?

MICHAEL: I don't know.

GRACIELA: Find out something. Do your homework.

MICHAEL: I'll take this with me.

GRACIELA: It's a library book. Bring it back. If I knew the right questions, I'd call myself. Maybe I should just—

MICHAEL: No, no. I'll do it, Graciela.

GRACIELA: Thanks. (*MICHAEL gives her a quick kiss goodbye.*) I felt it that time. Your little spark.

    Are they establishing a little routine?

MICHAEL: You shock me.

GRACIELA: You shock me.

MICHAEL: (*As he leaves.*) We're shocking.

    GRACIELA laughs.

SCENE 6

The morning of Cinco de Mayo. Lights quickly up on the Moreno home. GRACIELA ices ALEX's head. He is sprawled out on the couch. He is groggy.

ALEX: Not so hard.

GRACIELA: I'm not applying any pressure at all.

ALEX: I'm just a little dizzy.

GRACIELA: Is that why I found you lying face down on the bathroom floor?

ALEX: The tiles feel good on my face in the heat.

GRACIELA: It's not even summer yet. And I don't see you as the kind to roll around on tiles, like a dog, to cool off.

ALEX: (*A non sequitur.*) Mexican tiles.

GRACIELA: (*Doesn't understand.*) Yes, they're Mexican tiles. (*With humor.*) You look like shit. (GRACIELA *waits for him to give his standard response.*) Aren't you gonna say, "So do you"? (*Beat.*) You always say that.

ALEX: (*Truly not remembering.*) I do?

GRACIELA: Yes, you always say, "So do you." It's one of our routines.

ALEX: Routines?

GRACIELA: What happened to you last night? (AMÁ *enters. She plays with her new vacuum cleaner. A gift, it still has a red bow wrapped around it. She vacuums every part of the house while singing "I Feel Pretty." She even tries to vacuum* ALEX *and* GRACIELA *with the hose.* ALEX *just smiles as she runs over him. She grabs her necklace.*) Watch out! You could catch my cross in that thing. (*Screaming over the vacuum.*) He isn't well. Enfermo, Amá.

GRACIELA *clicks the vacuum off. Dead silence.*

AMÁ: ¿Qué qué qué?

GRACIELA: You're always off in your own little world.

AMÁ: I like my little world.

GRACIELA: Look at him. He isn't himself.

ALEX: (*Singing.*) "There's no business like show business like no business I know."

GRACIELA: (*To* ALEX.) Ever since we got home, you've been acting crazy like Amá.

This clearly offends AMÁ. ALEX *motions for her to come over. She kisses* ALEX *on the head.*

AMÁ: Is your head all better, mijo?

ALEX: You're the best, Amá.

ALEX *starts kissing her over and over on the cheek. It's a little much.*

AMÁ: (*To* GRACIELA.) Ella tiene celos. We got good stuff now.

ALEX: Yeah, we got good stuff.

GRACIELA: You're lucky that cabrón didn't break your—(*nose*).

ALEX: I lose one fight and look at you.

GRACIELA: I don't want you to fight anymore, Alex.

ALEX: Christ! A guy's allowed to get knocked out once in his life.

AMÁ: Yeah!

GRACIELA: You guys are driving me crazy.

ALEX: Go find yourself another family.

AMÁ: Yeah!

GRACIELA: I thought we agreed to not give her permission to do that.

AMÁ: Yeah!

GRACIELA: Stop it!

AMÁ: Yeah!

ALEX: Yeah yeah yeah yeah yeah yeah.

> GRACIELA *covers her ears, visibly upset.*

GRACIELA: I've got to get out of here. I've got a performance.

ALEX: Go. Go perform. (GRACIELA *steps out in her ballet folklórico costume. She wears a white dress with red trim and a fake braid. She balances a glass-encased candle, about three inches in diameter, on her head.*) That's just gonna fall off your head on the way to the car.

GRACIELA: Will not.

ALEX: Will too.

GRACIELA: (*To* AMÁ.) Aren't you gonna come watch me, Amá? It's Cinco de Mayo—the most high-paying Mexican holiday of the year. Kennedy Park. I used to make you proud before that little mocoso came around.

> ALEX *motions behind* GRACIELA'*s head, indicating to* AMÁ *that she needs to get* GRACIELA *to leave.*

AMÁ: I used to go watch you dance before the people got shot.

GRACIELA: Those were gang kids. The park has good security now.

> AMÁ *puffs her hair.*

AMÁ: I don't want to get any bullet holes through my hair.

> AMÁ *smiles, self-satisfied.*

GRACIELA: (*As she leaves.*) I'm outta here.

> GRACIELA *exits.* AMÁ *pulls* ALEX'*s boxing trunks out of her purse.*

ALEX: I thought she was never gonna leave.

> ALEX *puts his boxing trunks on.*

AMA: Are you too fat?

> AMÁ *drags out a scale.* ALEX *stands on it.*

ALEX: This is bullshit. I haven't eaten in three days, and I haven't had a glass of water in four hours.

Amá hands him a razor. Alex looks at it, confused.

AMÁ: Shave your hairs.

Alex drags the scale to the hallway, starts taking his trunks off. He stands on the scale again.

ALEX: That scale should be right. I bought it last week.

ALEX: (*Offstage.*) Thank God.

Graciela enters. The glass enclosing the candle on her headdress has indeed broken. She looks distressed, perhaps crying a bit.

GRACIELA: Amá, look. Do you have another candle?

AMÁ: Only on my *altar.*

Graciela looks with begging eyes. Amá resists.

GRACIELA: Just this once.

AMÁ: No, mija. That's for La Virgen. You want me to take her candle and give it to you? What's she going to think? That's our protection—para nuestra familia. ¡No!

GRACIELA: I promise you I'll buy you some nice ones at Walgreens. I'll borrow it just for this afternoon, so I can do this dance from Veracruz. La Bruja— the one where I have to dance completely solo with a pinche candle on my head. (*For Alex's benefit.*) I wouldn't have to do it if I had *a partner.*

AMÁ: OK. Just this once. (*Amá crosses to her altar and takes down a small pink candle, encased in glass. She hands it to Graciela.*) Don't break this.

GRACIELA: I won't, Amá. (*Alex enters, busily wrapping his hand with tape, in his own world.*) You're fighting?

ALEX: Cinco de Mayo. Most highly paid Mexican holiday of the year.

GRACIELA: (*To Alex.*) Tell her you can't do this.

ALEX: It's just this little weasel from Nogales. Nothing El Lobo de Magdalena can't handle. No te preocupes.

GRACIELA: Alex.

ALEX: You're doing your thing. I'm doing my thing, Gracie.

Graciela: OK, *wa,* but I think you should have your head examined.

Alex: It's my business.

GRACIELA: Whatever. Do what you want.

Graciela exits. Lights fade.

SCENE 7

The present. MICHAEL *arrives at the front porch.*

Michael: Am I late for class?

Graciela: So?

Michael: So what?

Graciela: Did you find anything out?

Michael: Yeah.

Graciela: And.

Michael: It's very complicated . . .

Graciela: Locked-in Syndrome?

MICHAEL seems surprised she knows about this.

Michael: What?

Graciela: I was up half the night trying to figure out the possibility that Alex has this Locked-in Syndrome thing—like it says in the book. It says that the patient can blink and that makes everybody, especially the family, think that the person's still in there but they're not.

Michael: He's locked inside his body. I'm sorry, Gracie.

Graciela: That's Alex's name for me. (*MICHAEL tries to hold her.*) People think, if you have a boyfriend, you really love him, and maybe you do, but your brother, that's someone who's been with you almost every day of your life—that's someone who stays with you no matter what—'cause he's your brother.

There is an awkward silence. MICHAEL *hands her a handkerchief. She wipes her eyes.*

Michael: You might want to think about letting him go. When you feed him, you keep him alive.

Graciela: Yeah.

Michael: Letting him die.

GRACIELA: Oh.

MICHAEL: Just think about it.

GRACIELA: He's got to be in there. Somewhere. (*Choking up at the end.*) I'm not going to starve my brother and make him suffer! He's going to be OK.

MICHAEL: I wish that were true.

GRACIELA: He's my little brother; I'm supposed to take care of him.

MICHAEL: I am so sorry this happened.

GRACIELA: (*Retreating to the daze of her mourning.*) I can still see him there. (*ALEX boxes behind the scrim, agile and healthy.*) Fighting that first fight.

Winning. He was beautiful to watch. The most beautiful boxer I've ever seen. It was because of the dance he was like that. I never found another dance partner like him after he quit. He moved like the wind. Have you ever watched the wind? The way it crawls into every little place unseen. And you know it's been somewhere because of how it changes everything around it.

MICHAEL: I'm sorry.

GRACIELA: (*Beat.*) They really loved him in México. El Lobo de Magdalena.

MICHAEL: I've heard tell.

GRACIELA: Where?

MICHAEL: I've been known to watch a little Spanish television.

GRACIELA: Since when?

MICHAEL: Since I met you.

GRACIELA: You've been trying to learn Spanish?

MICHAEL: Poquito.

GRACIELA: Why?

MICHAEL: (*Beat.*) I'm sorry to be the one to tell you the news.

GRACIELA: Well, I think maybe one of those little miracles you told me about might happen. You think?

MICHAEL: Sure.

GRACIELA: Say yes, Michael. It would really mean a lot to me if you said "yes" instead of "sure."

MICHAEL: (*More positive.*) Yes.

GRACIELA: You're very kind when you lie.

MICHAEL: Now, don't go and ruin it.

GRACIELA: You're very kind. (*Beat.*) Alex is never going to wake up again.

MICHAEL: (*Sadly.*) He can't.

GRACIELA: OK, *wa*.

Lights fade.

SCENE 8

The past, days before Cinco de Mayo. Lights come up to happy times on the beach in Kino Bay, Sonora, Mexico. Sound of waves splashing. GRACIELA dances folklórico on an upside down boat. She is trying to lift her brother's hand, so he will join her.

GRACIELA: C'mon. (*ALEX resists like hell. ALEX looks around. It appears that he might do it.*) It's not like anyone's going to see you.

ALEX holds his ground. He is not going to do it. GRACIELA slips, strad-dling the boat. It was not such a great surface to dance on anyway. They both break out laughing, especially ALEX.

ALEX: That was graceful, Gracie.

GRACIELA: You wanted to dance with me. (*ALEX lifts his hands up in defense. GRACIELA smacks him. He reacts. GRACIELA quickly leans against ALEX back to back. This is a game they've played before.*) Beat you to the ground. I'm faster.

ALEX: I doubt it. (*GRACIELA and ALEX lower their bodies, bending their knees. GRACIELA slides past ALEX easily.*) You cheated. (*GRACIELA lifts her hands in denial. They slide down back to back.*) Did I ever tell you I love you, Little Sis?

GRACIELA: Hey, I'm older.

ALEX: I'm taller.

The mood shifts as they relax.

GRACIELA: You did the right thing bringing Amá here. She loves the water.

ALEX: By the end of the month, we'll have lobster every day. Promise.

GRACIELA: You should save some of that money for yourself.

ALEX: It's for you guys.

GRACIELA: She'll suck you dry. She even wants a trip to the Canary Islands. She saw it on Telemundo and said, "It looks real pretty, mija." Papi would be ashamed if he knew. I can still hear him. (*Quoting him.*) "I am not a Mexican. I am not a wetback. You got to give me my minimum wage."

ALEX: What a jerk.

GRACIELA: I really believed that line about the welfare. Just an excuse to take off with that woman and her three kids.

ALEX: We're on vacation.

GRACIELA: Sometimes I think you live your whole life for him. Like all the hatred you have for him fuels you to want to be some big boxing champ. That is so twisted.

ALEX: I don't hate him. But I might be a little twisted.

GRACIELA: He'd be too embarrassed to come home.

ALEX: He's not coming home, Gracie.

GRACIELA: (*Wistfully.*) It would be nice. If he did.

ALEX: Let him go.

GRACIELA: (*Beat.*) Are you still fighting right before Cinco de Mayo even though you won in Hermosillo?

ALEX: Nope.

GRACIELA: Some guy from Brownsville got caught by the boxing commission playing both sides of the border and he lost his purse.

ALEX: Risk noted.

GRACIELA: Twenty-five K.

ALEX: Ouch.

GRACIELA: They repossessed the car he bought his mom. Had her grandson in the back seat and everything.

ALEX laughs.

ALEX: You'll believe anything, won't you? Hey, enjoy the water and chill.

GRACIELA: I can't believe you won again. What's it like—to always win?

ALEX: I don't always win. Just most times.

ALEX giggles.

GRACIELA: You're gonna be real famous someday.

ALEX: You think?

GRACIELA: Alex Moreno—the poster.

ALEX: Something for teenage girls to masturbate to.

GRACIELA: God, Alex.

ALEX: I fucked that guy up last night—kicked some Mexicano butt.

GRACIELA touches his face. Last night left some marks. She starts their routine.

GRACIELA: (*Affectionately.*) You look like shit.

ALEX: So do you.

GRACIELA laughs lightly. She starts embroidering one of three of ALEX's boxing trunks.

GRACIELA: (*Beat.*) Aren't you worried that people are going to figure out you're not from Mexico? If you keep making mistakes with your Spanish . . . It's not *la* boxeo—you sound like a sissy.

ALEX: And they love the Magdalena thing because of Colosio. "If Colosio hadn't been shot down in Tijuana while he was running for president, then everything would have turned out beautiful." Like if he would've been president, he would've cleaned up the pinche government.

GRACIELA: He would have.

ALEX: Don't tell me you believe that shit.

GRACIELA: That's why he got assassinated, pendejo, because he would have cleaned up the pinche government.

ALEX: OK, OK.

GRACIELA: So ignorant.

ALEX: Did you see those guys from Magdalena there acting like they knew me from school? They're like, "¡Órale, vato!" I love Mexico. It's OK to have a little pride. It's OK to lie to look good.

GRACIELA: I'm almost done.

ALEX reads the embroidery on the waistbands of his boxing trunks.

ALEX: (*He likes this.*) Mi vida loca. ¿Te quiero?

GRACIELA: Well, you guys are always up there hugging and shit.

ALEX: El bailador. I'm not wearing that. It's a total folklórico thing.

GRACIELA: No one will know what it means.

ALEX: You just want to make me look like a wuss.

GRACIELA: You do dance. That's what they said in *KO Magazine.* "He's got the grace of a dancer and the swing of a—"

ALEX: "Tiger."

GRACIELA: Why'd they say that?

ALEX motions with his hand, indicating that ex-boxers have scrambled brains.

ALEX: 'Cause they're written by ex-boxers. (*GRACIELA does not get it.*) They drag one leg, slur their words. Duh. Duh. Duh. You've seen los veteranos at the gym. You've seen Rainman.

GRACIELA: Rainman's not retarded?

ALEX: Hey, he had his day in the sun. He was regional champion. Three years in a row. But that was back when boxing was real dangerous. They used to schedule their fights too close together.

GRACIELA: (*Anxious.*) Muhammed Ali— (*got brain damage*)

ALEX: I thought we'd retired Muhammed Ali.

GRACIELA: Papi had those tapes of Ali, remember?

ALEX: I thought we'd retired Papi, too.

GRACIELA: "Float like a butterfly and sting like a bee." Ali was our hero and look at him now.

ALEX: Ali has Parkinson's.

GRACIELA: What makes you so special that you think it's not going to happen to you?

ALEX: Hey, I am not Muhammed Ali here. Cassius Clay had a huge fat ego. He let himself take too many hits. Whereas I wear boxing trunks that say "Te quiero." I am that macho. I am that confident. I am the only man con huevos en mi familia.

ALEX indicates his crotch.

GRACIELA: You're pretty enamored with your balls.

ALEX: I'm not enamored.

GRACIELA: You grab them like they're gold or something.

ALEX laughs a special laugh that will echo later.

ALEX: Hey, if I didn't have balls, I'd be a shitty boxer. And if I wasn't a boxer, we'd never get out of that hell hole. I'm gonna buy us a house far away from Barrio Hollywood. C'mon, a river with no water? Someone ought to condemn our entire street. I'm gonna give Amá everything she ever wanted and she'll forget about the past.

GRACIELA: Like everything with you has to be so profound.

They stand and brush the sand off themselves, walking away from the water. ALEX waves at AMÁ on the deck.

ALEX: Hey, Amá.

GRACIELA sees her and waves.

AMÁ: (*Offstage.*) That trip to the Canary Islands, Alex? Why don't we make it a cruise?

ALEX: Lo que quieras, Mami.

GRACIELA nudges him.

GRACIELA: Kiss up.

ALEX: You're cashing in on this, too.

GRACIELA: You know I don't care about money.

ALEX: What do you want for your thirtieth birthday?

GRACIELA: A dance studio with more room than the "Y," so I can teach my classes the steps I learned in Veracruz. Got enough money for that? And—

ALEX: What?

GRACIELA: You to dance folklórico with me again.

ALEX: Has it ever occurred to you to get someone else?

GRACIELA: Someone else isn't you. They don't understand.

ALEX: How do you know when you've never even looked for someone else. Take some risks, Lil' Sis. Get somebody new.

GRACIELA: They think it's wrong how much I love you, but I don't care. Just dance with me again, Alex. We dance so beautifully together. You know we do. C'mon.

ALEX: God, Gracie. Never. No fucking way.

GRACIELA: You don't have to hurt my feelings.

ALEX: Sometimes it seems like the only way to make you understand.

GRACIELA: OK, I promise to never bring it up again.

ALEX: I bet.

GRACIELA scoops up a handful of sand, sifts some of it into ALEX's hand.

GRACIELA: Here. (*He looks at it confused.*) A grain of sand for each promise. (*ALEX puts the sand in his pocket.*) What are you doing?

ALEX: Keeping track.

GRACIELA whacks him. They laugh. Lights fade on the beach.

SCENE 9

The present. Inside the Moreno home. Lights come up on AMÁ, who wears a large-brimmed straw hat and a Hawaiian short/top ensemble. She carries a suitcase. She sings to herself.

AMÁ: (*Singing.*) I love ME! Me. Me me.

GRACIELA enters.

GRACIELA: (*Singing.*) You you you.

AMÁ drops the suitcase.

AMÁ: I was just . . .

GRACIELA: Having a love fest? (*Beat.*) How's Alex doing?

AMÁ: He should be OK.

GRACIELA: Haven't you checked on him? I've got to get to rehearsal.

AMÁ: I poked my head in a few times. He was sleeping.

GRACIELA: Amá, he's been the same since he came home from the hospital. Unconscious. Where're you headed?

AMÁ: Nowheres.

GRACIELA: Do you always pack to go nowhere?

AMÁ: Just dreaming.

GRACIELA: You packed to dream?

AMÁ: I'm dreaming again about the Canary Islands. Sitting in the shade with the canaries looking down at me. I packed my bags, my bathing suit, the first day of May. Alex had already given me some money, but I waited four days to see him fight. Four days and he would have $25,000. (*Short beat; suddenly upset.*) I really want to go there.

GRACIELA: Maybe someday.

AMÁ: Maybe never. Because of Alex. (*Beat.*) Lo quiero tanto.

GRACIELA: We both love him.

AMÁ: Even if his mind took a little break like that Dr. Morris said. But these things, this mind, can come back again. It can reappear. It's gray and fuzzy so it goes away, and then one day, it comes back and it's bright like a painting, como el sol, or that lipstick at the bottom of my purse. Red and alive. Like breathing. I keep waiting for that. For the red to come back to his face. But I can't wait anymore. I can't look at him in bed like that anymore.

GRACIELA: Do you think I want to look at him? We have to, Amá.

AMÁ: For how long?

GRACIELA: Forever.

AMÁ: Maybe if I go away, he'll wake up, like when you are really hungry at a restaurant and you go to the bathroom and you come back and your food is already there. Like a miracle. (*Beat.*) Last night I turned him over. (*She points to her rear end.*) He had cuts right here. On his nalgas.

GRACIELA: I hope you put alcohol on those. They can get infected.

AMÁ: I—

GRACIELA: I'll do it.

AMÁ: I just can't—

GRACIELA: Shhh.

AMÁ: I'll go away, he'll get better. I know he will. (AMÁ *measures how small the vacation would be with her fingers.*) Un viaje corto. Para tu mamá.

GRACIELA: It would be OK with me if we didn't have to take care of Alex.

AMÁ: I was looking forward to things like that. Taking classes. Making things with my hands.

GRACIELA: I know.

AMÁ: I wanted things, too. Yo tenía sueños. Just like you want your dance studio. (*Short beat.*) I'll just be gone for a little bit. I can't help you anymore, mija. I can't help Alex. Let me go, so he can get better. I'll just close my eyes and God will make Alex well. Trust me, it will work.

GRACIELA: Don't leave us, too, Amá.

AMÁ: You have everything, mija. You have an Anglo doctor who loves you who won't run off with some puta.

GRACIELA: It's a little early to call it love.

AMÁ: You'd be crazy not to marry him. I won't be long.

GRACIELA: Amá, you have to stay. Don't leave me here alone. Please. (*No response. AMÁ gives up.*) Promise you'll be here when I come back.

AMÁ: I promise.

GRACIELA *exits.*

SCENE 10

That night. The lighting gives the effect that there is something unreal about this place. Perhaps MICHAEL *is framed in blue light or in sharp edges.* MICHAEL *wears pajamas and boxes fiercely. The only sounds we hear are* MICHAEL'S *grunts as he takes on a singular opponent.* ALEX *appears behind the scrim, boxing with a master's skill.* MICHAEL *and* ALEX *blend into one—a transference of power. Their physical movements, for a split second, mirror each other. It is as if* MICHAEL *is possessed by the spirit of* ALEX.

The sound of ballet folklórico music comes up. When the music begins, MICHAEL *is thrown off balance. Graciela dances La Negra. Her moves have a direct impact on* MICHAEL'S *and* ALEX'S *heads. The stomping of her feet becomes the pounding of their heads. The lines mimic what happens to them physically. It is no longer clear if* MICHAEL *has a singular opponent or multiple opponents as he takes hits from all sides.*

MICHAEL: Trapped. Inside my body. Want out. Want freedom. From hand to head, nothing happens. Know how to take a punch—how to give one. Body stuck. Mind locked inside. Stuck. No freedom—can't speak—no voice. Better to drive on outta here. Drift on away.

ALEX *disappears.* GRACIELA *enters in a white nightgown and lies down on the ground under a light cotton blanket.* MICHAEL *has joined her under the blanket as though they were asleep for the night. A boxing bell rings.* MICHAEL *jerks up, awakening from his dream.* GRACIELA *does not stir. Michael instinctively gets up to check on* ALEX. *Bleary-eyed and a little clumsy,* MICHAEL *crosses into* ALEX'S *room. He is gone for several seconds.*

MICHAEL: Graciela! (GRACIELA *stirs, rolling over onto her side.* MICHAEL *enters distraught.*) Graciela. (GRACIELA *looks up at him.*) Alex is dead.

GRACIELA *leaps to her feet, pacing with her hands on her head. She stops moving, gathers her composure.*

GRACIELA: Amá! Amá! (*Graciela goes to* AMÁ'S *room. She comes out pale and a bit spooked after a long beat.*) Oh my God. She's gone.

Blackout.

SCENE 1

The next day. GRACIELA *leans in front of the outdoor barrio altar—El Tiradito.* GRACIELA *lights candles. It's a private moment. She is distraught—visibly shaken. In fact, her hand shakes so hard, she can hardly light the candle. The match goes out. Flustered, she lights another match.* MICHAEL *enters.*

MICHAEL: Did you want me to get that for you? (*The match goes out when* GRACIELA *turns, startled, to look at him.*) I didn't mean to startle you.

GRACIELA: I—

MICHAEL: Shh.

GRACIELA: I—I can't . . . see—

MICHAEL: Shh.

GRACIELA: —Him.

    MICHAEL *holds her.*

MICHAEL: It's time, Graciela. The police are ready for us.

GRACIELA: I keep . . . looking. I don't . . . see him.

MICHAEL: (*Comforting.*) Shh.

GRACIELA: I saw him—every day. (*As if looking at* ALEX's *face.*) His face.

MICHAEL: I know.

GRACIELA: I never memorized him. (*She strikes her own heart.*) My heart . . . (*he holds her hand there*) forgot. (MICHAEL *takes her hands.*)

MICHAEL: Your mind remembers everything it's ever seen. It's the most amazing organ—the human brain.

GRACIELA: Not that amazing. When I get a scratch on my skin, my skin knows to grow back.

    GRACIELA *leans on* MICHAEL *as he leads her away.*

SCENE 2

Later that day. The police station. GRACIELA *sits in a chair on stage right.* MICHAEL *sits in a similar chair on stage left. It should be clear that these interviews are not happening in the same room although they are occurring simultaneously.*

GRACIELA: About 10 p.m. That's when I last saw Alex alive.

MICHAEL: Her brother basically died the night of the fight. Sure, when she came into the hospital that day, I fell in love with her. I'm not going to defend that.

GRACIELA: Then at about 10:30 my boyfriend, Michael, came to spend the night. (*Nervous laugh.*) I don't usually have men over—

MICHAEL: Her love for her brother devastated her. I wanted to be part of a person who could love like that.

GRACIELA: You're not thinking Michael did this, are you? There's no chance that he did it. You don't understand what was going on.

MICHAEL: Maybe God just found a way to set Alex free.

GRACIELA: (*Beat.*) But we didn't have the heart to do what he suggested.

MICHAEL: The doctor didn't bother to tell them what they could do.

GRACIELA: Maybe we should have. (*Beat.*) Don't you know?

> *GRACIELA looks up at them. They don't get it. She motions pulling an IV out of his arm.*

MICHAEL: To stop feeding him.

GRACIELA: Can you picture a family doing that?

MICHAEL: (*Agitated.*) It happened because his mother had propped him up to watch Saturday Night Boxing on Mexican TV. His head fell back and got caught between the rails of the headboard.

GRACIELA: (*Reality starts dawning on her.*) Oh, I have no idea where my mother went.

MICHAEL: (*Beat.*) She's scared. She sure as hell isn't going to come here to talk to you.

GRACIELA: We acted like we never smelled him, but we did.

MICHAEL: A beautiful woman like Graciela all closed up in that house. It was a waste.

GRACIELA: Maybe my mom just stepped out for some fresh air—to talk to God. She'll be back.

MICHAEL: (*In love.*) Graciela? How can anyone be objective about Graciela? You should see her dance. So much class. Like a queen. Made up perfectly like a photograph. Her hair pulled back tightly in a bun. And the eyes . . .

GRACIELA: (*Long beat.*) She wanted to believe.

MICHAEL: The way I see it is Alex's mother made a simple mistake and Alex choked on the headboard. That's why his windpipe collapsed. Now, those two nice ladies get to go on with their lives. The whole thing just makes you want to have faith.

GRACIELA: See, where I come from, if you have faith, God has pity on you and makes things better. It's like He reaches His hand into your head and captures whatever picture you hold there. And if you imagine it just right, He'll set his hand down on earth and set that picture free. He makes it real. But you've got to believe. That's the first rule of faith. (*Beat.*) My mother? She does what she wants. (*Realizing she's incriminated* AMÁ.) Well, she wants what's best for us. Me and Alex. That's all I meant.

MICHAEL: Look, I'm a doctor. If I'm not willing to deal with the sick, I'm a hypocrite. (*Beat.*) There is no murderer here.

GRACIELA: (*Upset.*) Murder? My brother was a VEGETABLE. (*Beat.*) Fucking chota. Here. Why don't you arrest me instead? If you have to blame someone, why don't you blame me?

GRACIELA offers her hands.

SCENE 3

Later that day. Lights shift to AMÁ, *who enters handcuffed. It is clear she is in a separate space from the other two.*

AMÁ: My son. My child is dead. And you blame me? He killed him. Michael took Alex's throat in his hands and he killed him. I saw the whole thing. That horrible man murdered my son. I *am* a witness! I want that man to go to the electric chair! I want him dead! Let him feel what it feels like to be murdered. (*More upset.*) My son was going to be fine. He had a difficult few months, but he was going to be fine. (*Short beat.*) I did not sneak off. I went out for some air. (*Short beat.*) No, I did not know he was dead when I left. I had no idea until you said it to me. What do you mean—contradicting myself? (*Beat.*) You already have ideas in your head. I can see them floating around in there. I can see that! I didn't go to school. I don't have perfect English like you, but I can see this. This is not right. (*Short beat.*) I saw everything. Don't pretend. When you know. (*Breaking down.*) The truth.

Let me see Graciela. She knows why this happened. (*To herself.*) Taking me from my church. From my prayers. When my God comforts me. That's who I love. That's who I listen to. Él siempre está conmigo. You and your fancy cars. You and your guns. You've never done nothing good for me. (*Short beat; yelling to someone as if he's leaving.*) Give me back my suitcase! My son gave me that. Para mi cumpleaños. For my birthday trip. He's giving it to me as a gift. When Graciela turns thirty, I turn forty-eight. Only two days apart. (*Getting emotional.*) I saw that pretty island on Channel 52. I saw it in *Spanich.* It was a beautiful place with canaries up in the trees. And water—bluer than your eyes. You can see little canaries there like lizards in the desert. Singing all the time. Making everybody happy. And everybody could be happy if some people let God do His job.

(*AMÁ starts crying.*) Simple things. That's all I ever wanted. (*Short beat.*) I didn't kill Alex with my hands but by wanting so much. And he wanted so much to give me those things. He fought when he was bleeding. When he couldn't see. He fought for money. But I kept wanting more. And you know how God feels about that! You must accept what He gives you. And smile. BECAUSE THAT IS HOW GOD WORKS! He makes the rules. He decides. And you take it. Whatever hand you're dealt. But you gotta keep your poker face on. You gotta look like you're winning or you lose that much more. My grandfather taught me that. He was a poker player from Chihuahua. He knew how to fool people into believing him. (*Quickly.*) That's not what I meant.

Blackout.

SCENE 4

A week later. Lights come up on the jail. AMÁ *and* GRACIELA *are separated by a clear screen.* AMÁ, *dressed in an orange prison jumpsuit, looks around for bugs.*

GRACIELA: Amá, it's private. They assured me. No bugs.

AMÁ: You never know. I saw a telenovela once where this woman said something to her daughter in the pinta and they used it against her in court. They gave her the electric chair. Her hair was sticking up to the ceiling. Like this. (*She motions and laughs nervously.*)

GRACIELA: They're not gonna give you the electric chair. This case is totally bogus.

AMÁ: Who said so?

GRACIELA: I said so.

AMÁ: (*Registers disappointment.*) They told me they want to put me in the prison. That I have to confess. I told them I'm guilty, but they want more. They want me to tell them every part. And I tell them, I don't remember. Every part. Only that I'm guilty, and I am, mija.

GRACIELA: We'll get you out of this.

AMÁ: How?

GRACIELA: We'll figure out a way.

AMÁ: I lied to them. I had to. Four hours they kept me in there. With no water. They didn't let me go to the bathroom. I had to pee! (*Beat.*) They just kept telling me to sign that little piece of paper and everything would be all right. But I'm too smart for them. Too smart to fall for their tricks. I know the police here *think* you're supposed to call them first when somebody dies, but I couldn't do that. You can't trust la chota.

GRACIELA: You can't.

AMÁ: (*Slowly, whispering.*) He was dead already when I left. But I don't think they need to know that. Why would they need to know? (*AMÁ looks around carefully to make sure no one is hearing her.*) That's why I went to the church. To talk to him. I missed him already. But we've missed him since Cinco de Mayo, ¿qué no? I just wanted to talk to him before all the craziness started. Before they took his body away. Because I saw this coming. I saw it ahead. Just like my amá used to see things and warn me before they happened. I could see the little pictures in my brain. And I didn't want them to be real for us. Para nuestra familia. But it's true. I put my hand on his neck and he was dead. His skin felt hard like a rock, and I lied about it.

GRACIELA: Why did you tell the police you saw Michael do it when you know he didn't?

AMÁ: I didn't stop him, mija. I didn't stop him because part of me wanted Alex to be dead. But it wasn't right. Alex should have died when God wanted him to die, not Michael.

GRACIELA: It wasn't Michael's fault.

AMÁ: He had ideas in his head. I hate him.

GRACIELA: I love him.

AMÁ: Promise me you'll never see him again. It's not right to turn your back on a sick person when you're supposed to be helping him.

GRACIELA: Maybe it was what had to be done—all that could be done. (*Tearing up.*) Don't tell me you believe Alex was going to spring back to life and shower you with gifts? And kiss you on the cheek like you liked him to. He wasn't. He wasn't ever going to wake up again.

AMÁ: Michael left no place for God to do His miracle work. And God owed me one. He did. God was doing a miracle for Alex to make up for the years I spent with your father. (*Breaking.*) He owed me that. And He was this close to doing it. I could feel it. He was thinking about doing something special just for us, and Michael had to come in and spoil everything.

GRACIELA: Don't blame Michael. Alex's head fell back by itself. I don't see why we have to blame someone. Why does someone always have to take the responsibility?

AMÁ: I'm not afraid of taking the responsibility. I'm not afraid of dying.

GRACIELA: (*Beat; offhandedly.*) Do you want me to just say that I did it so you can leave?

AMÁ: No. Don't lie to them. I already lied to them. We don't need you lying to them, too.

GRACIELA: Amá, I did—

AMÁ: It's a lie and I don't want to hear it again.

GRACIELA: It would get you free.

AMÁ: (*Firmly.*) No. I want to die. Maybe it would be a relief. I could just leave this earth. Like a breath.

GRACIELA: Don't say that.

AMÁ: I would see Alex again. At the end of a dark tunnel, there's a light. I read it in the *National Enquirer.* And all your familia waits for you there.

Heaven—it's beautiful. The mountains and the trees. I could see him there. Again. I do love him. (*Back to reality.*) Oh, I love you, too. You know that, don't you?

GRACIELA: I know.

AMÁ: Do you know how much?

GRACIELA: (*Crying.*) I think I might.

AMÁ: It's hard to show you when I feel frozen inside. Like the meat in the freezer with little bits of ice in the cracks of my skin. I don't like this feeling, mija, because it is no feeling. No siento nada. I try and try to push my tears out, but there is no water left inside me.

GRACIELA: We cried a lot when he first got hurt. That's when we said good-bye.

AMÁ: (*Sighs.*) I hate it here. They don't let me light my candles or nothing.

GRACIELA: I'll light one for you at home and at El Tiradito, too.

AMÁ: Would you?

GRACIELA: Of course. (*Crying.*) I light a candle for you every night. I pray for you. Because I know you are innocent and someday you will come home.

AMÁ looks up at the clock on the wall.

AMA: Thank you for visiting your amá.

GRACIELA: (*Beat.*) Let me change this.

AMÁ: You cannot change this.

GRACIELA: (*Beat.*) You know I can.

AMÁ: (*Firmly.*) You will not change this, Graciela.

GRACIELA: But—

AMÁ: (*Almost harsh.*) Don't.

It becomes clear AMÁ won't relent.

GRACIELA: (*Conceding.*) OK, wa.

AMÁ: Don't let him into our lives again, mija. You and I do much better on our own. We do. We don't need some gabacho telling us what to do. We don't need some gabacho killing us in the middle of the night. I'd sleep better if you just let him go back where he belongs. Over there. ¿Verdad? (*Beat.*) Please. Do what I say. (*GRACIELA begins to walk away.*) Graciela.

SCENE 5

Later that day. El Tiradito. GRACIELA is alone praying in front of the altar.

GRACIELA: You're not allowed to see me, so go away.

MICHAEL: That's not how you feel.

GRACIELA: Amá has her rules.

MICHAEL: You've broken them before. We made love in your bedroom. (*Short beat.*) Three-and-a-half times. (*Michael touches* GRACIELA. *Emotionally.*) You love me.

GRACIELA: You need to go.

MICHAEL: (*Beat.*) Does it bother you to feel something for me?

GRACIELA: I promised I wouldn't.

MICHAEL: You promised your mother you wouldn't love me? (*Beat.*) Because she hallucinated that I killed Alex? (*No response.*) You don't believe that bullshit, do you?

GRACIELA: (*Softens.*) I don't know what I know.

MICHAEL: (*Short beat.*) You love me.

GRACIELA: I was starting to. I could feel it in there, like a little sprout trying to burst through the hard earth. A little flower in my heart, but you killed it.

MICHAEL: Well, mine was more than a sprout. It was kind of like a whole tree.

GRACIELA: Do you think true love can grow that fast?

MICHAEL: All I know is what I feel for you is pretty damn special. I want to feel that way forever.

GRACIELA: (*Fishing; calm.*) Why'd you say Alex choked on the rails of the headboard?

MICHAEL: I didn't do it. You know I didn't.

GRACIELA: I just want to know why you said it.

MICHAEL: I was trying to protect your mother.

GRACIELA: (*Disappointed.*) Oh.

MICHAEL: Why do you think I said it?

GRACIELA: They should let her come home. She deserves that, don't you think?

MICHAEL: She confessed, Graciela. Jesus. Of course they're going to hold her.

GRACIELA: She confessed because she feels guilty. (*Yells.*) Because she has a conscience. Because of some fleeting thought she had one day.

MICHAEL: She feels guilty because she did it. It was her mistake.

GRACIELA: You don't understand us at all.

MICHAEL: I didn't want to see the police breathing down your throats because of some corpse with a heartbeat. That's why I made the head rail comment. I didn't off your brother. Frankly, I don't care why she did it. It was an asinine way to kill him. That is my only thought on the matter. (*Beat.*) Someday, we could have a really beautiful life together. You and me.

GRACIELA *kisses him on the side of the mouth.*

GRACIELA: (*Solemn.*) It's spoiled—paradise. It's like all the canaries have died and God doesn't live here anymore.

MICHAEL: You have no faith.

MICHAEL moves in closer to GRACIELA. She resists the attraction.

GRACIELA: It wouldn't work anyway. You don't understand my language.

MICHAEL: I'm studying Spanish.

GRACIELA: That's not the language I'm talking about, Michael. The language of my heart. (*Beat.*) My family moves in me. Like breathing itself.

MICHAEL: You're turning me down? (*GRACIELA remains tight, doesn't relent. MICHAEL remains in disbelief. Beat.*) I know how to love, Graciela. I'm a person who knows how to do that. You don't have a corner on love or family just because you're a Mexican. I have fought for your rights in this case. I have fought for the rights of your mother. I have fought. And if that isn't understanding the language of your heart, I don't know what is.

GRACIELA: Just leave.

MICHAEL: (*Long beat.*) So, you're just going to rot away doing your dance classes forever? You're going to do that when you're sixty and you're living in poverty here in this fucked-up place?

GRACIELA: This fucked-up place is my home.

MICHAEL: I didn't mean—(*that*).

GRACIELA: Sure, you meant that. (*Beat.*) I'm not going to be your pity-wife. (*Short beat.*) So leave. I can clean up my own family's mess.

MICHAEL: (*Realizing.*) Did you clean up your own family's mess?

GRACIELA: Leave.

MICHAEL: I love you anyway.

GRACIELA watches him walk off. Blackout.

SCENE 6

Lights up on GRACIELA at the police station. She has a bag full of visual aids. She pulls out specific items to punctuate her points. She is on stage alone facing the police detective.

GRACIELA: Detective, you've gotta see this. I really think there's been some confusion here. (*She pulls the IV apparatus out of her bag and sets it on the table.*) He ate out of this. (*She sticks the bedpan on the table.*) He shit in this. (*She pulls out a sheet with red bloodstains.*) And if we didn't turn him enough, he'd bleed all over this. (*Beat.*) You and your men combed my house for evidence. There just isn't any proof that my amá, or anyone, calculated in any way to kill my brother. What do you have? A head rail. Evidence of some fanciful murder. Alex had his pride. He wouldn't have wanted his sister cleaning his bedpan. What do all these things prove, Detective?

To live you have to think. You have to laugh to be alive. (*Beat.*) Alex was this miserable piece of flesh we prayed over. (*Beat.*) How could God sit up there in heaven and watch us go through this and do absolutely nothing? (*Up *to God.*) How dare you, God? How dare you? Oh, He's not there, I know, but I still like to pretend. (*Upset.*) Because He used to bring me comfort.

Blackout.

SCENE 7

Later that day. Lights shift. GRACIELA *is alone on stage in the semi-dark. She lights a candle with a picture of the Virgin of Guadalupe on it. She is in front of her altar.*

GRACIELA: Amá's free, Virgen. The cops let her go. Not enough evidence, I guess. I'm just letting you know what happened. In case you're not paying attention. In case you're too busy with India or the Middle East or something. In case other people in the world have problems that are so much worse than ours. Is it true, Virgencita? Do you always forgive like Amá says? Will the words I speak on earth be swept up with the wind and somehow catch your ear in heaven? (*Beat.*) You wouldn't punish me for wanting us to be free, would you? For wanting to dance—to hear their applause. Every time they put their hands together, I feel it in my heart like one very loud beat. (GRACIELA *claps her hands together, once and slowly.*) And I keep on living. (*Beat.*) I can't sleep. Not since that night. (*Beat.*) Do you really spy on us from behind your cloud like Amá says? (*Long beat.*) You could let me know if you do. You could bring me roses in winter or something. Like you did for Juan Diego. To help me believe. (GRACIELA *lifts the candle skyward.*) Can you see my little candle? It's just one tiny light and the world is so big. Free me. Like you did her. Free me. From that picture of what I did to him stuck in my mind. Virgen, I want you to know that I loved my brother. With everything inside me. And if there is any way in your great big heart that you can find a space for me, where I can sit and rest for a moment, I ask that you let me in there.

GRACIELA *closes her eyes in prayer.* ALEX *enters. They are now inside the Virgin's heart—red, pink, and beating.* GRACIELA *opens her eyes and sees him.*

GRACIELA: (*Hard to say.*) I . . . killed you.

ALEX: I thought I recognized that half-assed manicure job.

GRACIELA: It's not funny.

ALEX: You were praying for forgiveness.

GRACIELA: They would have left you unconscious forever. We would never have danced again. Could you see me with my feet pinned to the ground? You—pinned to a body that couldn't move?

ALEX: Heaven's better. Tougher boxers.

GRACIELA: (*In a tizzy.*) I'm imagining you, right? Because I haven't slept. I'm trying to get strong. Trying not to die. Dying seems so easy sometimes—dying seems like it sneaks right up on you when you're not paying attention.

Do you forgive me? (*ALEX nods. She touches ALEX.*) You're back. (*Beat.*) I can see you in my mind again. And you're not the way you were at the hospital at all. (*Delighting in the memory.*) But you're bright and awake. And we're laughing like we used to. We're getting ready to perform and we're standing in the dressing room and my hair is all stiff from the hairspray. And my face is red from the rouge. And you're putting on your pants, trying not to notice that every girl there, except me, is watching you buckle yourself. You tap your foot. That's my cue. It's just a simple tap at first. (*ALEX starts to tap his foot. It is the beginning of a simple folkórico step. GRACIELA begins to slowly tap in unison with him. She stops.*) I have to call the police. I have to turn myself in.

ALEX: I can see things now I never imagined. I can see your soul.

GRACIELA: Does it have like a big black stain on it?

ALEX: No. (*GRACIELA opens her mouth to protest.*) You'll just have to trust me on that.

GRACIELA: (*Beat.*) Did you ever feel like you failed the one person you loved most in the world?

ALEX: I was never going to wake up again. It was brave what you did, but you always were my protector—the one. The only one I could count on. In this life. For reals.

GRACIELA: I feel like you're leaving me.

ALEX: I am.

GRACIELA: In Barrio Hollywood, you will always be alive to me. Like a lively ghost. With hands and feet. Who sometimes likes to dance. Who strokes your face when you're crying. Who grasps your hand when you feel alone. (*Beat.*) Don't go yet.

ALEX: Gracie, we're dance partners. I'm a part of you, and you're a part of me.

ALEX strokes GRACIELA's face as she is crying and grasps her hand. He kisses her good-bye.

GRACIELA: Did I ever tell you I love you, Little Bro?

ALEX: (*Giggles. Beat.*) You know what would really make me happy, Gracie? If you let yourself love somebody else.

GRACIELA: But I love you.

ALEX: Somebody who isn't family.

GRACIELA: They don't understand—when they're not family.

ALEX: Somebody alive.

ALEX hands her some sand.

GRACIELA: (*Surprised.*) Sand? A grain of sand for each promise.

ALEX: You can do it. I know you can.

GRACIELA: (*As he walks off.*) Just one more dance, Alex. Just one more dance.

It is too late for him to answer, and the Virgin's heart disappears.

SCENE 8

Moreno home. MICHAEL *bumps into* AMÁ *while she is outside watering the plants.* AMÁ *crosses back into the house without saying a word.* GRACIELA *hangs up a paper cut-out streamer that says "Welcome Home."*

GRACIELA: Go back out there. I'm not done yet.

AMÁ: He's out there.

GRACIELA: I didn't invite him over.

MICHAEL: (*Still outside.*) I love her!

GRACIELA *hears this from inside the house. She can't help but smile.*

AMÁ: Screaming out there. For all the neighbors to hear. (GRACIELA *starts to leave.*) Don't— (go).

GRACIELA *opens the door.*

GRACIELA: I'm just gonna . . . tell him to leave. (GRACIELA *steps outside.*) Hi.

MICHAEL: Hi.

GRACIELA: You came back.

MICHAEL: Didn't know where else to go really. Just wandering around out there. In the desert. Driving.

GRACIELA: Do you wanna come in? Actually, let's just stay out here.

MICHAEL: OK. (MICHAEL *and* GRACIELA *sit on the top step of the wooden porch. The night sky has made a display of stars. He takes her hand.*) Feels good— holding your hand.

GRACIELA: Yeah.

MICHAEL: I'm sorry.

GRACIELA: No, I'm sorry.

MICHAEL: Most women would give up after a fight like that.

GRACIELA: (*Long beat.*) Do you think killing your little brother is love?

MICHAEL: It can be. The truest, purest act of love.

GRACIELA: "Thou shall not kill." One of the Ten Commandments.

MICHAEL: When they hang on like that, it can go on for years. And it's the family who suffers. You did the right thing.

GRACIELA: It was an asinine way to do it.

MICHAEL: You're a woman who knows how to love, Graciela. You're a person who knows how to do that.

GRACIELA: (*Touched.*) Stop. (*Beat.*) It's hard. To let yourself love somebody . . . different. (*Beat.*) It's hard. (*Beat.*) For me. (*Beat.*) But I love you. Phew! I've never said that to a man before.

MICHAEL: I don't believe that.

GRACIELA: (*An admission.*) It feels like I've never said it before.

MICHAEL: I love you, too.

GRACIELA: (*Beat.*) You're really different from us, but you know you are. That's what makes you special.

MICHAEL: (*Beat.*) Is your amá gonna have trouble if we get back together?

GRACIELA: Yeah.

MICHAEL: (*Disappointed.*) Oh.

GRACIELA: Just because it's hard doesn't mean we shouldn't do it.

MICHAEL: Does she know what really happened?

GRACIELA: Little girls don't commit murder. I'm supposed to agree that you did it.

MICHAEL: Wow.

GRACIELA: It's complicated family stuff.

MICHAEL: I understand.

GRACIELA: I don't think it will ever come up again if that helps.

MICHAEL: OK, *wa.*

 GRACIELA *laughs.*

GRACIELA: Now we got you saying "*wa.*"

MICHAEL: I've always said "*wa.*"

There's an awkward silence. Then, they relax more into the silence. They look at the sky.

GRACIELA: (*Beat.*) If you could do one thing in the whole world that you've never done before, what would it be?

MICHAEL: Let me think.

GRACIELA: C'mon, you're not supposed to think. You're supposed to just say it.

MICHAEL: I can't just say it. That's not the way my mind works.

GRACIELA: Come on. Blurt.

MICHAEL: (*Long beat.*) I'd learn to dance the dance with you. I'd hold my head in place and have that serious look, and have my hand against my waist right over my belt buckle, and you would find me attractive. And nobody would say, "What's that white guy doing up there dancing like that?" Nobody would even notice. They would just see two people dancing and they would know I'm a part of you and you're a part of me.

The echo of ALEX's *words moves* GRACIELA. GRACIELA *kisses him gently. A quiet moment.*

GRACIELA: (*Long beat.*) Listen. Can you hear . . . my little brother laugh?

MICHAEL strains to hear, gives up.

MICHAEL: I guess I don't live in the magical world that you do.

GRACIELA grabs MICHAEL's hand.

GRACIELA: Stay with me. And you will.

In the distance, there is the faint sound of ALEX's *laugh.* MICHAEL *registers it.* GRACIELA *stands and pulls* MICHAEL *toward her, teaching him the first steps of the folklórico dance she danced earlier with* ALEX. *In the Tucson night sky, a storm brews. The thunderous crack of a summer thunderstorm. Lightning lights up the sky. A light rain begins falling.*

As they dance in the rain, lights dim. ALEX's *laugh cracks again and grows faint, but they don't hear it because they are wrapped up in each other. Lights fade to black.)*

End of play

"YO, CASIMIRO FLORES"

SILVIANA WOOD

About the Play

Of all the plays in this anthology, *"Yo, Casimiro Flores"* is the most traditional when it comes to representing Chicano and Yaqui culture, reflecting decidedly Mexican values and popular celebrations.

This full-length play centers on the celebration of the Día de los Muertos, the Day of the Dead, a traditional holiday during which people remember and honor loved ones who have died. The commemoration consists of decorating their tombs or graves with colorful flowers and altars, preparing their favorite foods and beverages, and having a picnic at the cemetery. It is believed that the souls of those who have died return on the Día de los Muertos to eat the food that has been prepared in their honor.

"Yo, Casimiro Flores" starts with the main character having a nightmare and regretting the fact that four of his friends died when they all tried to cross the border illegally. Casimiro had the opportunity to help one survive, but his fear paralyzed him. On this Day of the Dead, Casimiro plans to set up the altar in memory of those fallen friends and to bring their favorite foods and drinks to their burial places, but instead he gets drunk, wishes to die, and, as the saying "be careful what you wish for" suggests, Death pays him a visit. Death in this case is not the typical grim reaper; instead it is the Aztec god of the dead, Mictlantecuhtli, and his sidekick, Calavera Nurse, both of whom are equipped with beepers. Mictlantecuhtli gives Casimiro an opportunity to redeem himself, and in the process the latter encounters a variety of characters ranging from those in traditional folklore tales, such as La Llorona, to popular real-life Mexican "legends," such as Cantinflas.

Through the use of numerous theatrical devices and symbolic images, *"Yo, Casimiro Flores"* reflects the hybridity of Chicano culture from the time of the Aztecs to the present day. The play teaches not only about a traditional Mexican holiday but also about Mechicanos' lives, the concept of the afterworld, and, above all, the rich culture that makes Chicanos, Yaquis, and Mexicans unique.

The development and first production of *"Yo, Casimiro Flores"* at the historic Guadalupe Theater in San Antonio, Texas, was made possible by the Guadalupe Cultural Arts Center under the Gateway Project funded by the Ford Foundation. The original music used in the play was composed by Raúl González Guzmán, and the production was directed by Richard Talavera.

About the Author

A native of Tucson, Arizona, Silviana Wood received her MFA in creative writing from the University of Arizona and has been involved in the local theater community since the 1970s. She is known for her bilingual comedies and dramas as well as for her work as a professional storyteller, actor, director, and teacher of literature and Chicano theater. For many years she appeared in *Reflexiones*, a program on the University of Arizona's PBS station KUAT-TV, as the feisty Doña Chona, an elderly woman who had an opinion on everything and who without hesitation would call the White House collect to give advice on running the country.

Wood is the author of many plays, including *Anhelos por Oaxaca, Amor de hija*, and *A Drunkard's Tale of Melted Wings and Memories*, and her works have been produced in Arizona, California, Texas, Colorado, New York, and Massachusetts. *And where was Pancho Villa when you* really *needed him?*, about a high school dropout's remembrance of fifth grade and her language difficulties and "failure" to assimilate, was published by the University of Arizona Press in *Puro Teatro, A Latina Anthology* (Alberto Sandoval-Sánchez and Nancy Saporta Sternbach, eds.). It was performed at the Henry Street Settlement/Abrons Art Center Urban Youth Theater in New York City and at the TV Studio, Mendenhall Center for the Performing Arts, Smith College, Northampton, Massachusetts.

Silviana Wood has twice won the Chicano/Latino Literary Prize from the University of California, Irvine: once for short story, and once for drama. In 1993 she was awarded the Arizona Arts Award from the Tucson Community Foundation. She has also received playwriting fellowships and done several residencies at the Guadalupe Cultural Arts Center in San Antonio. She has been a member of TENAZ (El Teatro Nacional de Aztlán), Teatro del Pueblo, Teatro Libertad, and Teatro Chicano and is a founding member of Mujeres Que Escriben, a Latina writers' group that was formed in 1991 and is comprised of professional women whose poetry and fiction have been published in various anthologies. She recently completed her first novel, *La Quinta Soledad*, which will be published by Aztlan Libre Press in 2014.

CHARACTERS

Except for CASIMIRO, ROCKY ROAD, MAD DOG, XOCHIL, DON PRISCILIANO, and MICTLANTECUHTLI, most roles may be doubled, depending on blocking and costume changes.

CASIMIRO FLORES:	a Yaqui in his late thirties
EL COYOTE:	any age
MIGUEL:	mid- to late teens
JESÚS:	mid- to late teens
CARLOS:	mid- to late teens
MARIEL:	age fifteen
DON REMIGIO:	a Yaqui maestro, very old, strong in appearance and bearing
THE HUNTER/BORDER PATROL AGENT:	any age
MICTLANTECUHTLI:	costumed and masked, tall, imposing, ageless
CALAVERA NURSE:	preferably chubby, in her forties or older
ROCKY ROAD:	twenty-five
MAD DOG:	very thin, young teen
XOCHIL:	fourteen, soon-to-be fifteen
DON PRISCILIANO:	old man, in his seventies
ALLEGORICAL DANGERS:	boulders, blades, winds, jaguars, and lizards
CANTINFLAS:	Need we say more? Rent and watch his movies.
LA LLORONA:	any age
CÉSAR CHÁVEZ:	dignified bearing, in his sixties
EHECATL:	costumed and masked, any age
MARÍA ISABEL:	chubby, in her seventies
EL TANQUE:	an obese, huge teen
EL PEEWA:	a runty, skinny teen

Also, recorded offstage voices of MANUEL, CASIMIRO'S MOTHER, XOCHIL'S MOTHER, MAD DOG'S FOSTER MOTHER, and ROCKY'S SUGAR DADDY.

TIME

The present, a combined Halloween and Día de los Muertos, but note that CASIMIRO's dream takes place in 1977, somewhere at the border between Mexico and the United States.

PLACE

The basement of an understaffed, underfunded general hospital near a barrio somewhere in the Southwest.

SET

There are many hospital or office room-dividers in various stages of disrepair and abandonment, overhead water/heating pipes, plastic bags filled with garbage, several laundry duffel bags, a few old Halloween decorations, and a ramp or step unit, preferably at center upstage, that leads to upstairs. There is a small, cramped rest area for CASIMIRO's coffee breaks: a small table with a large bowl of Halloween candies and the makings for instant coffee; a small portable TV near an old, beat-up recliner covered with a sarape; one or two chairs; and a box filled with a photo, pom-pom, food and drink, flowers, candles, etc., for the altar that CASIMIRO will set up on the table. GERALDINE, CASIMIRO's best friend, is a discarded classroom skeleton that hangs on a nearby stand, dressed in her vintage Goodwill finery; a cigarette dangles from her upraised hand or from her mouth. The set does not change during ACT ONE.

TECHNICAL NOTES

The transitional lights between scenes should be down and up quickly even though the actors may not be completely in place. The music may start sooner than is indicated on script. An off-stage actor or technician will be needed for GERALDINE's movements. The friends' dialogue in ACT ONE, Scenes 2 and 3 may be prerecorded for ethereal effect.

SCENE 1 ■ CASIMIRO'S DREAM

The introductory music is mysterious, dreamy. Lights come up as a soft moonlight is seen; on CASIMIRO at center stage, shadows. CASIMIRO is acting out his dream. He is dressed in his janitor's uniform with his hospital identification badge over his shirt pocket, but he is wearing parts of the Yaqui deer dancer's costume: a deer head with a red scarf tied across its antlers over a folded white handkerchief, cocoon rattles on his ankles, and a gourd in each hand. He is crouched, wary. The music changes to indigenous music or "la Danza del Venado." CASIMIRO dances; his movements should be hesitant and unskilled, but determined. EL COYOTE, wearing border cowboy clothes and a coyote mask, enters and joins the dance, stalking CASIMIRO. They hear a noise and EL COYOTE hides.

The music now changes to the same mysterious and dreamy introductory music from before. CASIMIRO's four friends, MIGUEL, CARLOS, JESÚS, and MARIEL, enter. They are holding hands, helping each other in the desert darkness, and they are dressed for travel, carrying mochilas with their few clothes and containers of food and water.

CASIMIRO: (*Urging them.*) ¡Aquí, Miguel! Apúrate, Carlos. Cuidado con los nopales. ¡Miguel! Ayúdale a Jesús. Mariel, ¡dame la mano!

EL COYOTE comes out of his hiding place, hands out for his money. Everyone pays EL COYOTE. The four friends sense danger, but CASIMIRO reassures them and they follow him and EL COYOTE. Unseen by them, EL COYOTE gives a signal and quickly hides again. Gunshots are heard; lights become jumpy and erratic, following the running figures who are trying to hide and escape from the bullets. CASIMIRO and his friends run.

CASIMIRO: ¡Mariel! ¡Corre conmigo! (*Goes toward MARIEL.*)

MARIEL: ¡Casimiro! No puedo ver; ¡dame tu mano!

MARIEL puts her hand out to CASIMIRO. He goes to MARIEL and is ready to take her hand, but hesitates. He moves away from her quickly and hides. Louder gunshots are heard. CASIMIRO's friends are trapped, cornered. They are shot, and they fall to the ground, dying and wounded. CASIMIRO reacts but stays hidden. Music abruptly changes to joyous, lively music. EL COYOTE and CASIMIRO come out of hiding, and EL COYOTE gives CASIMIRO half of the money. They embrace and dance happily, waving the money in the air. A loud, sharp drumbeat is heard. The music is indigenous, blended with violin. DON REMIGIO enters, beating a drum. He's dressed completely in black, with a ragged black poncho over his pants and shirt, an old beat-up cowboy hat, and boots.

CASIMIRO: ¡Tata Remigio! (*Shows him the money.*) Mire, ahora sí tengo dinero para—

DON REMIGIO angrily pushes CASIMIRO's hand aside, and the money falls to the ground. CASIMIRO kneels and starts to pick up the money.

DON REMIGIO: (*Pointing at EL COYOTE accusingly.*) ¡Coyote maldito!

EL COYOTE slinks away with guilt. DON REMIGIO turns to exit.

CASIMIRO: (*Stands up.*) Tata Remigio, espere. (*Pleads, almost childlike.*) No se vaya; mire, ya mero aprendo su danza; mire, abuelito. (*Starts to dance.*)

Once again, the indigenous music or "la Danza del Venado" is heard. CASIMIRO dances but DON REMIGIO remains unimpressed, disapproving. THE HUNTER enters. He is armed and dressed in either military or Border Patrol uniform. CASIMIRO continues dancing and THE HUNTER stalks and shoots CASIMIRO. A gunshot is heard. CASIMIRO starts to fall. Freeze. Music goes up for the freeze, then down, then continues and blends with the drum beating. CASIMIRO falls to the ground; THE HUNTER takes the deer head as a trophy, and EL COYOTE takes the money and the gourds. THE HUNTER and EL COYOTE exit on very good terms.

DON REMIGIO: (*Begins to sing or chant a Yaqui prayer.*) Vesate sewau hotekate; sewa valikai, sewau hotekatee.

FOUR FRIENDS: (*Rise. In unison, repeat slowly in Spanish as they cross to CASIMIRO.*) Ya nos sentamos a la flor; para recibir la flor, nos sentamos a la flor. (*They kneel around CASIMIRO.*)

MARIEL: (*Repeats in English as she removes the handkerchief from CASIMIRO's head.*) Already we sit down to the flower; to receive the flower, we sit down to the flower.

DON REMIGIO: (*Still beating drum softly, repeats prayer.*) Vesate sewau hotekate . . . (*kneels next to CASIMIRO*) sewa valikai . . . (*lays drum down*) sewai hotekatee . . . (*Cradles CASIMIRO's head on his lap.*) Ne Casimiro Flores: . . .

FOUR FRIENDS: (*Pray in unison.*) Yo, Casimiro Flores: . . .

They pick CASIMIRO up and carry him to his recliner chair. They remove the cocoon rattles and cover him with his sarape as they continue repeating the prayer and place an old book in his hands.

DON REMIGIO: (*Louder.*) Ne Casimiro Flores: sewa walikai, sewai hotekatee. (*Gives one last, hard beat.*) Ne Casimiro Flores:—

Lights go out. La Danza del Venado or indigenous music with violin increases in volume. Then out.

SCENE 2

Immediately after the dream. All lights up on stage. Ambulance or police sirens are heard. A Western television theme emanating from a TV set is heard. CASIMIRO is sleeping restlessly, mumbling. The same four friends who were in his dream are now visiting CASIMIRO. They have returned from Mictlan to visit the altar that CASIMIRO sets up for them every year, and they are watching him intently as he tries to wake up. Note: Except for some comedy "bits," the four friends will not be seen or acknowledged by CASIMIRO, and they can either start or finish his sentence or thought and complete his actions for him.

CASIMIRO: (*Still dreaming.*) Yo, Casimiro Flores . . . para recibir la flor . . .

MIGUEL: Ya, Casimiro, never mind las flores. (*Crosses to CASIMIRO and yells near his ears.*) ¡Despierta, Casimiro! It's time to set up our altar, c'mon, wake up! ¡Tenemos hambre!

CARLOS: Déjalo, Miguel. He'll be waking up soon.

The sounds of galloping horses emanating from the television set, then gunshots are heard.

CASIMIRO: (*Sits up, half awake and half asleep.*) ¡Mariel! ¡Dame tu mano!

JESÚS: (*To MARIEL.*) Pobre, he'll never stop dreaming that night.

MIGUEL: La misma pesadilla de siempre, pero tonight at least it wasn't so bad. Mictlantecuhtli sent Don Remigio to help him.

CARLOS: ¿Don Remigio? ¿El maestro de los yaquis?

MARIEL: Don Remigio is his grandfather; he will be the best guide for Casimiro's journey. (*Crosses to CASIMIRO. Caresses his brow. Softly.*) Despierta, Casimiro, despierta.

CASIMIRO: (*Very loudly.*) ¡Mariel! ¡Dame tu mano! (*Awake now.*)

The FOUR FRIENDS move away and watch. CASIMIRO sits up and tosses the book aside. Beat. He turns off the TV, drinks water, and relaxes. CASIMIRO continues.

CASIMIRO: (*To GERALDINE.*) Ah, Geraldine, my love. Buenos días, nalgas frías. (*Takes her hand and kisses it. Removes her cigarette.*) Cuántas veces te he dicho: smoking can kill you.

JESÚS: (*Nervously, to ease tension.*) You can say that again.

FOUR FRIENDS: (*Repeat admonishment to audience.*) Smoking can kill you. (*Giggle.*)

CASIMIRO: Oyes, sweetheart, ¿sabes qué holiday es esta noche?

FOUR FRIENDS: (*In unison. Teasing.*) Halloween!

They quickly pick up four orange plastic jack-o'-lanterns and hold them out for treats.

FOUR FRIENDS: (*In unison.*) Trick or treat; give us something good to eat!

CASIMIRO: (*To* GERALDINE.) No, no, Geraldine. No Halloween, no trick or treat.

Disappointed FOUR FRIENDS *put the jack-o'-lanterns down and move away agüitados.*

CASIMIRO: (*Continues.*) Anyway, tú sabes que ni vienen aquí los trick or treaters. They're afraid porque saben que aquí en el basement del hospital ponen todos los dead bodies conmigo. Pobrecitos, tienen miedo.

CARLOS: ¿Qué pasa, pues? I'm dying of thirst; why hasn't he set up the altar with my Tecate beer?

CASIMIRO: (*Removing the sarape from the recliner.*) Esta noche, Geraldine, es Día de los Muertos, and it's time to set up my altar again.

FOUR FRIENDS: (*In unison.*) ¡A trabajar, muchachos!

They cross to CASIMIRO *and help him cover the coffee table with the sarape.*

CASIMIRO: (*Takes a framed photo from the box.*) Primero, la foto. (*Stares intently, in reverie.*)

MIGUEL, *bien metiche, peers over* CASIMIRO's *shoulder.*

MIGUEL: (*To others.*) Es la foto que nos tomó Manuel, ¿se acuerdan? Aquel día después del soccer game.

MIGUEL, CARLOS, *and* JESÚS *quickly pantomime some energetic soccer moves.* CASIMIRO *places the photo on the table and, remembering that day, seems to be seeing his friends when the photo was taken.*

CASIMIRO: ¡Tenemos que ganarle a Navajoa!

Crosses to his friends and joins in soccer moves. MARIEL *crosses to the box and takes out a bedraggled pom-pom.*

MARIEL: (*Cheers with pom-pom.*) A la bim, a la bum, a la bim-bum-bah, Nogales, Nogales, rah-rah!

A goal is scored.

ALL: (*In unison. Long, drawn-out.*) G-O-L! (*Jump and hug.*)

MARIEL: ¡Vengan, pronto! Manuel nos va a sacar una foto.

JESÚS, MIGUEL, *and* CARLOS *run to* MARIEL *and strike a hugging pose while* CASIMIRO *watches.*

MARIEL: (*Continues.*) ¡Casimiro! ¡Ven! No vamos a sacar la foto sin ti. Espérate, Manuel. ¡Casimiro! Ven; ¡apúrate!

CASIMIRO *runs to his friends and gets in the middle of them. He places his arms around* MARIEL *and* CARLOS. *All pose with serious looks. A recorded line from the unseen amateur photographer,* MANUEL, *is heard.*

MANUEL: Pero no tan serios, you're not at a funeral. ¡Sonrían!

ALL: (*Smiling and in unison.*) ¡Enchiladas!

> *They freeze. Beat. A camera flash. Lights down as a corrido norteño is heard.*

SCENE 3

> *Lights up and music down.* CASIMIRO *has placed the photo on the table. As he continues to speak and to place the other items on the table or around the room, his four friends, still unacknowledged by* CASIMIRO, *will continue to either start or finish his sentence or thought and complete the action for him.*

CASIMIRO: Un six-pack de cerveza Tecate para el tragón de Carlos, tequila con sal y limón—

JESÚS: Tequila? He's never put out tequila for us before.

CASIMIRO: El tequila es para mí. To celebrate my twentieth anniversary working in this hospital. (*Continues taking out items.*) Un bucket de Kentucky fried chicken para Mariel y Miguel—

MARIEL: La pechuga es para mí, Miguel, y que sea "extra crispy."

CASIMIRO: Y como siempre—el chop suey es para Jesús.

JESÚS: ¿Y los egg rolls? Casimiro, you know that I love egg rolls; ¿por qué nunca me compras egg rolls?

MIGUEL: He can't remember everything; no seas necio. Let's help him with the flowers.

CASIMIRO: (*Snaps fingers.*) ¡Las flores! I almost forgot the flowers. Lots of strong-smelling marigolds cempasuchiles bien apestosas—

FOUR FRIENDS: (*Smell the flowers. In unison, holding their noses.*) ¡Fuchi!

CASIMIRO: —so that the muertos can smell them and find their way back to—

FOUR FRIENDS: Mictlan!

CASIMIRO: —wherever they go.

> CASIMIRO *and his friends put bouquets of marigolds in the plastic jack-o'-lanterns and place them on a path leading to the ramp or step unit at center upstage.*

CASIMIRO: (*Takes out four candles.*) And finally, las velas.

FOUR FRIENDS: (*In unison.*) So los muertos can see what they're eating! (*Giggle and light candles.*)

> CASIMIRO *lies on the recliner, legs crossed, hands behind his head, pleased with himself as he surveys the altar.*

Casimiro: (*To* Geraldine.) Geraldine, mi amor; tú sabes que por more than twenty years I've been setting up this altar con las ofrendas for my dead friends, sin saber if I was doing it right or wrong—

Carlos: ¿Y el libro, pues?

The friends scatter around, looking for the old book until one of them finds it and hands it to Casimiro.

Casimiro: —pero mira, according to this book, estoy haciendo todo bien. I found it anoche, right before my last coffee break, en la basura. Maybe one of the new candy-stripers threw it away by mistake—

Jesús: No era "mistake." ¿Te acuerdas, Miguel? Mictlantecuhtli said Casimiro had to read it in preparation for his journey when his heart—

Casimiro: Anyway, I started to read it, y lueguito pensé en mi tata Remigio. People used to call him "el maestro" because he knew everything about the Yaqui people. (*Beat.*) I'm Yaqui, ¿sabías? (*Reflective.*) I thought about the times he wanted me to learn la Danza del Venado—

Miguel: The deer dance—es bien difícil. Not just anyone can learn to dance it.

Casimiro: It was a manda, a promise he made when I was very sick one time . . . but I couldn't learn it; it was just too hard for me.

Mariel: Casimiro, una manda se tiene que cumplir. You should've learned the dance. If not for you, then for your grandfather, Don Remigio.

Casimiro: Anyway, me dio sueño and I guess I fell asleep. And then I had the dream, el mismo sueño de siempre. But this time, my tata Remigio was in my dream, and I tried to dance. (*Beat.*) Mira. Este libro te dice todo de los aztecas.

Stands up, crosses to Geraldine, *and shows her the book, as the friends cross to him and peer over his shoulder.*

Casimiro: (*Reads title.*) "Peregrinación a Mictlan en el Día de los Muertos."

Four Friends: (*In unison.*) "Journey to Mictlan on the Day of the Dead."

Lights flicker. Spooky but playful organ music, like "The Monster Mash."

Four Friends: Uuuuh, se 'sta poniendo spooky.

Casimiro: Parece que no hicieron pay la 'lectricity otra vez. Qué nuevas. (*Beat.*) A ver, a ver, where was I? (*Reads title again.*) "Peregrinación a Mictlan en el Día de los Muertos." (*Looks around to see if lights go out again but they stay on.*) OK, maguey. "Peregrinación" means journey. To Mictlan. OK, so where's this Mictlan place? (Jesús *licks his finger, then leafs through pages for him.*) Aha, aquí 'sta. (*Reads.*) "Mictlan: place of the dead; the dwelling of—"

Four Friends: (*In unison. Fearful.*) Mictlantecuhtli!

CASIMIRO turns to his friends. Comedy bit as he tries to see if he can see them. One time he almost sees one who gets scared at seeing CASIMIRO seeing him, peek-a-boo, etc.

CASIMIRO: (*Reading. Pronouncing very slowly.*) "Mic-tlan-te-cuh-tli, the Aztec god of the dead!"

Lights flicker. Same organ sound, louder.

CASIMIRO: I knew it! No pagaron la luz, Geraldine. Y last week we almost didn't get paid porque el payroll ran out of money. (*Continues reading.*) "Mic-tlantecuhtli. One of the most powerful of the Aztec gods. Mictlantecu—" (*Looks around.*) Nah, I'm not gonna say that name again. (*Beat. Then mockingly to friends.*) El Mictlante-cu-cui!

FRIENDS jump back, both fearful and enjoying the word play.

FOUR FRIENDS: (*In unison.*) Te va 'garrar el cu-cui!

CASIMIRO: (*Gets daring.*) El mero chingón de los dioses. (*Beat.*) (*Suddenly.*) ¡Un brindis! (*Serves himself a shot of tequila. To photo.*) A shot of my tequila, mis amigos, con sal y limón, si me lo permiten. Salud, amigos: Jesús, Miguel, Carlos y . . . Mariel.

The FOUR FRIENDS quickly serve themselves a shot of tequila and gather around him. The toasts, clinking of glasses, lemon and salt will be done with very synchronized movements.

CASIMIRO: Salud. (*Toasts.*)

FOUR FRIENDS: ¡Salud! (*Toast.*)

CASIMIRO: Otro brindis. (*Serves himself another shot.*)

The FOUR FRIENDS serve themselves.

CASIMIRO: (*Toasts.*) Salud, amigos; salud, amor y pesetas.

FOUR FRIENDS: (*In unison.*) ¡Y tiempo para gastarlas! (*All drink a shot of tequila.*)

CASIMIRO: (*Pouring himself another shot. Toasts photo.*) I drink to your happiness and eternal peace.

Drinks it alone.

FOUR FRIENDS: (*Toast and drink.*) Un brindis para nuestra felicidad y la paz eterna.

Music, both melancholy and aggressive.

CASIMIRO: (*Becoming bitter.*) Dichosos los muertos; they only have to be here for one or two days, then back to Mictlan with the mighty Mictlantecuhtli. (*Drinking the tequila straight from the bottle now.*)

JESÚS: O, o, ya está comenzando el rencor. (*Refilling glass shots.*)

MIGUEL: Yeah, that's what tequila always does to you. Makes you mean and bitter. Wátchalo.

CASIMIRO: (*Continues drinking. Increased aggression.*) So who needs an Aztec god anyway? (*Gets abrasive.*) ¿Me oístes, Mictlantecuhtli? ¡No compones nada!

CARLOS: (*A bit righteously.*) See? That's why I never drink tequila; yo prefiero mi Tecate. (*Drinks tequila anyway.*)

The friends put down shot glasses and move away from CASIMIRO, *fearful.*

CASIMIRO: (*Puts bottle down and crosses to center.*) Mictlantecuhtli! I dare you to come and take me and put an end to my miserable existence! (*Arms up in defiant supplication.*) Si eres el dios tan poderoso que te crees, ven por mí. (*Repeats very loudly.*) ¡MICTLANTECUHTLI! ¡VEN POR MÍ!

The music is discordant. Lights flicker. Spot on GERALDINE, *who is now moving spasmodically, unseen by* CASIMIRO. *Conch shell. Aztec/indigenous music. Lights down and up on* MICTLANTECUHTLI *on top of the ramp or step unit.* MICTLANTECUHTLI *is standing tall, arms akimbo, in full costume, headdress, and face makeup. He carries a beeper/cellular phone on his waist. The* CALAVERA NURSE, *wearing a nurse's uniform and cap or green hospital operating scrubs and calavera face makeup is next to* MICTLANTECUHTLI. *She is holding a container of burning copal.*

MICTLANTECUHTLI: Aquí estoy, Casimiro Flores. I am Mictlantecuhtli, god of Mictlan, the land of the dead, or . . . (*walking down*) as you so eloquently put it . . . (*stops midway*) el mero chingón. A tus órdenes. (*Nods smartly.*)

CASIMIRO *faints. The friends exit quickly. As lights go down, music goes up.*

SCENE 4

Immediately after. The theme from a popular soap opera is heard. MIC-TLANTECUHTLI *has removed his headdress and is lying down on the recliner, eating the old Halloween candies, and watching TV. The* CALAVERA NURSE *has spread out her latest, state-of-the-art communication gadgetry (iPod, beeper, Blackberry, laptop, portable video camera, Kindle, etc.) all over the basement and is now kneeling over* CASIMIRO, *attempting to revive him.*

CALAVERA NURSE: Look, Mictlantecuhtli; parece que 'sta reviving. Pobrecito, you really scared him.

MICTLANTECUHTLI: (*Too engrossed to turn to her.*) ¿Pues quién le manda salir con sus babosadas?

CASIMIRO *sits up and looks intently at* CALAVERA NURSE. *He doesn't see* MICTLANTECUHTLI *behind him. Beat.*

CASIMIRO: (*Stalling.*) Ehhh, trick or treat, right? (*To* GERALDINE.) Geraldine, can you believe it? We finally got some trick or treaters here. (*To* CALAVERA NURSE.) No offense, calaca, pero you look kinda old for trick-or-treating. Don't get me wrong; Geraldine y yo estamos bien happy to finally see someone down here with us. Anybody. (*Beat.*) ¿Quieres candy? (*Stands up, goes to table, and looks for candies.*)

MICTLANTECUHTLI: I have the rancid candies. Ten. (*Extends the bowl to* CASIMIRO.)

CASIMIRO: (*Afraid to turn around. To* CALAVERA NURSE.) ¿Quién es? Otro trick-or-treater?

MICTLANTECUHTLI *gets up and stands behind* CASIMIRO. *Taps him on the shoulder.*

MICTLANTECUHTLI: Turn around and face me, Casimiro. ¿O me tienes miedo?

CASIMIRO: (*Still won't turn.*) ¿Quién eres?

MICTLANTECUHTLI: Ay, Casimiro. What a short memory you have. ¿Que no te acuerdas que me llamaste? (*Mimics.*) "Mictlantecuhtli, ven por mí." ¿Qué más? Ah, sí. "Mictlantecu-cui." Remember? ¡Qué imprudencia! Pues, here I am. (*Forcefully turns* CASIMIRO *around to face him.*) Y la Calavera Nurse is my administrative assistant, a bit inept, pero what can I do? Good workers are so hard to find.

CALAVERA NURSE: My job is to keep track of every single person in the universe. See? (*Shows* CASIMIRO *her gadgetry.*) This is for this town. Antes, no era tan difícil to keep track of everybody, when everybody stayed put en el pueblo donde nacieron, pero ahora con el upward mobility, es una chinga keeping it up to date. Aquí tengo todos los nombres, con su número, and a brief description. When someone kicks the bucket, o como dicen ustedes, cuando cuelgan los "tenis," Mictlantecuhtli gets a call on his beeper, then we come and take the body to Mictlan.

CASIMIRO: I am honored to meet both of you, y les pido disculpa por mi . . . imprudence, pero you can leave now. Los dos se pueden ir.

CALAVERA NURSE: It's not that easy, Casimiro. Once Mictlantecuhtli comes for a body, that's it; no podemos regresar a Mictlan sin el cuerpo.

CASIMIRO: You need a body? In less than an hour, when the new interns on the midnight shift come on duty, tendrán todos los cuerpos que quieran. You can take them!

MICTLANTECUHTLI: Qué listo eres, Casimiro, para intercambiar lo que no es tuyo. Sorry, Casimiro, you called me, begging me to take you, pues aquí estoy and I'm ready to take you with me.

CASIMIRO: Pues, I refuse to go.

MICTLANTECUHTLI: (*Patiently.*) Casimiro, believe me, soy uno de los dioses más poderosos, just like the book says. I can easily give you a fatal heart attack, end this discussion, and take you to Mictlan.

CASIMIRO: (*To CALAVERA NURSE.*) Can he really do that?

CALAVERA NURSE: Aha, he sure can. (*Reading from her Rolodex, describing CASIMIRO.*) "Casimiro Flores, age—" (*To CASIMIRO.*) Thirty-seven? (*CASIMIRO nods yes.*) (*Keeps reading.*) "Employed as janitor in a hospital for twenty years; cruzó la frontera en mil novecientos setenta y siete, with his four friends, Jesús, Carlos, Miguel, and Mariel—

MICTLANTECUHTLI: —and led them straight into an ambush." Write that down.

CALAVERA NURSE: (*Obeying. Writes.*) "—and led them straight into an ambush."

CASIMIRO: I didn't know that the coyote would betray us! There was nothing I could do but run to save my life. We all had to run; it wasn't my fault. We had all agreed to take our chances in the desert that night. (*Repeats.*) It wasn't my fault.

MICTLANTECUHTLI: Maybe not. (*Crosses to altar. Derisively.*) But now, do you really think que un container de chop suey is a fair exchange por una vida de un ser humano?

CASIMIRO: No! No lo es. But what of the twenty years I've spent here, alone, in this god-forsaken basement; sin ningún amigo, with no one to talk to but that stupid skeleton; ¿eso no cuenta?

MICTLANTECUHTLI: ¡No, eso no cuenta! You've buried yourself in this basement porque eres un cobarde! (*To CALAVERA NURSE.*) Add this: "For that betrayal, Casimiro diligently sets up an altar en el Día de los Muertos—" (*Picks up the photo and studies it.*) (*Beat.*) Pero, you didn't really think that placing this altar, con las ofrendas, velas y flores, would ease your guilt? Que ese dolor que cargas en tu alma would disappear like magic, con un trago de tequila?

CASIMIRO: Maybe not; la traición no tiene perdón. But there was nothing else I could do, was there?

A beeper goes off.

MICTLANTECUHTLI: Parece que ya llegaron tus interns, Casimiro. (*Reads the number on his beeper.*) The number's not too clear; pero we may soon have the body you were so ready to exchange for yours. (*Beeper goes off again. Reading beeper.*) It's still not clear, pero parece 587-6614. ¿Quién es?

CALAVERA NURSE: 587-6614? (*Reading from her Rolodex.*) Es la Rocky Road. (*Tense, worried.*) ¿Y Don Prisciliano? Where is he? ¿Que no la ve? He's always there—

MICTLANTECUHTLI: (*With power to see beyond.*) Don Prisciliano isn't looking up. He doesn't see Rocky. Está platicando con Xochil. She's describing her upcoming quinceañera fiesta to him.

CALAVERA NURSE: (*Fervently.*) Look up, Don Prisciliano, look up; no le quite la vista a Rocky.

MICTLANTECUHTLI: (*Still seeing beyond.*) Bullets. Wayward bullets and blood running in the street. Parece que es initiation night. I see El Tanque y El Peewa de la pandilla del Southside—habrá muchas, muchas balas.

CALAVERA NURSE: Xochil! (*With urgency.*) Mictlantecuhtli, you must take Xochil away from the bullets.

MICTLANTECUHTLI: (*Angry.*) ¡Sabes bien que no puedo! She cannot escape her destiny. (*Beat.*) It's gonna be a busy night, Calavera. Too busy for just the two of us; we'll need help. (*They exchange meaningful looks, then both look at* CASIMIRO.)

CASIMIRO: (*Beat.*) ¿Qué?

CALAVERA NURSE: (*Doubtful.*) Mictlantecuhtli, I don't think that he can—

MICTLANTECUHTLI: Why not? The trip must be made, alone or with company; either way, he'll have to do it, no? He may as well earn it.

CASIMIRO: Earn what? I'm not working overtime! El bookkeeper ya no quiere authorize nada de overtime.

MICTLANTECUHTLI: Overtime? ¿Y cómo a mí nadie me paga overtime, eh? (*Beat.*) A while ago you were talking about betrayals and forgiveness, Casimiro. Those are very difficult concepts for me to understand, la traición, el perdón y la redención. How can we correct the mistakes we made in the past?

CASIMIRO: Don't you think I've asked myself that over and over? ¡No podemos cambiar el pasado!

MICTLANTECUHTLI: Yo sí puedo cambiar el pasado.

CASIMIRO: Can you really change the past?

MICTLANTECUHTLI: Most of the time. But it's the future that's a bitch. (*Beat.*) You wanted me to come and take you to Mictlan, no? Para mí, eso también es muy fácil. I can take you to Mictlan right now, con o sin el perdón de nadie. Or . . .

CASIMIRO: Or what?

MICTLANTECUHTLI: Or you can take four bodies to Mictlan for me and return bien perdonado. A fair exchange, no crees? Cuatro cuerpos por los cuatro amigos que traicionaste. (*A beeper goes off.*) So, Casimiro, what will it be: tu vida o ese perdón que buscas?

Aztec or indigenous music is heard. Lights go down and the sound of a beeper gets louder.

SCENE 5

Lights up. The theme from the Oprah Winfrey Show is heard. MICTLANTECUHTLI *and the* CALAVERA NURSE *are drinking tequila, watching TV.* CASIMIRO *is cleaning up.*

MICTLANTECUHTLI: (*To* CALAVERA NURSE.) La Oprah Winfrey. Qué mujer. Today she's gonna try to turn these ugly ducklings into beautiful women con un "makeover." Lots of luck, Oprah, porque están más feas que mi wife, Mictecacihuatl. (*Shudders.*)

CASIMIRO: Bueno, pues, since I've agreed to take your next four bodies to Mictlan, I think you should explain your beeper system to me mientras que esperamos los cuerpos, ¿no?

MICTLANTECUHTLI: (*Shows* CASIMIRO *his beeper.*) You see, Casimiro, everything's high technology now. Tú sabes, high tech. Todos tienen sus beepers, ¿no? (CASIMIRO *nods yes.*) Pues, yo también: caller ID, call waiting, cellular phones, conference calls, call forwarding, tengo todo. So that makes my job much easier. Este número es de la Rocky Road.

CASIMIRO: Rocky Road? La nieve?

CALAVERA NURSE: No, no es la ice cream. Asina se llama, Rocky Road. Bueno, más bien es un nickname que se puso ella misma . . . (*Reads description from her Rolodex.*) "Rocky Road, age twenty-five, but looks younger—or older—depending on makeup. Somehow manages to live dangerously and to fall in love with rats. Married rats. She's a 'party animal,' dances salsa—or punk—all night, smokes, drinks tequila, has a black belt in karate, hang-glides, bungee jumps—"

MICTLANTECUHTLI: Bungee jumps? ¿Qué es eso?

CALAVERA NURSE: Pos, the way I understand it, se suben en un platform—bien alto—y se ponen un harness, un cinturón, yo creo, y luego—brincan!

MICTLANTECUHTLI: ¿Brincan? ¿A poco? (*Beat.*) Just like the voladores de Papantla, ¿no? It pleases me that something has endured from the greatness of the Aztecas (*with sarcasm*) even if it's only jumping off high platforms.

CASIMIRO: (*Curious.*) This Rocky Road sounds like a real interesting person. Me hubiera gustado conocerla.

MICTLANTECUHTLI: Oh, don't worry; you'll be meeting her soon enough; they're bringing her here, to this hospital. (*Musing.*) La Rocky Road. (*To* CALAVERA NURSE.) Lo que no dice en tu Rolodex es que she has a special laugh that sounds like bells ringing. And a throaty voice. She likes to give a "dramatic pause" and makes circling motions with her hand while she searches for just the right word.

CALAVERA NURSE: Asina: "Death is just an (*stops; makes three circling motions*) . . . experience." Pero, this time, you might say she took a (*stretches word*) l-o-n-g dramatic pause and died before she found the word she wanted! (*Giggles at her wit until* MICTLANTECUHTLI'S *glare stops her.*)

MICTLANTECUHTLI: "An experience." Pero no se crean; at the end, they're all afraid. And they exit kicking and crying. Chillones. Pero como dice mi paisano, José Alfredo Jiménez: "la vida no vale nada."

CASIMIRO: (*Suddenly, to break silence.*) ¡Un brindis! (*Quickly pours three shots of tequila.*)

ALL: (*Toast.*) ¡A la vida! (*Drink tequila with salt and lemon with very synchronized movements.*)

They keep drinking and immediately become sentimental drunks.

CASIMIRO: (*Singing.*) "No vale nada la vida, la vida no vale nada—

CALAVERA NURSE: (*Hugs him and sings with him.*) "Comienza siempre llorando, y así llorando se acaba—

MICTLANTECUHTLI: (*Hugs CASIMIRO on other side and also sings.*) "Por eso es que en este mundo—

ALL: "La vida no vale nada."

They end the song with more hugs and maudlin statements of love and friendship. Beeper goes off.

MICTLANTECUHTLI: (*Sobers up instantly. Reflectively.*) La Rocky. So she finally did it. Vayan por el cuerpo de Rocky Road; está en el corridor outside the Emergency Room. Y tú, Casimiro . . . (*Referring to CALAVERA NURSE.*) Cuídala. She loves to go into the Intensive Care Unit and play with the heart defibrillators.

CALAVERA NURSE: (*Still tipsy.*) O, sí. Especially when it's full of chief executive officers. (*Demonstrates.*) Agarro los defibrillators—asina—place them over the heart, como el doctor George Clooney en *E.R.* y luego: z-z—z-z-z-z-z-z-zz!

MICTLANTECUHTLI: ¡Apúrense! You've wasted enough time already.

CALAVERA NURSE: (*Saluting like a soldier, but still drunk.*) Adelante, mi coman-dante. (*Takes CASIMIRO by arm.*) Vamos, Casimiro. ¡Por el cuerpo de la encantadora Rocky Road!

CASIMIRO and CALAVERA NURSE: (*Exit, embracing, singing and staggering.*) "Por eso es que en este mundo, la vida no vale nada."

Lights down and music up. TV still on and the Oprah theme is heard.

SCENE 6

Lights up. CASIMIRO is standing over a covered body on a gurney. The CALAVERA NURSE is standing next to him, holding the old book, giving CASIMIRO instructions. Applying what he learned on the Oprah Show, MICTLANTECUHTLI is raptly giving himself a "makeover."

CASIMIRO: (*Repeating an invocation, hands over the body.*) "Les imploro: al dios Mictlantecuhtli y a la diosa Mictecacihuatl—"

MICTLANTECUHTLI: (*Applying makeup.*) Mi wife, la Mickey. Hijo, que si me hace nag. All day long. (*Mimics.*) Mictlantecuhtli, go see why Huitzilopochtli and Quetzalcoatl are fighting; las milpas de aguacate no tienen agua porque Tlaloc trai pleito casado con el señor César Chávez y—

CALAVERA NURSE: "—que Cantinflas se puso de tour guide, pero se la lleva platicando and ends up getting lost, y que los babies en Chichihuacuauhco no tienen Pampers—" (*Stops sheepishly. To CASIMIRO.*) Sorry, sigue.

CASIMIRO: (*Continues invocation.*) "To the water gods, Tlaloc and Chalchi—salchichas!"

MICTLANTECUHTLI: (*Correcting him.*) Chalchihuiticue.

CASIMIRO: Esto es demasiado difícil. I can't even pronounce these gods' names. Chal-chi-hui-ti-cue. Why don't you just say "water gods"?

MICTLANTECUHTLI: (*Angry, explosive.*) ¿Y como si puedes pronunciar los nombres de los dioses aquí? The powerful gods of capitalism? El poderoso (*pronounces as one word, Aztec-sounding*) let's-go-shopping-charge-it-Jerry-McGuire-get-the-money-get-the-money god?

CALAVERA NURSE: (*To* CASIMIRO, *placating.*) Go on; los nombres de los dioses get easier the more you say them. (*Reads.*) "Al dios de las flores, Xochipilli—"

MICTLANTECUHTLI: Xochipilli, my favorite. God of the flowers. Did you know, Casimiro, that every flower here on earth is someone's soul?

CASIMIRO: No, no lo sabía. Pero it makes sense. Somehow. Mi abuelito, Tata Remigio, always talked about a flower world. La sea ania. (*Beat.*)

CALAVERA NURSE: (*Reading.*) "Y Iztapapalotl—"

MICTLANTECUHTLI: "God of the butterflies." ¿Sabías que de ahí viene la palabra papalote? Kites. And that our warriors who die in battle return to earth as hummingbirds or butterflies after traveling with the sun por cuatro años?

CALAVERA NURSE: Mictlantecuhtli, he's never going to finish the invocation si nomás lo estás interrupting.

Beeper is heard.

MICTLANTECUHTLI: (*Reads number on beeper.*) 578-1311. ¿Quién es?

CALAVERA NURSE: (*Puts down the old book and reads from her Rolodex.*) Es "el Mad Dog Sánchez."

MICTLANTECUHTLI: "Mad Dog?" ¿Estás segura que no es el número del dog pound? Muy pronto hasta los perros van a trair sus "beepers." Ya ni la friegan.

CALAVERA NURSE: (*Defensively.*) Hey, I don't make these names up; nomás estoy reading what it says here: el Mad Dog Sánchez.

MICTLANTECUHTLI: Bueno, Florence Nightingale; no te agüites. With a name like that tiene que ser un bona fide gang member, o otro stupid "wanna be."

CALAVERA NURSE: Neither one. Ni gang member, ni "wanna be." Era un "gonna be." He was supposed to prove himself tonight. Pero, he didn't make his initiation. You could say que one of the other gang's members—El Peewa o El Tanque—put Mad Dog to sleep. (*Giggles.*)

MICTLANTECUHTLI: Vamos por él. (*He and* CALAVERA NURSE *start to exit.*)

CASIMIRO: Hey, wait! ¿Pa' dónde creen que van? You can't leave me with . . . her. (*Gestures to body on gurney.*)

MICTLANTECUHTLI: ¿Y por qué no? She's dead; ¿qué te va a hacer? (*Beat.*) Maybe if you had met her when she was alive, de seguro she would've broken your heart, Casimiro. ¿Pero muerta? Here, you can do the invocation without help. (*Tosses the old book to him.*) Page 287.

CASIMIRO: ¡No! No puedo y no quiero.

Throws book down. A horrified CALAVERA NURSE *quickly picks it up and hands it to* MICTLANTECUHTLI.

MICTLANTECUHTLI: (*Unruffled.*) You really don't have any choice, do you? We have to go pick up this "Mad Dog" for you, and you can continue the invocation and bring her back to life, or, quédate con ella así—muerta. (*Beat.* CASIMIRO *takes the book.* MICTLANTECUHTLI *continues, giving instructions.*) You start by imploring to the gods, you call their names as you called mine—pero no les digas dioses chingones, they're not as tolerant as I am—and then . . . you wait. (CALAVERA NURSE *and* MICTLANTECUHTLI *start to exit.*)

CALAVERA NURSE: (*Stops and turns to* CASIMIRO.) Oh, one more thing, Casimiro. Use maracas. The gods love to hear maracas. Cha cha cha. (*Both exit.*)

CASIMIRO: (*Mimics.*) "The gods love to hear maracas." Chistosa. Page 287. (*Finds page.*) Órale, Rocky, here goes. (*Reads.*) "Les imploro: al dios Mictlantecuhtli y a la diosa Mictecacihuatl . . ." (*Looks down at* ROCKY. *Nothing. Continues.*) "Al dios de las flores, Xochipilli, and to the god of the butterflies, Itzapapalotl—" (GERALDINE *moves convulsively.*) "Yo, Casimiro Flores, implore you to lift this body—" (*Unseen by* CASIMIRO, ROCKY *sits up.* CASIMIRO *continues the invocation*) "—and take it to Mictlan, the land of the dead."

Beat. ROCKY *falls back.* CASIMIRO *looks away from the book and looks at* ROCKY *lying down. Gives* ROCKY *a dirty look, crosses to the table, and starts to put all of his ofrendas back into the box. The photo of his friends is the last item and* CASIMIRO *holds it, meditatively.*

CASIMIRO: (*Continues. Turns to* ROCKY.) Mictlantecuhtli said you would break my heart, pero he was mistaken; no tengo corazón. ¿Me oístes, Rocky Road? ¡No tengo corazón!

ROCKY ROAD, *hearing her name, sits up, sheet to her waist, and looks around.*

ROCKY ROAD: Ya pues, you don't have to shout; aquí estoy, mi rey.

ROCKY *jumps off the gurney, flinging the sheet aside. She is wearing a striking outfit of tiger, leopard, or zebra skin.*

ROCKY ROAD: (*Continues directly to audience.*) Órale, raza; it's party time! (*Toward sound booth.*) ¡Música, maestro, o me voy!

A sensual danzón plays in the background.

ROCKY ROAD: (*Hand out to* CASIMIRO, *invitingly seductive.*) ¿Bailamos, mi amor?

Lights go down as music goes up.

SCENE 7

Danzón continues. ROCKY ROAD *and* CASIMIRO *are dancing,* ROCKY *is leading. Danzón ends.* ROCKY *lets go of* CASIMIRO *abruptly; he almost falls but catches his balance.*

ROCKY: Not bad, partner; pero you do need more practice.

ROCKY looks around, sees the tequila, serves herself a shot, and drinks it expertly and with great thirst. Picks up the photo.

ROCKY: (*Continues.*) Cute; están guapos los . . . chavalones. ¿Quiénes son? Parecen part of a soccer team. Ah, there you are. Te ves bien joven; when was this picture taken? (*Reads the date on the back.*) April 1977. How old were you? Fifteen, sixteen? Uuuuh, you've got your arm around someone. ¿Quién es la cheerleader? (*Shows* CASIMIRO *the picture.*)

CASIMIRO: (*Tightly.*) Mariel.

ROCKY: (*Laughs her tinkling laugh, which annoys* CASIMIRO.) Mariel. Bonito nombre; I like it. Sounds . . . cosmic. ¿Es tu girlfriend?

CASIMIRO doesn't respond but takes the photo from her and places it the box. ROCKY *checks out* CASIMIRO.

ROCKY: (*Continues.*) ¿Y tú? What's your name?

CASIMIRO: (*Somewhat formally.*) Casimiro Flores, para servirle. (*Puts out his hand for her to shake but she ignores it.*)

ROCKY: Casimiro? Sounds . . . traditional. (*Puts her fingers around her eyes like eyeglasses. Teases.*) Doctor Oculista, casi miro, pero no miro. I think I need glasses. ¡A lo mejor estoy ciego!

CASIMIRO: ¿Y a poco crees que tu nombre está muy pretty? Rocky Road. Mejor te hubieras puesto pistachio nut.

ROCKY: (*Ignores his remark.*) Bueno, si . . . Mariel no es tu novia, entonces (*crossing to* GERALDINE) maybe she is . . . (*Facing* CASIMIRO.) ¿Cómo se llama mi rival? (CASIMIRO *refuses to answer her.*) Anda, don't be mad. (*Referring to* GERALDINE.) No está fea, pero she looks like she's been on a diet too long. (GERALDINE *hits* ROCKY *on her shoulder.*) Ow! (*To* GERALDINE.) No es pa' tanto, cara de espanto. (*To* CASIMIRO.) Parece que 'sta jealous la girlfriend. C'mon, she's gotta have a name; ¿Cómo se llama?

CASIMIRO: (*Blurts out.*) Geraldine. Nomás Geraldine.

ROCKY: (*Laughing.*) Geraldine! Qué . . . precious. Well, I hate to kiss and run, pero there's no action here, so ya me voy. Arrivederci. (*Crosses to exit.*)

CASIMIRO: (*Very quickly.*) ¿A cuál kiss?

ROCKY: Dices bien; no hubo kiss, just a dance and good tequila. Pero eso se remedia easily, ¿no?

(*Crosses to* CASIMIRO, *dips him backwards, and gives him a nice, long, passionate kiss. He is too astounded to respond and almost falls when she finally lets go of him.*)

ROCKY: There. Para que no digas que no pagué por el tequila.

ROCKY heads toward one of the room dividers leaving an open-mouthed CASIMIRO. Gets confused when she can't find an exit.

ROCKY: Hey, where's the exit? ¿Por dónde salgo? Where am I, anyway?

CASIMIRO: En el basement del hospital.

ROCKY: Hospital? (*Beat. Starts to remember slowly. Crosses to* CASIMIRO. *Points upward.*) Allá arriba 'sta el Emergency, ¿no? I remember waiting hours and hours before . . .

ROCKY: (*Continues.*) . . . they finally got around to pumping my stomach, para sacarme las píldoras. But it was too late, ¿verdad?

CASIMIRO: (*Nods yes. Beat.*) Why did you take the pills?

ROCKY: ¿Por qué? Why does anyone take too many pills? (*Crosses to gurney.*) Because I wanted to die; I was ready to die. And maybe I thought that the old viejito downstairs would see me in time, but he didn't look up. (*Climbs up on the gurney.*) He was enjoying Xochil's visit, probably describing his aches and pains to her. (*Starts to cover herself with the sheet.*)

CASIMIRO: I still don't understand why you—

ROCKY: ¿Sabes qué? You're boring me, and if I had wanted to be bored, I wouldn't have taken the pills. Life bored me, OK? So, déjame en paz. (*Lies down, covers her face with sheet. Beat. Sits up again. Uncovers her face.*) And one more thing, Casimiro; I know that this . . . dump ain't heaven or hell, so don't you dare bring me back, unless you've got a good reason. ¿Me oístes? A damn good reason. (*Covers head and lies down.*)

Lights go down as Danzón music goes up.

SCENE 8

Lights up. MICTLANTECUHTLI *and* CALAVERA NURSE *wheel in* MAD DOG, *who is covered with a hospital sheet, and place him next to* ROCKY ROAD.

MICTLANTECUHTLI: (*To* CASIMIRO, *referring to* ROCKY.) ¿Qué pasó? Didn't you try the invocation?

CASIMIRO: (*Calmly drinking coffee.*) Oh, I got her up alright, pero she got mad y se volvió a acostar.

MICTLANTECUHTLI: (*To* ROCKY.) ¿Es cierto, Rocky? (ROCKY *nods yes under the sheet.*) Ay, ¿qué voy hacer contigo? I know you're gonna raise hell in Mictlan if I don't find something to occupy your time there. (ROCKY *nods another yes.*)

CALAVERA NURSE: Why don't you introduce her to Selena? Ella siempre está complaining que en Mictlan nadie tiene rhythm y que los concheros need to update their steps—

Beeper sounds.

MICTLANTECUHTLI: You were right, Casimiro; we'll have four bodies very quickly. (*Reads number on beeper.*)

CALAVERA NURSE: ¿Otro gang member? ¿El Tanque? ¿El Peewa?

MICTLANTECUHTLI: (*Very sad.*) No. I don't have a complete number yet, pero no es un gang member; it's one of the Innocents.

CALAVERA NURSE: Es Xochil, ¿verdad?

MICTLANTECUHTLI: (*Nods yes.*) It won't be long now, le falta poco. (*Gets angry.*) Parece que'l mentado Mad Dog wasn't satisfied to seek his death alone, también se lleva a una de las inocentes, one who wasn't even expecting death. (*To* CALAVERA NURSE.) Vamos, we don't have much time, pero maybe we can still help. (*Both start to exit.*)

CASIMIRO: (*Stops them.*) Hey, wait! You can't just keep waltzing in here with dead bodies and leaving them here with me. Este hospital—believe me—tiene proper procedures con el required paperwork, processing, death certificates—

Beeper goes off.

CALAVERA NURSE: ¿Xochil?

MICTLANTECUHTLI: (*Without reading beeper number.*) Sí, es Xochil.

  CALAVERA NURSE *and* MICTLANTECUHTLI *cross to exit.*

CASIMIRO: ¿Y ahora pa' dónde creen que van?

MICTLANTECUHTLI: (*Softly.*) A recoger una flor. Xochil Martínez. (*Rhetorically.*) Would you believe it? A flower blossoming aquí, entre las espinas de tu barrio? (*Suddenly very angry.*) Una flor, cut down by a bullet aimed at this scum: el Mad Dog Sánchez. (*Pushes gurney toward* CASIMIRO *and exits with* CALAVERA NURSE *following him.*)

Lights down.

SCENE 9

ROCKY: (*Sitting up.*) Uhhhh, he sure is mad.

CASIMIRO: I thought you weren't getting up again.

ROCKY: Te dije que nomás for a good reason, remember? Besides getting to finally meet Selena, yo digo que finding out who got Mictlantecuhtli so pissed off is a damn good reason, verdad? Let's meet el Mad Dog Sánchez! (*Jumps off gurney.*) Levántalo, Casimiro.

CASIMIRO: Oh no; Yo no levanto a nadie. Never again.

ROCKY: Ándale, don't be such a . . . piss-ant all your life. (*Looks around for the book and finds it.*) ¿Qué page?

CASIMIRO: (*Reluctant, but curious.*) 287.

ROCKY: 287? Aquí está. (*Reads.*) "Les imploro: al dios Mictlantecuhtli y la diosa Mictecacihuatl—"

CASIMIRO: (*Crossing to her.*) That's his nagging wife, la diosa regañona. Can you believe it? She sends Mictlantecuhtli to buy Pampers.

ROCKY: Good. All husbands should be sent to buy Pampers. Shhh. (*Continues reading.*) "Created by Ometeotl; les imploro a los water gods, Tlaloc y—"

CASIMIRO: (*Pronounces expertly to show off.*) "Chalchihuiticue."

ROCKY/CASIMIRO: (*Together.*) "Al dios de las flores, Xochipilli, and the god of the butterflies, Iztapapalotl." We, Rocky Road and Casimiro Flores, implore you to lift the body of Mad Dog Sánchez (MAD DOG *rises*) and lead him to Mictlan!

MAD DOG jumps off gurney. He is dressed in typical "cholo": plaid flannel shirt, baggy pants, neutral-color headband, shades, etc.

ROCKY/CASIMIRO: (*Together.*) We did it! (*High five.*)

In the background, rap music is heard.

MAD DOG: (*Rapping and break dancing.*) Yo soy el Mad Dog Sánchez, and that's easy to say; me gusta matar people in a major way. Yeah, I know that killing's no game, but here in the barrio, it's the quickest road to fame; un hero no llora so don't mention my pain, when you're writing a poem or a very triste canción, just remember my name; ask me no questions and I'll tell you no lie, I don't know the reason, so don't even ask why, I just know that today El Tanque y el Peewa will have to die!

MAD DOG whips out a knife and advances toward CASIMIRO and ROCKY. CASIMIRO places ROCKY behind him in a protective gesture, but ROCKY steps around him.

ROCKY ROAD: (*Executing fancy preliminary karate steps, yells.*) Ki-ya! (*Ready to knock the knife out of MAD DOG's hand.*)

Lights go down as a contemporary rap plays in the background.

SCENE 10

Lights up and music down. CASIMIRO is reading the old book, ROCKY is pacing impatiently, and the CALAVERA NURSE is placing an ice pack on MAD DOG's wrist. He is sitting on the gurney.

MAD DOG: (*Wincing in pain.*) Owwww! That hurts.

ROCKY: Don't be such a . . . puppy dog. You sound just like the cowardly lion in *The Wizard of Oz*. (*Mimicking.*) "Am I bleeding? Am I bleeding?"

MAD DOG: Lady, you're dangerous; you shouldn't be allowed out on the streets.

ROCKY: Neither should you—without your rabies shots. (*To* CALAVERA NURSE.) Pues, ¿cuándo regresa Mictlantecuhtli? He should've already been back, no? How come you came back by yourself?

CALAVERA NURSE: He'll be here soon. It's just taking him longer porque Xochil was one of the Innocents.

ROCKY: Innocents? Who are they?

CALAVERA NURSE: Los inocentes son the ones you least expect to die. Or that you think shouldn't die porque they haven't really lived their lives, nor reached their potential. Están floreciendo, dice Mictlantecuhtli.

ROCKY: Pues, why do they die?

CASIMIRO: Who knows why anybody dies? Maybe es como dijía mi tata Remigio cuando no sabía la answer: nomás porque sí. Just because.

MAD DOG: Or like one of my foster mothers always said: quien te manda. Shit, that would make me mad. No matter what happened to me, she would just say: quien te manda. She could never explain anything.

CALAVERA NURSE: Oh, sometimes it can be explained. An unknown virus, bad luck, human error, a drunk driver, or, in Xochil's case (*directly at* MAD DOG), a stray bullet meant for someone else.

MAD DOG: Hey, it wasn't my fault! El Tanque y El Peewa started to shoot wild—Don Prisciliano tried to stop Xochil—

CALAVERA NURSE: (*Ignores him.*) And, when it can't be explained, there's always the "Pobre, ya le tocaba."

ROCKY: El "ya le tocaba." That sounds so . . . existentialist.

CALAVERA NURSE: (*Continues explaining.*) The Innocents are always confused, scared. And angry. Por eso it's taking Mictlantecuhtli so long to bring Xochil. She's very angry, but he'll calm her down; van a ver. He has a way with words.

ROCKY: Well, you'd think that by now, a god as powerful as Mictlantecuhtli—or any other god—would've figured out a way to protect the Innocents, no?

CALAVERA NURSE: (*Beat.*) Yes, you would think so. Pero nadie puede proteger a los inocentes. Not even a god as powerful as Mictlantecuhtli. (*Sensing without seeing.*) Ya viene Mictlantecuhtli con Xochil.

Soft music is heard in the background. All stand and turn toward ramp/ step unit as MICTLANTECUHTLI *leads* XOCHIL *by the hand. She is dressed in a school uniform. A calm and smiling* XOCHIL *looks around* CASI- MIRO's *room.*

CALAVERA NURSE: ¿Qué les dije? Xochil ya no está tan enojada como estaba before Mictlantecuhtli had his talk with her.

XOCHIL, *still smiling beatifically, crosses to* MAD DOG *and gives him a resounding slap that knocks him down.*

CALAVERA NURSE: Well, I did say not as angry, didn't I?

MICTLANTECUHTLI: Sorry, Mad Dog, I did have to promise her that one slap. (*Beat.*) Bueno, you have a lot of things to do before you leave—

CASIMIRO: Pero nomás son tres cuerpos; didn't you say I had to take four? (*Gets suspicious.*) Hey, I'm not gonna be the fourth body, am I?

MICTLANTECUHTLI: No, Casimiro, trust me; you're not the fourth body. (*Beat.*) As I was saying, you have a lot of things to do before you leave, pero primero, let's introduce ourselves. Como los gringos en sus meetings: (*With accent.*) "Give us your name and tell us a little something about yourself." (*Beat.*) Ya saben quien soy yo. (*Nods to* ROCKY *to begin.*)

ROCKY: My real name is Raquel Castillo, but I changed it to Rocky Road. Not for the ice cream, pero for my philosophy on life. It's a rocky road; get it?

MAD DOG: Yo soy el Mad Dog Sánchez. And let me tell you right now antes que somebody else decides to give me another karate kick or a slap. I never meant to hurt anyone. I was ready to join the gang nomás porque no soy un coward. With my luck I figured I was gonna get killed before I killed anyone—just like it happened. And if I was gonna get killed, pues at least maybe someone in the 'hood would write a corrido about me.

XOCHIL: You went out to shoot someone for a corrido? Pues why didn't you just go fix a horse race instead? Como en "el moro de Cumpas."

MAD DOG: The who?

CALAVERA NURSE: "El moro de Cumpas." El moro was a very famous horse from el pueblito de Cumpas, en Sonora. (*Singing. Pantomimes riding a horse.*) "El diecisiete de marzo, en la ciudad de Agua Prieta, vino gente de 'onde quiera—"

XOCHIL: I remember that song. It's my Dad's favorite corrido, porque él era de Cumpas. He claims to have been there, at the horse race, when the horse, "el moro," won—or lost, I forget which. But he always said he thought that the race was fixed. (*To* MAD DOG.) Anyway, I can't believe I'm here, stuck with a bunch of losers, just because you wanted a corrido named after you.

MAD DOG: Who you calling a loser? ¿Qué te crees? You and your friends. Stuck up como si you owned the world. I used to watch you, en la elementary, before you transferred to your fancy private school, but you never once looked at me. Un día, we were gonna have a test, and the vieja teacher said we had to use a number two pencil. Pues, I didn't have a pencil—number two or any other number—so I asked you to lend me one of yours and you just looked at me like you were smelling a fart.

All turn to XOCHIL, *who has a fart-smelling pose.*

MAD DOG: Yeah, just like you're doing now.

XOCHIL: (*Quickly changes her fart-smelling expression and smiles sweetly. To the others.*) My name is Xochil Martínez—

CASIMIRO: Named for the god of the flowers, Xochipilli!

XOCHIL: No, I wasn't! Me nombraron por la "Panadería Xochil," where my mom worked when she got pregnant with me. Anyway, as I was saying, my name is Xochil Martínez; tengo catorce años, pero soon to be fifteen—I'm already planning my quinceañera . . . (*Beat. Realizing.*) No, I guess not. Fourteen. There, I'm done.

MICTLANTECUHTLI: Bueno. You are now heading to Mictlan, place of the dead. Your journey will be long and difficult, pero las ofrendas de su familia y amigos will help you. (*Lectures.*) In our world, how you died determines where you'll end up in Mictlan. Xochil, you're going to be with the children en Chichihuacuauhco—

XOCHIL: Yo no quiero estar con los niños; I'm too old for that, and I don't want to be stuck babysitting.

ROCKY/MAD DOG: (*Together.*) ¿Y nosotros?

MICTLANTECUHTLI: Ay, Rocky y Mad Dog, todavía no sé where you'll be porque we don't have a place in Mictlan for persons who die como ustedes dos: de puro stupidity.

CASIMIRO: Bueno, let Mictlantecuhtli finish lo que 'sta diciendo, so we can leave. Yo tengo mucho que hacer and you're holding me up. Mictlantecuhtli, sigue.

MICTLANTECUHTLI: Before reaching Mictlan, you must cross nine levels—eight, really, because your life here, on earth, is the first level. You will encounter many dangers: eight deserts without water; ocho montañas de alturas peligrosas; and you must cross eight rivers. Encontrarán jaguares, winds as sharp as obsidian knives, flechas que vuelan por el aire, green serpents and lizards, and in Teocoyllqualoyan, your hearts will be eaten—

Beeper sound is heard.

CALAVERA NURSE: (*Annoyed.*) ¡Ay! Just when he was getting to the good part! (*Sadistic. Demonstrates.*) En Teocoyllqualoyan les arrancan el corazón—

MICTLANTECUHTLI: (*Reading beeper.*) 893-43—

CALAVERA NURSE: (*Interrupts and completes the number by memory.*) 36. It's 893-4336. (*To* MICTLANTECUHTLI.) Es Don Prisciliano.

XOCHIL: Don Prisciliano? I know him! (*To others.*) He lives down the street from me, and he's always sending me to the tiendita to buy things he needs. Rocky, you know him, too; he lives downstairs, across from your apartment.

ROCKY ROAD: ¿El viejito que se la pasa siempre sentado afuera? Is that his name, Don Prisciliano? I could always see him from my window. Just sitting there. Watching the world go by. I always had this weird feeling that he was looking out for me, you know, that he worried about me when no one else gave a damn.

CALAVERA NURSE: Pues, he *was* looking out for you. Don Prisciliano's a very caring person.

MAD DOG: Oh, yeah? He's always hated my guts. When I walk by, he always mumbles in Spanish: "desgraciado pachuco." What's that, anyway?

CASIMIRO: (*Impatiently.*) Bueno, pues, is this Don Prisciliano the fourth body we're waiting for?

CALAVERA NURSE: Maybe. Don Prisciliano siempre se anda muriendo—

MICTLANTECUHTLI: But he never dies! Puro false alarms. Los paramedics ya ni quieren ir a su casa.

CALAVERA NURSE: Mictlantecuhtli, it looks serious this time. Tiene pneumonia.

XOCHIL: No wonder his chest hurt! And that's why he was sending me to the tiendita to buy him some Vicks. Pobrecito. This time he was really sick.

CALAVERA NURSE: Aquí está, en el Emergency. I don't think he's gonna make it this time.

MICTLANTECUHTLI: Bah. Siempre dices eso; but the old man ya me cansó. Casimiro needs to take four bodies to Mictlan. Aquí están tres; Don Prisciliano will be the fourth one.

CALAVERA NURSE: But, Mictlantecuhtli, he's not dead!

MICTLANTECUHTLI: Not yet, pero he will be. This time, Don Prisciliano, ready or not, I'm taking you with me!

Lights go down.

SCENE 11

Lights up. Something similar to "la Danza de los Viejitos" from Michoacán is heard. DON PRISCILIANO is walking down the ramp or step unit, pushing a metal walker with very slow turtle steps. He is wearing a hospital gown, slippers, and his old black hat; a sign stating "Do not resuscitate" is hanging from his neck. DON PRISCILIANO finally reaches the bottom and does not see MICTLANTECUHTLI step up behind him. MICTLANTECUHTLI is wearing surgical greens and a stethoscope around his neck. DON PRISCILIANO continues to walk around the room, looking out for MICTLANTECUHTLI, not knowing that MICTLANTECUHTLI is behind him, matching him step by step. All the others quietly move in behind MICTLANTECUHTLI, also stalking DON PRISCILIANO, until he is surrounded. DON PRISCILIANO finally turns and sees MICTLANTECUHTLI behind him. He is startled and starts to run slowly up the ramp/step unit.

MICTLANTECUHTLI: (*Forcefully.*) Don Prisciliano, stop!

DON PRISCILIANO stops and walks down.

MICTLANTECUHTLI: (*Gently.*) ¿Por qué corre? (*Points to the sign.*) Aquí dice "Do not resuscitate."

DON PRISCILIANO: (*Looking down at the sign and trying to read it upside down.*) Sí, eso dice. (*Beat.*) Pero—I changed my mind.

Picks up the ends of his hospital gown, leaps up, and starts to run again, but MICTLANTECUHTLI grabs him.

MICTLANTECUHTLI: Pues you changed your mind too many times before, pero esta vez, lo siento, pero you finally died, and now you're to going Mictlan. (*DON PRISCILIANO gets dejected.*) Ande, Don Prisciliano, no se ponga triste. You've been wanting to die for over sixty years, ¡pues hasta que se le hizo! Come and meet the others who are going with you. (*Takes DON PRISCILIANO to the others.*) Les presento a Don Prisciliano.

DON PRISCILIANO: (*Talkative like most viejitos.*) Sí, es cierto, hace más de sixty years que mi vida terminó. My fiancée, María Isabel, and I were planning our wedding. We were novios for three years, mientras yo trabajaba, saving our money for the wedding. Y la noche antes de la boda, we all went swimming a las pompitas, the irrigation canals near Oracle. I kept going (*yelling to her*) "¡No te vayas a lo hondo! ¡No te vayas a lo hondo!" You see, she didn't know how to swim, but she wouldn't listen to me. Y se ahogó. Right in front of my eyes, she drowned. (*Beat.*) I tried to save her; I wanted to save her, pero no pude.

MAD DOG: And why not?

DON PRISCILIANO: ¡Porque yo tampoco sabía nadar!

MICTLANTECUHTLI: Pero anímese, Don Prisciliano. You'll be seeing María Isabel very soon. Está en Tlalocan. The land of Tlaloc, the water god. (*Beat. Giving orders as he removes the surgical gown and stethoscope.*) Bueno, you must make preparations for your journey. You'll need plenty of water, your favorite foods, pots and pans for cooking—pronto!

A lively polka is heard. Energy rises as the CALAVERA NURSE equips them for the trip with water, backpacks, etc.

DON PRISCILIANO: (*Mostly putting on a pair of pants behind a chair. Complaining.*) Pues yo digo, que no es proper que una señorita, como Xochil, haga travel sola, sin chaperone, con hombres—

ROCKY: Oh, Don Prisciliano, don't be so . . . prissy.

DON PRISCILIANO: (*Steps out.*) No soy prissy, but in my time—

ROCKY: (*Crosses.*) Han cambiado los tiempos since you were engaged. (*She links her arm through his.*)

XOCHIL: (*Also crosses to him.*) I've never ever gone on a trip, with or without men, Don Prisciliano. In fact, I never did get to do much of anything. And now, I'm ready to go to Mictlan. (*Links arms on his other side.*)

MAD DOG: (*Crosses next to* ROCKY.) And I will protect you! And if I can't—I've got this!

MAD DOG takes out a little toy dog from inside his shirt and places it on the floor. The dog has batteries that make him wiggle.

CASIMIRO: Good thinking, Mad Dog. The book says que ningún viajero a Mictlan puede caminar sin un perrito amarillo.

MICTLANTECUHTLI: Sí, es cierto. And in case que les dé hambre, you can always make him into taquitos de escuincles!

All react, horrified.

MICTLANTECUHTLI: (*Continues.*) Just kidding. But it would be one way to finish off that odious dog in the commercial: "Yo quiero Taco Bell!"

MAD DOG: (*Picks up the dog.*) Not this perrito. (*Links arms with* ROCKY.) Ready? (*Beat.*)

Music similar to The Wizard of Oz theme is heard. XOCHIL, ROCKY, MAD DOG, *and* DON PRISCILIANO *link arms, skip, hop, and sing in unison, to the tune of "We're off to see the wizard": "Vamos a ir a Mictlan, the wonderful world of the dead! The dead, the dead, the dead! O! Hermoso mundo Mictlan!"*
Lights go down as music goes up.

SCENE 12

Lights up and music down. XOCHIL, ROCKY, MAD DOG, DON PRISCILI-ANO, *and the* CALAVERA NURSE *have exited.* MICTLANTECUHTLI *is putting on his headdress.*

MICTLANTECUHTLI: Your friends are waiting for you; listo?

CASIMIRO: No son mis friends; I don't even know them.

Soft music, as in the beginning of CASIMIRO's *dream.*

MICTLANTECUHTLI: No? (*Beat.*) Casimiro, te dije que el perdón y la redención eran conceptos que yo no comprendía muy bien, perhaps they're concepts that are too modern for me to understand. También te dije que puedo cambiar el pasado—

CASIMIRO: ¡El pasado no me interesa!

MICTLANTECUHTLI: Then why are you forever dreaming of the past?

CASIMIRO: Porque nadie puede dirigir sus sueños. Not even you, the mighty Mictlantecuhtli.

MICTLANTECUHTLI: (*With sarcasm.*) Hello? Who do you think brought your Tata Remigio into your dream last night? And not only can I direct your dreams, I can bring the past to you. Now! Casimiro, listen carefully: sit down, close your eyes, put your head down, and start counting while your Tata Remigio hides from you. (*CASIMIRO follows his orders. Calls out to beyond.*) Vamos a su pueblito en México cuando eras un niño, many, many years before the tragedy at the border.

Lights down. The sound of a conch shell and indigenous music is heard.

MICTLANTECUHTLI: (*Continues.*) Casimiro, you're now very young; un chamaco, jugando en el monte, entre los nopales. Your grandfather's hiding from you, y tú lo buscas porque te prometió un cuento si lo encuentras. Find him!

CASIMIRO: (*Raises his head and finishes counting. As a young child.*) Veintiocho, veintinueve . . . ¡treinta! (*Runs around.*) ¡Tata Remigio! ¡Quiero mi cuento! (*Runs to slightly offstage and pulls DON REMIGIO forward.*)

Offstage voice of CASIMIRO'S MOTHER.

CASIMIRO'S MOTHER: ¡Casimiro, déjate de juegos y cuentos! Tienes que ir a ayudarle a tu padre en el molino.

CASIMIRO: (*Responding to offstage voice.*) I still have time! (*To DON REMIGIO.*) Please tell me a Yaqui legend, please, Tata. We still have time antes que entreguen el maíz al molino. Please.

DON REMIGIO: Bueno, hijo. Te platicaré de nuestra religión yaqui; but then you must go and help your father. You know that he needs your help. (*Sits down.*)

CASIMIRO: Sí, Tata Remigio, I will. (*Kneels on the floor next to DON REMIGIO.*) Abuelito, tell me about the seyewailo.

DON REMIGIO: Mijito, la seyewailo is the Yaqui convergence of time, place, direction, and quality of being—donde todo de la vida se junta, ¿me entiendes?

CASIMIRO: Sí, Tata, seyewailo also means "the earth covered with flowers," no?

DON REMIGIO: Mijo, óyeme bien. This is very important. Para llegar a seyewailo, un yaqui debe ser de buen corazón. With good heart. Some Yaquis have a very special power: seatakaa, the flower body. Sólo las personas de buen corazón tienen seatakaa. Only those persons that would never harm another person have this special power.

CASIMIRO: (*Impatiently.*) Sí, sí, Tata. A Yaqui must be with good heart to reach seyewailo—ahora, tell me about the sea ania—

DON REMIGIO: Again? Bueno. La sea ania is the essence of the Yaqui world of flowers. Someplace in the east—en un lugar "beneath the dawn"—está nuestra sea ania. And there, toda la belleza natural del Sonoran Desert may be seen. Las flores, el agua—abundancia de todo—pájaros, insects—all the animals live there. And especially the deer—

CASIMIRO: I know! I know! The Yaqui word for deer is malichi, ¿que no?

DON REMIGIO: (*Laughs. Proud that CASIMIRO remembers.*) Sí, hijo. Malichi. Our sacred deer. (*Starts to sing popular song.*) "Soy un pobre venadito que habita en la sea ania." (*Beat. Reflecting.*) Casimiro, hijo mío, last year, cuando estabas tan enfermo con una fiebre, I made a promise that I would teach you our deer dance and that you would dance it at our ceremonies.

CASIMIRO: Abuelito, teach me la Danza del Venado now; I know I can learn it. I'm ready. Mire.

(Tries to dance.)

MICTLANTECUHTLI: Dispense, Don Remigio, but we don't have time. Se nos terminó el tiempo; we must return to the present. Es la hora que Casimiro tiene que caminar hacia Mictlan.

Sound of conch shell once again and lights up. DON REMIGIO is standing at the top of the ramp.

DON REMIGIO: Ven, hijo mío, I will help you on your journey to Mictlan. You won't see me, but on every step of the way I will be with you, guiding you. (*Puts his hand out to CASIMIRO.*)

CASIMIRO, almost trancelike, starts to walk slowly up to DON REMIGIO.

DON REMIGIO: Escúchame bien, Casimiro: Life here on earth is a journey. And you are now embarking on a journey que sigue en este camino peligroso. On one side of this road, there is an abyss. (*CASIMIRO looks to one side of the ramp.*) En el otro lado del camino, otro abismo. (*CASIMIRO looks to the other side.*) You must walk without falling on either side; andando siempre en el mero centro del camino. Always, right in the center.

CASIMIRO centers himself and holds out his hand to DON REMIGIO. DON REMIGIO pulls CASIMIRO to him and embraces him.

DON REMIGIO: (*Continues.*) And at the end of your journey . . . (*His voice breaks. Beat. He is unable to continue.*)

MICTLANTECUHTLI: Siga, Don Remigio. And at the end of his journey—what?

DON REMIGIO: (*Turns to MICTLANTECUHTLI. Forcefully.*) Mictlantecuhtli, this time, he will not fail; Casimiro will fulfill his obligation and his destiny. (*Turns to CASIMIRO and places his hands on CASIMIRO's shoulders.*) And at the end of your journey, Casimiro, you will dance la Danza del Venado, y cumplirás la manda y tu destino.

Lights go down as la Danza del Venado music is heard.

TIME

Sometime in the beyond.

PLACE

Mictlan, which is rather brown and desolate. The center ramp or step unit now has a carpet runner with an Aztec design. There are two platforms with sloping ramps on each side of the stage and possibly some side-decorated pillars.

TECHNICAL NOTES

ACT TWO is one long scene and is not divided into traditional format; it should have a dream quality of seamless unconnectedness. Please note that the set does not change during ACT TWO.

The ALLEGORICAL DANGERS—BOULDERS, BLADES, WINDS, JAGUARS, and LIZARDS—are dressed in surrealistic costumes and masks and are positioned in place.

The ending will consist of two parallel scenes on the platforms that take place at the same time: the shooting at the border in 1977 and the gang shooting on the barrio street in 1997. Precise coordination of lights, sound cues, music, blocking, dialogue, repeated lines, pantomime, and freezes is required and is not always marked in the script.

Lights come up as indigenous Aztec music is heard. Then there is a soft drumbeat during MICTLANTECUHTLI's monologue.

MICTLANTECUHTLI is standing at the top of the center ramp or step unit, very much as he was in his first entrance in ACT ONE. The ALLEGORICAL DANGERS are simply lounging and making very slight, menacing movements. They will be choreographed to follow MICTLAN-TECUHTLI's descriptions.

MICTLANTECUHTLI: (*Directly to audience, almost chanting.*) En Apanohauyan, the water crossing place, los viajeros a Mictlan cruzaron el río on the back of a dog . . . (*an aside to the disbelieving audience*) . . . believe me, they did. (CASIMIRO, ROCKY, MAD DOG, XOCHIL, *and* DON PRISCILIANO *enter, tired and staggering from their arduous trip.*) Y en Tepetlimonamiquiyan, the place where mountains come together, las montañas golpearon a todos los viajeros. (BOULDERS *knock them around.*) En Itztepetl, the knives as sharp as obsidian blades made them bleed. (BLADES *cut them.*) Y en Ehecayan, the wind place, los fuertes vientos brought out the fierce jaguars and green lizards. (JAGUARS *and* LIZARDS *attack them.*) Pasaron por Pacoecoetlacayan, and in Temiminaloyan they were repeatedly shot by arrows. Y en Teo-coyllqualoyan, the place where one's heart is eaten, their corazones were ripped out. (*Any of the* DANGERS *can cut out their hearts. Another aside to audience.*) Créanmelo, you must suspend your disbelief, así pasó. (*All* DANGERS *exit.*) Hasta que por fin llegaron a Izmictlan, Apochcalocan, the place with no chimneys, o simplemente, el lugar sin escape. (*Starts to exit, sternly. Stops. Turns.*) Oh, what the hell. There is an escape. But I'll leave that to my compadres, Cantinflas and Quetzalcoatl.

A final sharp drumbeat is heard. Lights go down and MICTLANTECUHTLI *exits.* CASIMIRO, ROCKY, MAD DOG, XOCHIL, *and* DON PRISCILIANO *are huddled in a dead heap on the ground. Lights go up. They get up slowly, helping each other. They look around, trying to get their bearings.*

CASIMIRO: Bueno, parece que ya estamos en Mictlan.

XOCHIL: This is Mictlan? (*Disparagingly.*) Ghet-to heaven.

ROCKY: If it is, it looks like I'll need to take more pills!

DON PRISCILIANO: Casimiro, ¿qué hacemos ahora?

CASIMIRO: I don't know what you'll do, Don Prisciliano, pero I'm heading back to the hospital. Mictlantecuhtli just said I had to bring you here, to Mictlan. Pues aquí están.

MAD DOG: But where's Mictlantecuhtli? Shouldn't he be here? How are we supposed to know where to go now?

DON PRISCILIANO: Casimiro, yo no pienso que nomás te puedes ir and just leave us here. Alone.

All ad lib, worried and complaining.

CASIMIRO: Quiet, everybody! Everyone, stay here, and I'll try to find him. (*Exits.*)

CANTINFLAS: (*Enters as* TOUR GUIDE. *To* TRAVELERS.) Bienvenidos a Mictlan, my sweethearts. (*He places arms around* XOCHIL *and* ROCKY's *shoulders in a very familiar manner.*) Let me give you a brief overview of your new residence, el merito Mictlan.

LA LLORONA: (*Enters, crosses, practicing her wailing.*) ¡Ay, mis hijos! Where are my children?

(*Stops, takes a can of hair spray from a shopping bag, and sprays her hair. Continues wailing as she exits.*)

ROCKY: (*In wonder.*) Es la Llorona. All my life I've been afraid of her and now I finally get to see her.

CANTINFLAS: La Llorona? There's really no reason to be afraid of her; she just has a bad reputation. Como dice el refrán: cobra fama y acuéstate a dormir. Es la best friend de la goddess Chocaciuatl. Y las dos son bien chillo-nas. Actually, there's three crybabies. (*Begins to cry as he gives lecture.*)

Chocaciuatl was the first of all mothers to die in childbirth, forever wandering, forever wailing for her lost baby and her own life. La tercera chillona es the goddess Cihuacoatl, que siempre se viste de blanco and also roams the earth, weeping and wailing, predicando guerras y miseria. (*Blows his nose loudly.*) But we should be the ones weeping and wailing, porque fue Ciuacoatl who gave mankind the tools of labor: el azadón and the tumpline—

DON PRISCILIANO: Herramienta para que el hombre trabajara como un buey—

CANTINFLAS: (*Abruptly continues his tour lecture.*) El calendario azteca is divided into . . . (*he takes out pad and pencil, licks the pencil, and writes as he talks*) eighteen months, each with twenty days, porque mire usted, dieciocho por veinte equals three hundred and sixty days, and it's very clear that the year has three hundred and sixty-five days, ¿verdad, chato? Sí, pero no. Vea usted, ahí 'sta el detalle, compadre. Sobran cinco días. Entonces, in these leftover five days, useless and inservibles, porque dígame usted, Don Prisciliano, what do we need these five days for? (*DON PRISCILIANO opens his mouth to answer, but CANTINFLAS merely takes a deep breath and continues.*) Es bueno el cilantro, pero no tanto, y no todo en el monte es orégano, ¿verdad? Pues por eso mismo le digo, that's precisely why we have días de los muertos. To use up these five days. Pero, llegaron los españoles y lueguito metieron la pata, con sus santos y misas y qué sé yo, y luego los gringos con su "Halloween" y "trick or treat." Bueno pues, lo que se va a pelar que se vaya remojando. Caminen, caminen, no se haga bola.

CÉSAR CHÁVEZ: (*Enters, reading his notes.*) Tenemos que organizar a todos los trabajadores en Tlalocan. We have to demand better wages, an eight-hour day, breaks, clean and sanitary bathrooms.

CANTINFLAS: Es el señor César Chávez, el presidente de los United Farmworkers. He and I came to Mictlan almost at the same time. Fíjense nomás, when he was alive, he was always organizing, organizing, organizing. Y desde que llegó a Mictlan, ¿qué creen ustedes que se la pasa haciendo? Organizing! He hasn't stopped organizing. Listen to him; está preparando su speech para los aguacateros, newly arrived de por allá de Chula Vista, California, y que bien lo saben son rabble-rousers criados en Oaxaca donde se conocen sus derechos, not like the mensos en Tlalocan. Pay attention.

CÉSAR CHÁVEZ: (*Repeats. Louder.*) Tenemos que organizar a todos los trabajadores en Tlalocan. We have to demand better wages, an eight-hour day, breaks, clean and sanitary bathrooms . . . (*XOCHIL moves away from the other TRAVELERS and moves closer to hear CÉSAR CHÁVEZ.*) Vacaciones con pago, agua fresca, todos los días de fiesta pagados o double pay if they have to work on holidays. Aguacateros, ¡sálganse de los files! (*Starts to exit.*)

XOCHIL: Mr. Chávez! Please wait; who are the aguacateros?

CÉSAR CHÁVEZ: They are the avocado pickers, m'ija. They have very dangerous jobs, way up in the trees, cutting avocadoes with sharp knives—vente conmigo, I'll introduce you to them. (*Starts to exit with* XOCHIL. *Stops.*) Ah, but what's your name?

XOCHIL: Xochil Martínez.

CÉSAR CHÁVEZ: Xochil? (*Leading her.*) Wait until you see the flowers in Tlalocan. They are the most beautiful flowers on earth—pero we must organize the nursery workers—

XOCHIL: (*Stops in her tracks.*) Nursery? With babies? I distinctly told Mictlantecuhtli that I wouldn't be stuck babysitting in Chichihuacuahco—

CÉSAR CHÁVEZ: No, no. This is a nursery for plants and flowers and they need tender care just like babies, pero Tlaloc tiene un foreman . . . (*CÉSAR CHÁVEZ continues talking as he and* XOCHIL *exit.*)

ROCKY: Oh, no! Did you hear what he said about the avocado workers? He wants them to go on strike! And if they go on strike, we won't have guacamole for the Super Bowl fiesta tonight and I must find Selena and convince her to let me help her choreograph the half-time dance . . . (*Her attention is caught by* EHECATL's *entrance.*)

EHECATL *enters, in full costume and mask, carrying his bench and a bag filled with "PowerBall" numbered balls. He sits down and starts to throw the balls around.*

MAD DOG: Who's that vato?

CANTINFLAS: Ese "vato" es Ehecatl, god of the wind. Bueno, technically he's another aspect of our great Quetzalcoatl, pero eso es demasiado metaphysical to explain to mere mortals, so never mind.

MAD DOG: What's he doing with those balls?

CANTINFLAS: Picking the PowerBall winner. Ehecatl loves to roam the earth—y aquí en Mictlan—dressed in rags, sentadito en su banco.

MAD DOG: Why does he do that?

CANTINFLAS: If I knew that, no anduviera aquí de tour guide. Pero lo que sí sé, es que si you catch him, he'll grant you a wish and a long life to enjoy it.

MAD DOG and ROCKY: (*Together as they exchange looks.*) Un wish?

CANTINFLAS: Aha, un wish. (*Continues as* TOUR GUIDE.) Por aquí tenemos Tlalocan, the land of water, filled with corn, frijol—all kinds of beans—squash, and chili. Chili, pues pa' que les cuento: chili colorado, chili del árbol, serrano, jalapeños, chili piquín, chili poblano—

DON PRISCILIANO: Déjese de chilis, Señor Cantinflas. I'm dying to see my fiancée—bueno, ya murió—and Mictlantecuhtli said that María Isabel, mi novia, está aquí, en Tlalocan, because she died by drowning. (*To others.*) Verán cuando la vean; she's so beautiful and—

CANTINFLAS: ¿Se ahogó? Ah, pues sí, todos los ahogados llegan aquí, a Tlalocan. Y ahí les va algo muy interesante que yo sé que no sabían porque apenas lo supe yo, pero not only do the drowned ones end up here in Tlalocan, but also the ones que les pegó un rayo, or that died from water-related enfermedades like gout o pulmonía y—

DON PRISCILIANO: ¿Pues dónde está? Yo quiero ver a mi novia ahorita mismo. Where is she?

CANTINFLAS: Ay, Don Prisciliano, pues where else do you think she'd be? (*Points offstage.*) Allí, en aquel swimming pool, taking swimming lessons, pues no faltaba más . . . (*continues without pause*) sigamos a Chichihuacuahco, land of infants and children, where el árbol chichihuacuahitl nourishes them with milk from its leaves. Caminen, caminen, no se hagan bola. Walk this way.

All follow CANTINFLAS—*comedy bit, imitating his famous walk—and exit.*

DON PRISCILIANO: (*Stops. To himself.*) Yo no tengo que ir a ningún Chichihuacuahco; yo voy a buscar a mi María Isabel en la alberca. That shouldn't be hard; I remember exactly how she looked that night she drowned. Recuerdo muy bien como se veía, con su bathing suit—modesto, no disoluto—so beautiful, so young. (*Starts to sing.*) "Coje tu sombrero y póntelo, vamos a la playa, calienta el sol. Chiviriviri—" (*Exits.*)

EHECATL *glances up and sees that he's now alone. Stands and picks up his bench and starts to cross, stealthily. Entering from the opposite side that they exited,* ROCKY *and* MAD DOG *sneak up behind* EHECATL, *match their steps to his, and grab him.* EHECATL *puts up a struggle, but he is quickly subdued and forced to sit down on his bench.* MAD DOG *holds him down on one side and* ROCKY *holds him down on the other side.* DON PRISCILIANO *enters, sputtering, with a chubby* MARÍA ISABEL, *who is wearing a very old-fashioned bathing suit and cap.*

DON PRISCILIANO: (*Still sputtering, indignant.*) Esta . . . dice . . . que es . . . María Isabel.

ROCKY and MAD DOG: (*Together, introduce themselves but do not release* EHECATL.) Mucho gusto, Rocky Road y Mad Dog, a sus órdenes.

DON PRISCILIANO: ¡No! ¡No! No es mi María Isabel. Esta es una vieja; mi María Isabel is seventeen.

MARÍA ISABEL: I was seventeen, but Prisciliano, that was over sixty years ago.

DON PRISCILIANO: Yes, but now you're so . . . old.

MARÍA ISABEL: Well, viejo chorro, have you looked in the mirror lately? (*Exits in a huff, sputtering insults.*)

ROCKY: Se fue bien enojada, Don Prisciliano.

DON PRISCILIANO: (*Somewhat remorseful.*) I'm sorry, but did you see her? My María Isabel was so beautiful, and so—

EHECATL: Young?

DON PRISCILIANO: ¿Y a usted quien le dio permiso pa' que se metiera en la conversación?

MAD DOG: (*Quickly.*) Don Prisciliano, this is the god Ehecatl. ¿Se acuerda? The Cantinflas dude told us he can grant wishes.

DON PRISCILIANO: ¿Un deseo? (*Gets idea.*) Hmmm.

EHECATL: Yes, but only if you let me get up. I'm not going to run away, ¿qué creen? ¿Que soy un leprechaun?

ROCKY and MAD DOG release him.

DON PRISCILIANO: Señor dios Ehecatl, yo quisiera que—

EHECATL: Ay, Don Prisciliano, I'm sorry. I know what your wish is, but I can't grant it. I cannot make your María Isabel young again. Don Prisciliano, todos estos años, you've been in love with a memory, and now it's time for you to fall in love with the present.

DON PRISCILIANO: Y entonces, ¿de qué demonios sirve?

Exits grumbling about useless gods. XOCHIL enters, carrying a flower.

XOCHIL: (*To EHECATL.*) Can you really grant us a wish?

EHECATL: Sí, I can grant wishes. Bueno, within reason. Pero before you ask me for anything, think about it. Above all, consider your reasons. Ya vieron a Don Prisciliano, his was a purely selfish wish, pero everyone does that at first. I'll give you some time to reflect on your wish. Piénsenlo muy bien; and one more thing: you must justify your wish. (*Exits.*)

XOCHIL: Think about it? That'll take forever! Where do I start? I never got to do anything!

ROCKY: And I already did everything! I don't need a wish. (*Exits.*)

MAD DOG: And everything I did, I did for the wrong reasons.

XOCHIL and MAD DOG share brief awkward moment, neither knowing what to say next. The same music as when XOCHIL entered in ACT ONE continues during this dialogue.

XOCHIL: Well, if neither Rocky nor Don Prisciliano get to make a wish, I guess that leaves just you and me, no? But how does this work? Do we really get to wish anything?

MAD DOG: Remember, he said "within reason" and "justified." You know, like in those social science exercises: you're in a spaceship or a raft in the middle of the ocean, and you have room for only six persons, do you throw out the prostitute or the matches?

XOCHIL: Oh, forget about the matches. I never went out on a date, much less a spaceship. (*Plays with her flower nervously.*) I never danced with a boy, and I never, ever . . . got kissed.

MAD DOG: (*Beat.*) We might end up having the same wish. (*Crosses to her.*) I never went out on a date (MAD DOG *takes the flower from* XOCHIL's *hand*), danced with a girl (*holds her other hand*), or ever . . . kissed (*kisses the flower*) a girl. (*He then brushes* XOCHIL's *lips with the flower.* XOCHIL *takes his hand and both look into each other's eyes.*) Would you vote to throw me off the raft in the middle of the ocean?

XOCHIL: Depends. Is the ocean filled with sharks?

MAD DOG: Sharks, barracudas, giant squid, piranhas—

XOCHIL: Piranhas? In the ocean? I thought they were somewhere in the Amazon—

MAD DOG: OK, the Amazon. Would you throw me off the raft and keep all the water for yourself?

XOCHIL: (*Teasing.*) Maybe.

MAD DOG and XOCHIL *lower hands. Soft kiss.* EHECATL *enters. Sighs. MAD DOG and* XOCHIL *break apart quickly. Beat.* MAD DOG *and* XOCHIL *exchange looks.*

MAD DOG and XOCHIL: (*Together.*) Dios Ehecatl, we have our wish; we want to—

EHECATL: (*Sadly.*) Sí, yo sé. But your wishes cannot—

Interrupted when ROCKY ROAD *enters with* LA LLORONA *in tow; she is wearing something obviously borrowed from* ROCKY *and pink plastic rollers in her hair.*

ROCKY: Mr. Ehecatl Quetzalcoatl, I've been networking with this lady, and we need to deal with her depression and self punishment. Sure, she did wrong, pero even the prisoners on death row can get out on appeals, entonces, ¿por qué esta pobre mujer no? Y nada de Prozac. We've decided that Chichihua-cuahco, where all the babies are at, needs to be reorganized. The children there do nothing but drink milk from that immense . . . chichi tree—well, you tell him our plans, Chillona.

ROCKY *pushes* LA LLORONA *forward.*

LA LLORONA: Queremos establish un beauty shop for all the working moms and a day-care center para los niños, con música, theater, arts and crafts. Y vamos a tener poetry readings, plays—muchas cosas—para los aguacateros con el Señor Chávez, y—

DON PRISCILIANO *and* MARÍA ISABEL *enter, holding hands.*

DON PRISCILIANO: ¿Gran dios Ehecatl? (*Embarrassed slightly.*) My wish is—to marry María Isabel!

MARÍA ISABEL: I have forgiven his unkind words and have agreed—again—to be his wife.

EHECATL: Bueno, let me review your wishes. Raquel Castillo, is this your wish then, to work with the niños en Chichihuacuahco? (*ROCKY nods yes.*)

XOCHIL: And my wish is I want to—

MAD DOG: It's the same as mine. We both want to—

EHECATL: Wait, Xochil and Mad Dog. (*To ROCKY.*) ¿Estás segura? It'll be a drastic change from your life when your T-shirt's slogan was "Life is too short to dance with ugly men," ¿no te parece?

ROCKY: Oh, that was the shallow Rocky Road. You know, dios Ehecatl, when I was alive I never realized that the best thing, the very best thing about life, is that we can always . . . (*Trying to think of the word.*)

ALL: (*Impatiently.*) ¡¿Qué pues?!

ROCKY: (*Calmly.*) Change. If I had, I guess I never would've taken those pills.

MAD DOG: Our wish is to—

EHECATL: ¿Y usted, Don Prisciliano? Your wish is to marry María Isabel and stay here?

DON PRISCILIANO: Sí. Dijo bien, I was in love with a memory, pero ya veo que la María Isabel that I knew and loved is still the same one, underneath the old body here.

MARÍA ISABEL: Sí, Prisciliano, and even though our bodies get old and wrinkled, our corazones don't get old.

DON PRISCILIANO: Es cierto; our corazones siempre recuerdan el "first love."

CANTINFLAS: (*Enters and crosses.*) Bueno, si vamos a tener una boda y una fiesta, tenemos mucho que preparar. Lo que se va a pelar, que se vaya remojando. Vente, Chato.

Exits with DON PRISCILIANO and MARÍA ISABEL.

ROCKY: If there's going to be a fiesta, we have to find Selena. She promised me that I could choreograph one of the halftime dances at the Super Bowl. (*To LA LLORONA, giving her "bad hair day" tips.*) Mira, Chillona, con el humidity que tenemos aquí, necesitas un buen mousse; I know how to make an excellent moisturizer from the nopal, sí, el cactus, es un secreto, pero I'll share it with you, just don't be a crybaby anymore, OK?

ROCKY and LA LLORONA exit. MAD DOG and XOCHIL exchange uneasy looks. EHECATL is clearly uncomfortable.

XOCHIL: It looks as though Don Prisciliano's and Rocky Road's wishes are to remain here, in Mictlan.

EHECATL nods yes.

MAD DOG: Well, that takes care of two of the wishes. What about our wishes? You can't keep stalling around—

CÉSAR CHÁVEZ: (*Enters.*) Xochil! You must come quickly. The meeting you had with Tlaloc's foreman—¿qué le dijiste?—he has agreed to start negotiations, and you must be at these meetings to—

Starts to exit with XOCHIL.

XOCHIL: Wait, Mr. Chávez. Mad Dog, come with us; we need all the help we can get.

MAD DOG: (*To* EHECATL.) I know there's something wrong here that you don't want to tell us.

CÉSAR CHÁVEZ: Xochil, we have to go before the foreman changes his mind.

XOCHIL: Please, Mad Dog.

MAD DOG: All right, I'll go with you, but I'm not gonna carry no picket sign. That would ruin my image. (*Crosses to them, strutting. Stops. To* EHECATL.) But I'll be back and I'm getting my wish.

XOCHIL, MAD DOG, *and* CÉSAR CHÁVEZ *exit.*

CASIMIRO: (*Enters.*) Well, that should make it easier for you, no? Sólo te quedan los wishes de Xochil y Mad Dog.

EHECATL: Sí, pero there's a problem; they both have the same wish: to return to the living.

CASIMIRO: (*Impressed.*) Can you do that?

EHECATL: ¿Yo? No. Sólo Mictlantecuhtli puede regresar los muertos a la vida. And only in very special cases. Es algo muy difícil: the circumstances, the timing, el . . . sacrificio.

CASIMIRO: Sacrifice?

A special light goes on MICTLANTECUHTLI. *Drums and conch shell sounds are heard. The same Aztec or indigenous music as before is also heard.* MICTLANTECUHTLI *is standing exactly as when he first appeared to* CASIMIRO *in* ACT ONE, *and next to him, an assistant is burning copal.*

MICTLANTECUHTLI: Sí, el sacrificio. Before I can return someone who has died back to the land of the living, another living being must be willing to die and take that person's place aquí en Mictlan.

CASIMIRO: Die?

MICTLANTECUHTLI: (*With sarcasm.*) Sí, dying is usually enough. Una vida por otra vida, you might say. So, qué dices, Casimiro, would you be willing to give up your life for one of your friends? For Xochil or Mad Dog?

CASIMIRO: ¡Ya te dije que no son mis friends! I only helped them because you made me. I've done what you wanted, now let me go back. Es demasiado lo que pides. No one can be expected to give up his life for a stranger. (*Starts to exit.*)

MICTLANTECUHTLI: No, I guess not. Pero entonces, ¿qué tal si la conoces? (*CASI-MIRO stops in his tracks.*) It's been a long time, Casimiro—twenty years to be exact—but surely you remember . . . Mariel?

MARIEL: (*Enters. Calls him to pose for the picture.*) ¡Casimiro! ¡Ven, apúrate! Manuel nos va a tomar una foto.

CASIMIRO: Mariel!

MARIEL: ¡Ven, Casimiro! (*Holds her hand out to CASIMIRO.*)

MICTLANTECUHTLI: (*Taunting.*) Anda, ve, Casimiro.

CASIMIRO starts to go to MARIEL, holding out his hand to her.

MICTLANTECUHTLI: (*Continues.*) Ahora sí le puedes dar la mano. After all, it's just for a photo, no? ¿Por qué, no se la diste aquella noche en el desierto? (*CASIMIRO hesitates.*) Take Mariel's hand!

CASIMIRO: No, no puedo. I know what you're asking me to do, but I'm not ready to die.

MICTLANTECUHTLI: Casimiro, Casimiro. ¿De veras no ves? You're already dying, Casimiro. ¿Me entiendes? You're dying, there on the recliner, with my book on your chest; y el sueño que tuviste de tu abuelo y Mariel was to be your last dream. You're just like Don Prisciliano, living in the past.

CASIMIRO: Maybe the past is safer.

MICTLANTECUHTLI: Maybe. (*Beat.*) Pero, Casimiro, ¿sabes qué es lo más triste? That you're gonna lay there, dead, día tras día, hasta que someone finally notices that the hospital garbage is piling up, porque nobody will notice that you're gone, Casimiro. Nobody. Oh, but I'm forgetting your sweetheart, Geraldine. Ella sí va a derramar muchas lágrimas—

DON REMIGIO: (*Enters. Forcefully.*) ¡Mictlantecuhtli! ¡Ya déjalo! No trates a mi nieto como un ratón entre las garras de un gato. You told him he only had to bring the four bodies to Mictlan; he's done that. Ahora, déjalo que regrese.

MICTLANTECUHTLI: (*Chastened.*) Perdóneme, Don Remigio, dice bien. Go, Casimiro, and get your water and food for your journey back.

CASIMIRO starts to exit.

DON REMIGIO: ¡Hijo! Espera—prove to Mictlantecuhtli and to yourself que sí tienes seatakaa, the flower body. Que sí eres de buen corazón. Help Mariel now and forever change your past.

CASIMIRO stops and turns to MARIEL, giving her a thoughtful look. Beat.

CASIMIRO: No, Abuelito. Lo siento, pero yo no tengo seatakaa. Yo sí he lastimado a otras personas. I am not of a good heart. (*Exits.*)

MICTLANTECUHTLI: I'm sorry, Mariel; you must remain in Mictlan.

MARIEL exits.

Don Remigio: Estaba segura que Casimiro—

Mictlantecuhtli: Give up, Don Remigio; he's failed again.

Don Remigio: No tuve bastante tiempo para prepararlo con sólo una noche. Mictlantecuhtli, I need more time!

Mictlantecuhtli: But we don't have more time! Ya es demasiado tarde para Mariel, but there's still hope for Xochil.

Don Remigio: Only Xochil? Are you forgetting that Mad Dog wants to return also? Son dos almas, dos cuerpos. You need two bodies.

Mictlantecuhtli: Yes, I know, but there's also the special consideration for exceptional bravery. Yo creo que'l Mad Dog—

Don Remigio: Mad Dog? (*Beat.*) Yes, I see what you're planning. And if Casimiro—

Mictlantecuhtli: Forget Casimiro! Él es un cobarde, and I'm sending him back to his Geraldine.

Starts to exit.

Don Remigio: Casimiro is not a coward!

Mictlantecuhtli: ¿No? ¿Que no lo vio, Don Remigio? Ni el gran amor que le tiene a Mariel fue suficiente.

Don Remigio: Mictlantecuhtli, tú nunca has sido cruel. Give him another chance.

Mictlantecuhtli: Another chance? ¿Para qué?

Don Remigio: Para que encuentre ese perdón que busca.

Mictlantecuhtli: You know that the foregiveness he seeks must come from himself.

Don Remigio: Nosotros vemos eso; pero él no lo ve. We must help him see this.

Mictlantecuhtli: (*Beat.*) There's only one way left to find out.

Don Remigio, realizing what Mictlantecuhtli means, nods his head slowly.

Don Remigio: Sí, volveremos al pasado.

Mictlantecuhtli: Bueno. We will let the events of those nights reoccur.

A conch shell is heard. Mysterious lights dance across the stage. The music is a blending of previous music, almost jarring, as when a sound technician is trying to find a cue.

Mictlantecuhtli: (*Continues.*) Esta será la última vez que Casimiro podrá cambiar su destino. There will not be another.

Lights go down.

Don Prisciliano: (*Enters with his chair. Talks at times to himself and at other times to audience.*) Sí, I saw everything. Bueno, almost everything. I didn't see Rocky take the pills or I would've called the paramedics, although no sé si hubiera servido de nada porque los paramedics don't want to go to my house after . . . Yo, como siempre, estaba sentado afuera—ahí. (*Points and crosses.*) Just watching people go by. Nomás sentado ahí, looking across the street at a vacant lot, wondering: when did it become a vacant lot? Una vez era un negocio, lots of trucks in and out, mucho ruido . . . (*Sits down.*)

The sounds of trucks, etc., are heard.

DON PRISCILIANO: (*Continues.*) Muchos trabajadores, and then one day—nothing. (*The sound stops abruptly.*) Not even one brick. (*Beat.*) Primero, Xochil came down the street.

XOCHIL: (*Enters, talking to someone offstage.*) How come I always have to go for his tortillas?

Freeze.

DON PRISCILIANO: I knew that she would stop and talk to me. Siempre que la mandaban a la tiendita de la esquina, y le dijían que se hiciera "hurry up," ella siempre hallaba tiempo para platicar con este viejo. Not like that pachuco, Mad Dog, strutting como un gallito del gallinero. I'm not sure if Xochil really liked to stop to talk to me or if she only did it to make her father mad for making her go to the store all the time. Anyway, I always enjoyed our pláticas.

XOCHIL breaks freeze and crosses to DON PRISCILIANO.

XOCHIL: (*Dreamy.*) For my quinceañera, Don Prisciliano, I'm gonna have fourteen madrinas and they're gonna each carry a bouquet of white roses with pink and lavender ribbon streamers—my favorite colors—

DON PRISCILIANO: (*On his own usual subject, his health.*) Todo el día he tenido un dolorcito right here on my chest. It hurts more when I take a deep breath—like this. (*Breathes deeply.*)

XOCHIL: And their caps come over their foreheads, like this, pointing down, in a triangle, you know, sorta like from Romeo and Juliet's time, with little pearls hanging—

DON PRISCILIANO: Xochil, dime una cosa: when did that building across the street disappear?

MARIEL: (*Enters, leading a cheer with her bedraggled pom-pom.*) A la bim, a la bum, a la bim, bum, bah—

Freeze.

XOCHIL: Disappear? It didn't "disappear." Don Prisciliano, lo tumbaron last year, ¿que no se acuerda? You sat here every day and watched the wrecking crew from sunup to sundown. Remember?

DON PRISCILIANO: Sí, ya recuerdo. But what I said about the building disappearing, yo sé que it didn't just "disappear." Pero tengo miedo que someday alguien va mirar pa'ca and see this empty chair and wonder, when did that old man disappear?

XOCHIL: Oh, Don Prisciliano, don't worry; you're not gonna "disappear." (*Back to her usual subject, without dropping a beat.*) And I haven't decided if the dresses will have hoops, like in *Gone with the Wind*, you know? But probably not, 'cause all my madrinas say they won't wear them, but I tell them: whose quinceañera is it, yours or mine?

DON PRISCILIANO: (*Continues on his subject.*) Maybe not "disappear," but what if I die someday?

MARIEL: (*Breaks freeze, finishing her cheer.*) "Nogales, Nogales, rah, rah rah!" (*Jumping up and down.*) ¡Ganamos, ganamos! (*Freeze.*)

XOCHIL: You're not gonna die. Besides, if you do, I'll always think of you when I have to go to the store for my Dad's tortillas. I promise. (*Starts to leave.*) Con su permiso, do you need anything from the tiendita?

DON PRISCILIANO: Sí, hija. Cómprame un frasquito de Vicks. No se te olvide. Vicks. I don't want Mentholatum. Tiene que ser Vicks. (*Stands up to get the money from his pants' pocket.*)

A danzón is heard. ROCKY ROAD *enters carrying a cellular phone and pacing nervously. She carries a large purse on her shoulder as though ready to leave the house.*

XOCHIL: Look, Don Prisciliano, up there. See? La Rocky Road. What's she doing?

DON PRISCILIANO: (*Looks up at* ROCKY ROAD.) Pues, what she's been doing all week, m'ijita. Walking back and forth with that newfangled telephone, waiting for the llamada.

XOCHIL: Who calls her?

ROCKY: (*Willing phone to ring.*) Ring, dammit, ring. (*Freeze.*)

DON PRISCILIANO: Quién sabe, pero I think it was someone that used to call her every day, a todas horas, and she'd jump in her car and run all over town with him, probably. Pero luego, las llamadas stopped. Pobrecita.

A contemporary rap is heard. MAD DOG *enters, strutting.*

XOCHIL: (*Turns toward* MAD DOG.) Here comes that loser, Mad Dog. (*Freeze.*)

DON PRISCILIANO: (*Also turns.*) Desgraciado pachuco, perro callejero; stay away from him, Xochil.

Freeze.

MAD DOG *gives his monologue as he finishes dressing in a ritualistic manner, similar to a matador—buttoning shirt, combing hair, folding handkerchief, putting it on as a headband, shades, etc.—as all are in freeze position, watching him, hypnotized like spectators seeing a cobra coming out of a basket.*

MAD DOG: (*Getting ready to face rival gang.*) After I beat up my foster mother's real kid, the welfare said they were going to have to put me in another foster home. And nobody ever asked me why I beat up the punk. He used to go into the room and sit across from me, drinking this big glass of ice-cold milk. The rest of us foster kids weren't allowed to get into the milk 'cause it was just his milk, she said. Just some cheap fruit punch she got with the food stamps was what we had to drink.

The recorded voice of MAD DOG'S FOSTER MOTHER *is heard in the background.*

MAD DOG'S FOSTER MOTHER: Mad Dog! Vente a comer, and don't you dare say nothing about it just being baloney y papas, qué crees, que the welfare money is for millionaires?

MAD DOG: I bet you've never tasted baloney con papas, tomato sauce, and onions. Tastes like shit.

Freeze.
The recorded voice of XOCHIL'S MOTHER *is now heard.*

XOCHIL'S MOTHER: ¡Xochil! ¡Apúrate! Your dad's waiting for his tortillas!

XOCHIL: (*Breaks freeze. To* DON PRISCILIANO. *Repeating previous lines.*) For my quinceañera, I'm gonna have fourteen madrinas and they're gonna each carry a bouquet of white roses with pink and lavender ribbon streamers—my favorite colors—marching like this . . . (*Freeze.*)

DON PRISCILIANO: (*Breaks freeze. Repeating previous lines.*) Todo el día he tenido un dolorcito right here on my chest. It hurts more when I take a deep breath—like this. (*Breathes deeply. Freeze.*)

EL COYOTE enters. He is not wearing the coyote mask. He is counting money and talking to an unseen "associate."

DON REMIGIO: (*Enters.*) ¡Coyote, maldito! (*Freeze. Angry, fist up.*)

EL COYOTE: Yo le dije a Casimiro que les cobraría "group rate"! It's not worth the risk to cross with less than ten persons, pero ya llevan más de tres años juntando el dinero. I'll make an exception just this once. Cruzar a los cinco a la noche. There's five of them: Casimiro and his four friends. (*Freeze.*)

MAD DOG: (*Breaks freeze.*) So I wrote a letter to my sister, BeeBee, in California, asking if I could go live with her and her husband. She says they live in some apartments that have a swimming pool for everybody to use. A swimming pool. It took her over two months before she finally answered my letter. "Sorry, but Brian thinks that you'd be a bad influence on our younger kids." Can you believe that? Bad influence? Me? (*Freeze.*)

The sound of a telephone ringing insistently is heard.

ROCKY ROAD: (*Breaks freeze. Continues pacing with phone but doesn't answer it.*) I know exactly what he's gonna say. (*Quoting her* SUGAR DADDY'S *litany of excuses.*) "Sorry, sweetheart, but you know how it is, in-laws came into town, had to take them and wife and kids to Sea World, the baby has a temperature, too much sun, I guess, you understand, don't you? Ah, c'mon, don't be like that—"

Throws telephone into her purse. Freeze.

MARIEL: (*Breaks freeze.*) Nogales, Nogales, rah, rah, rah! (*Jumping up and down.*) ¡Ganamos! ¡Ganamos! (MIGUEL, JESÚS, *and* CARLOS *enter and join* MARIEL'S *jumping and hugging.*) ¡Casimiro! ¡Ven, apúrate! Manuel nos va a tomar una foto. (MARIEL *and the* MALE FRIENDS *group themselves as in the photo on* CASIMIRO'S *altar. Insistent.*) Casimiro, ven. No vamos a sacar la foto sin ti. Manuel, espera. ¡Casimiro!

CASIMIRO *enters, crosses to* MARIEL *and* FRIENDS, *and joins them in the pose for the camera. He places one arm around* MARIEL. *The previously recorded line from the unseen amateur photographer,* MANUEL, *is heard.*

MANUEL: Pero no tan serios, you're not at a funeral. ¡Sonrían!

CASIMIRO AND FOUR FRIENDS: (*In unison. Smiling.*) ¡Enchiladas de pollo!

The flash of a camera is seen. CASIMIRO *and* FRIENDS *freeze as though in a photograph.* NOTE TO DIRECTOR: *By now everyone should be in a freeze position. Some, but not all, of the freezes will break with sound cues. Also, some of the lines are intentionally repeated and out of order, overlapping, fast-paced, and without pauses. The repeat recorded voice of* XOCHIL'S MOTHER *is heard.*

XOCHIL'S MOTHER: ¡Xochil! ¡Apúrate! Your dad's waiting for his tortillas!

XOCHIL: (*Breaks freeze. To* DON PRISCILIANO. *Repeating previous lines.*) For my quinceañera, I'm gonna have fourteen madrinas and they're gonna each carry a bouquet of white roses with pink and lavender ribbon streamers—my favorite colors—marching like this—

The repeat recorded voice of MAD DOG'S FOSTER MOTHER *is heard.*

MAD DOG'S FOSTER MOTHER: Mad Dog! Vente a comer, and don't you dare say nothing about it just being baloney y papas, qué crees, que the welfare money is for millionaires?

MAD DOG: (*Breaks freeze. Gets gun out.*) So. Fuck the baloney con papas.

The recorded voice of ROCKY'S SUGAR DADDY *on the telephone is heard.*

ROCKY'S SUGAR DADDY: (*Caressingly, sexy.* ROCKY *breaks freeze and rummages through her purse, taking out bottles of pills.*) Sorry, sweetheart, but you know how it is, in-laws came into town, I had to take them and the kids to

Sea World, the baby has a temperature, too much sun, I guess, you understand, don't you? Ah, c'mon, don't be like that—

EL COYOTE: (*Breaks freeze. Gun in his hand. Defensively.*) Hey! It's a job; someone's gotta do it.

DON REMIGIO: (*Breaks freeze.*) ¡Coyote, maldito!

MAD DOG: I'm going out to waste either El Tanque or El Peewa. Maybe both.

DON PRISCILIANO: (*Breaks freeze. Repeats line.*) Desgraciado pachuco.

EL COYOTE and MAD DOG put guns into waistbands in same movement.

EL COYOTE: (*Crosses to CASIMIRO. Familiarly.*) Casimiro! Amigo mío. (*He pulls CASIMIRO out of the pose and others remain in freeze.*) ¿Ya tienes el dinero pa' cruzar la frontera a la noche?

CASIMIRO: Sí, I have the money.

EL COYOTE: Pues, it's about time. Ya llevas más de tres años saving for the trip. ¿Y tus amigos? Did you convince them to cross with you?

CASIMIRO: Sí, there's five of us now. Ellos también tienen el dinero.

EL COYOTE: (*In an aside.*) ¡Cinco pollos!

DON PRISCILIANO: (*Repeats previous lines.*) Xochil, cómprame un frasquito de Vicks. Tengo un dolorcito right here on my chest. No se te olvide. Vicks. I don't want Mentholatum. Tiene que ser Vicks.

XOCHIL and EL COYOTE take the money.

EL COYOTE: (*To CASIMIRO.*) Hicistes bien, Casimiro, porque así les cobro "group rate"! It's not worth the risk to cross with less than ten persons, but for you, I'll make an exception this time. Cruzaré a los cinco a la noche. I'm taking a loss, tú sabes, pero como eres amigo mío . . . (*Turns to FOUR FRIENDS.*) ¡A la noche, muchachos, a los United States of America!

FRIENDS and EL COYOTE break freeze. They prepare for the crossing, putting on pre-set jackets, mochilas with a few clothes, and water. Talk turns to food: fried chicken, chop suey, etc.

MARIEL: ¡Manuel! Otra foto, anda, no seas malo. ¡Pa' que te acuerdes de nosotros!

CASIMIRO and FRIENDS group themselves again, unsmiling. A different recorded line from the unseen amateur photographer, MANUEL, is heard.

MANUEL: Pero no tan serios, you're not at a funeral. Se van a hacer ricos en los United States of America.

MARIEL: ¡Tú también, Coyote!

EL COYOTE joins them. Recorded line from MANUEL.

MANUEL: Smile!

CASIMIRO, FRIENDS, and EL COYOTE: Cheeseburgers! (*End with a smiling, silly camera pose.*)

Camera flash. CASIMIRO, FRIENDS, *and* EL COYOTE *freeze.*

DON REMIGIO: Casimiro, mijo, aquí puedes cambiar tu destino; don't listen to him, quédate en México.

CASIMIRO: (*Breaks freeze and crosses to* DON REMIGIO.) ¿Para qué, Abuelo? So that I can end up like my father? Ni tiene los cuarenta años y ya lo ve jorobado como un viejito de noventa, his back bent from carrying los costales de maíz sixteen hours a day. Y yo y mis hermanos sufriendo hambre, eating week-old tortillas—tengo que irme a los Estados Unidos. I'll find a job, fácil. And I'll send all my money to my father, se lo juro. (*Turns to his* FRIENDS.) We'll all find a job. ¡Esta noche, nos vamos a los Estados Unidos!

A blending of CASIMIRO's *and* MAD DOG's *rap music is suddenly heard and then* OUT. *Lights go down and then shadows.* MICTLANTECUHTLI *enters and stands at the top of the center ramp or step unit. Spot on* MICTLANTECUHTLI.

MICTLANTECUHTLI: Volveremos al pasado. Don Remigio, empezamos.

Spot on DON REMIGIO.

DON REMIGIO: (*Praying.*) Vesate sewau hotekate; sewa valikai, sewau hoteka-tee. (*Starts to beat his drum and crosses to his place at the border shooting. Repeats softly as he continues to beat his drum.*)

JESÚS, MIGUEL, CARLOS, AND MARIEL: (*Break freeze. Together.*) Nomás queremos trabajar.

They position themselves as in CASIMIRO's *dream and start to move slowly, repeating this line softly. The repeat offstage voice of* XOCHIL's MOTHER *is heard.*

XOCHIL'S MOTHER: ¡Xochil! ¡Apúrate! Your dad's waiting for his tortillas!

XOCHIL: For my quinceañera, I'm gonna have fourteen madrinas and they're gonna each carry a bouquet of white roses with pink and lavender ribbon streamers. (*Crosses to her place in the street for the barrio shooting and repeats softly when in place.*)

The repeat offstage voice of MAD DOG's FOSTER MOTHER *is heard.*

MAD DOG'S FOSTER MOTHER: Mad Dog! Vente a comer; and don't you dare say nothing about it just being baloney y papas, qué crees, que the welfare money is for millionaires?

MAD DOG: All I want is for someone to write a corrido about me. (*Struts to his place in the barrio shooting and keeps repeating softly.*)

DON PRISCILIANO: Tengo un dolorcito right here, and it hurts when I take a deep breath. (*Sits down on his chair and keeps repeating softly.*)

ROCKY: Ring, phone, ring. (*Pacing, repeating softly.*)

EL COYOTE: Hey! It's a job; someone's gotta do it, ¿que no? (*Gun in hand, moves stealthily and positions himself, repeating line softly.*)

All should now be in their places for the barrio street shooting and the Mexican/U.S. shooting. Each is repeating his/her lines softly at the same time, almost chanting or praying as DON REMIGIO *beats the drum. Beat. Volume increases. Beat.* DON REMIGIO *gives one last loud drumbeat and all stop chanting at exact same time. Lights go up.*

DON PRISCILIANO: (*Stands up suddenly and with energy.*) ¡Xochil! ¡Cuidado! ¡Ahí vienen otros desgraciados pachuco gang members!

El TANQUE *and* EL PEEWA *enter strutting, menacing.* EL TANQUE *is huge, and* EL PEEWA *is a skinny runt. They are dressed almost identical to* MAD DOG *with guns showing at their waists.*

XOCHIL: ¡El Tanque y El Peewa!

Comedy bit. EL TANQUE *is on* EL PEEWA's *left side. On* XOCHIL's *line, they look at each other, point to selves, and see that they are not in the correct order, so they do-si-do and change position so that* EL TANQUE *is now on* EL PEEWA's *right side.*

EL TANQUE *and* EL PEEWA: (*Together.*) ¡Ese, Mad Dog Sánchez!

MAD DOG *turns to them, defiant and without fear.*

MAD DOG: That's my name; don't wear it out.

EL TANQUE: Wrong. It was your name—

EL PEEWA: Pero te vamos a hacer into dog food, so now it's Dead Dog. (*Nervous giggle.*)

MAD DOG, EL TANQUE, *and* EL PEEWA *take out their guns in one quick movement.* JESÚS, CARLOS, MIGUEL, *and* MARIEL *get separated.*

MARIEL: ¡Casimiro! No puedo ver; ¡dame tu mano!

DON PRISCILIANO: ¡Xochil! ¡No cruces la calle!

XOCHIL *is confused and crosses toward* EL TANQUE *and* EL PEEWA. *Turns to* MAD DOG.

XOCHIL: Mad Dog! Look out!

A shot is heard. MAD DOG *is wounded.* XOCHIL *starts to cross to* MAD DOG.

DON PRISCILIANO: ¡No, Xochil, no!

MARIEL: ¡Casimiro, dame tu mano!

EL COYOTE aims at MARIEL, and EL PEEWA aims at XOCHIL.

DON REMIGIO: Casimiro! Take Mariel's hand!

MICTLANTECUHTLI: Mad Dog, you're wounded, but you still have time. (*Commands.*) Salva la vida de Xochil.

CASIMIRO starts to cross slowly to MARIEL, and MAD DOG starts to cross slowly to XOCHIL. Both move with almost identical movements. Both stop. NOTE TO DIRECTOR: By now CASIMIRO and MARIEL should be on one of the ramps, and MAD DOG and XOCHIL should be on the other ramp.

DON REMIGIO: Hijo, prove to Mictlantecuhtli and to yourself que sí tienes seatakaa, the flower body. Help Mariel now, con buen corazón, and forever change your past. ¡Casimiro! ¡Salva a Mariel! Save her, m'ijo!

CASIMIRO and MAD DOG move closer to MARIEL and XOCHIL. At the precise moment that the bullets are fired, CASIMIRO and MAD DOG reach MARIEL and XOCHIL and move them so that CASIMIRO's and MAD DOG's backs are now to EL COYOTE and EL PEEWA, who are ready to shoot. Gunshots. CASIMIRO and MAD DOG get shot at the same time. XOCHIL and MARIEL try to support and hold the bodies.

MICTLANTECUHTLI: We have the sacrifices: dos almas y dos cuerpos.

Conch shell sound. Lights down. JESÚS, MIGUEL, CARLOS, EL TANQUE, EL PEEWA, DON PRISCILIANO, ROCKY, and EL COYOTE exit. Lights up.

MICTLANTECUHTLI: Mariel, you may return to the land of the living—to that night twenty years ago. You will work in Manuel's camera shop and eventually become a professional photographer there in your pueblo and buy him out.

MARIEL: (*Slowly letting go of CASIMIRO as he falls to the floor.*) Casimiro, you've been too hard on yourself. All these years, blaming yourself for what happened. Tú no sabías que el coyote nos iba a traicionar; besides, it wasn't your fault. We were to blame, too. We were young and caught up in the excitement of crossing the border, and we took that risk. (*Exits.*)

MICTLANTECUHTLI: Xochil, you will return to the land of the living, take your father his tortillas before his sopita de fideo gets cold, and help your mother with all those silly table decorations you want for your quinceañera fiesta.

XOCHIL: (*Teasing. As she crosses.*) They're not silly! They're pink and lavender Jordan almonds wrapped in white veil with a good-luck charm.

MICTLANTECUHTLI: And you, Mad Dog Sánchez, stand up!

MAD DOG stands up.

MAD DOG: I know; you don't have to tell me, I'm not going back.

MICTLANTECUHTLI: No, you're not going back; only Mariel and Xochil can return.

Mad Dog: But you said there was no place here in Mictlan for people like me. Stupid.

Mictlantecuhtli: Sí, es cierto, te dije que there was no place for you here in Mictlan, but that was before you saved Xochil. Now there is a place for you, a very special place. Ven. (*Mad Dog crosses to Mictlantecuhtli.*) I want you to know that I'm making a great exception here. (*He removes Mad Dog's headband and tosses it aside.*) Gang members who kill each other or who kill innocent bystanders do not come to Mictlan, much less to be among the brave guerreros who die in real battle.

Mad Dog: Guerreros? I'm gonna live with the warriors?

Mictlantecuhtli: Sí, porque you've done a very heroic act, más o menos; by taking that second bullet aimed at Xochil, you will now reside in Tonatiuhilhuicac and ride with the sun god, Tonatiuh, on his daily journey across the sky for four years. (*Places magnificent headdress of sun rays on Mad Dog's head.*)

Mad Dog preens proudly.

Xochil: (*Exits, looking over her shoulder.*) Uuhhh, Mad Dog, you look like a god!

Mad Dog: The name's Daniel. Daniel García.

Xochil: Uuhhh, Daniel García, you look like a god!

Mictlantecuhtli: Después de los cuatro años, you will return to earth as a hummingbird or a butterfly. If you're really lucky, you'll end up in Xochil's garden!

Lights down and indigenous music, with violin.

Don Remigio: (*Crosses to Casimiro, prays as he removes Casimiro's shoes.*) Vesate sewau hotekate/sewa valikai/sewai hotekate/ne Casimiro Flores, sewa walikai, sewai hotekatee. (*Casimiro stands up slowly.*) Ahora sí, mijo, puedes bailar la Danza del Venado.

The music from la Danza del Venado starts. Casimiro starts to dance. At first slowly, then faster, assured and skillfully.

Mictlantecuhtli: Already we sit down to the flower, para recibir la flor, we sit down to the flower—

Don Remigio: (*Continues praying.*) Vesate sewau hotekate; sewa valikai, sewau hotekatee.

Casimiro: Yo, Casimiro Flores—

Music goes up. Flower petals and blossoms float down. Slowly, lights go down and out.

End of play

WE LOST IT AT THE MOVIES

(WITH A SPECIAL APPEARANCE BY ROCK HUDSON)

GUILLERMO REYES

About the Play

he first time I saw *We Lost It at the Movies*, I very much liked the humorous, intelligent, and screenplaylike quality of the dialogue. I was also intrigued by the main character, a single mother who enjoys classic movies—or rather, the movies of her time that in today's society have become classics and who has one-on-one conversations with Rock Hudson, not because she is delusional, but rather because Hudson is her idol and she's able to call upon him whenever she needs him.

This play, like many of Reyes's works, presents a family in crisis, but it is not one of his typical dramas. Instead, *We Lost It at the Movies* is a comedy offering dramatic and sentimental moments and a great mix of one-liners. The family drama Reyes created is not a "kitchen-sink drama." Instead, the author presents us with a mother and a son who move from Chile to the United States, ending up in—where else?—Hollywood.

The move is made, as in the case of many immigrants, with the hope of a better life, and the main character, Rosalinda, will have to sacrifice a lot in order to make it in the United States. But this woman is not a soft, "in-the-kitchen" type of mother; rather, she's a very smart woman who knows what she wants, what she needs, and how to get it.

Like any other recent arrival, Rosalinda discovers her employment opportunities are limited, but she doesn't settle for just anything. She prefers to work for rich families, taking care of their children as a nanny. Yet she makes a point of saying that she isn't a maid; she has some education, and that separates her from other domestic help.

Rosalinda refuses to let anyone stand between her and a successful life, and we get to witness this determination when her bigamous late husband's other wife comes into the picture. It is in these types of confrontational scenes that Reyes brings to life likeable characters who are full of conviction and strength, separating them from the weak or hopeless. And although Rosalinda becomes manipulative, cold, and merciless, we understand her and we know her circumstances.

In contrast to this strong, driven, and almost cold character, Rosalinda's son is easygoing and wants to become a director of small budget films. It is through the son that we get to experience how two people who have a love for movies can be so different and yet so alike. And we accept them both because we share their humanity as they try to survive and adapt to a strange culture in a foreign country where the language is unfamiliar.

For cast and production information, see Appendix B.

About the Author

uillermo Reyes is a Chilean-born writer whose plays include *Men on the Verge of a His-Panic Breakdown, Deporting the Divas, The Seductions of Johnny Diego, Mother Lolita,* and various others. Two of his plays, *Places to Touch Him* and *Miss Consuelo,* were featured in the anthology *Borders on Stage: Plays Produced by Teatro Bravo,* published in 2008 by L&S Books. His autobiographical work, *Madre and I: A Memoir of Our Immigrant Lives,* was published by the University of Wisconsin Press in 2010.

Madison, a historical comedy, won first prize in the Premiere Stages New Play Development award competition and was produced at Premiere Stages in Union, New Jersey, in 2008. Other productions include *Blend,* which was performed at Theatre Three's One-Act Festival; *Mend,* performed at the Sands Theater in Deland, Florida, in February 2008; *Farewell to Hollywood,* which debuted at Bloomington (IN) Playwrights Project; *The Suspects,* which premiered at the Guthrie Theater in Minneapolis in April 2005; and *Sunrise at Monticello,* a historical comedy about Thomas Jefferson, which appeared at the Playwrights' Theater of New Jersey in October 2005. A sketch comedy entitled *The Hispanick Zone* was produced at Teatro Bravo in Phoenix, Theatrikos in Flagstaff, and East L.A. Rep in Los Angeles in September 2007.

Earlier productions include *Chilean Holiday,* which was produced at the Actors' Theater of Louisville and published in *Humana Festival '96: The Complete Plays,* and *Men on the Verge of a His-Panic Breakdown,* which won Theater L.A.'s Ovation Award for Best World Premiere Play and Best Production in 1994. It has since played across the country, most importantly in New York City, where it also won the 1996 Emerging Playwright Award and was produced off-Broadway at Urban Stages and at the 47th Street Playhouse.

In the Phoenix area, Reyes founded the bilingual theater company Teatro Bravo, where he has produced and directed dozens of productions, including the recent *American Victory* by José Zárate. Based on the autobiography by Olympic wrestler Henry Cejudo (with Bill Plaschke), it premiered at Arizona State University before playing at Teatro Bravo. In 2012 Reyes received a Best Director nomination for this production from the Phoenix ariZoni Awards.

Guillermo Reyes received his MFA in playwriting from the University of California, San Diego. He is currently a professor in the School of Theater and Film at Arizona State University in Tempe, where he heads the Dramatic Writing program.

CHARACTERS

ROSALINDA | aging from her early 20s to her 40s

MEMO/NARRATOR | a young man in his early 20s

NORMA | aging from her 30s to her 50s

ARMANDO | a man in his 30s

VLADIMIR/ROCK HUDSON | played by same actor, around his mid-30s

GRANDMA/DOROTHEA/FEMALE PRIEST/POLICEWOMAN/HELENA/OTHER ENSEMBLE PARTS | played by same actress

Memo (Aaron Wester). *Photo: Jon Simpson*

Armando (David McCormick) and Memo (Aaron Wester). *Photo: Jon Simpson*

Clips of famous films—luscious lovemaking at the beach in From Here to Eternity, *Yuri and Lara bid farewell in* Doctor Zhivago, *Maria runs through the hills in* The Sound of Music, *Rhett kisses Scarlett on the bridge in* Gone with the Wind, *lovers are torn apart in* Casablanca, *Bette Davis and Paul Henreid have their final smoke in* Now, Voyager, *and any other movie with a lover waving goodbye from a moving train, and so forth, not necessarily in this order, and perhaps including many other clips depending on the designer, all creating a kaleidoscope of longing. These films should go up to 1965 and no later. Two women,* ROSALINDA *and* NORMA, *can be seen sitting on stools shucking corn. Enter* NARRATOR.

NARRATOR: Santiago, Chile, 1965. On the world scene: Vietnam, the Beatles, the Berlin Wall, Fidel, Che Guevara, the Cold War, and in the kitchen of a modest home in this South American capital, a major controversy of universal importance erupts unexpectedly:

ROSALINDA *speaks to her friend* NORMA. *They both shuck corn while they do this. If they're done too early, they can slice off the kernels to get them into a pot.*

ROSALINDA: Audrey Hepburn was not even nominated!

NORMA: Well, Julie Andrews should have gotten the part to begin with.

ROSALINDA: But I think Audrey did a great job as the fair lady.

NORMA: Audrey Hepburn can't sing worth shit.

ROSALINDA: But—!

NORMA: Julie Andrews did the role on Broadway, and when they didn't cast her, it was downhill from there. She was robbed! We were robbed!

ROSALINDA: Look, I like Julie Andrews, too, but Audrey Hepburn—

NORMA: Julie would have sung her heart out, but there's no justice. Fuck Hollywood and the CIA; they're all connected!

ROSALINDA: Such language! I have a child!

NORMA: Don't you give me that! All that sweet innocence and you still let some man get you pregnant!

ROSALINDA: Moving on to Mary Poppins . . .

NORMA: What about the bitch?

ROSALINDA: Ah . . . Julie Andrews got to do Mary Poppins, which made up for the loss of *My Fair Lady*, and there's a new musical coming out with her in the lead.

NORMA: Something about a stupid rebellious nun! I'd rather see *Lolita* again—

ROSALINDA: And again and again. How many times is that?

NORMA: James Mason reminds me of my first boyfriend—

ROSALINDA: He plays a pervert.

NORMA: Don't matter, I could have married the guy, but no, I was too young, too stupid, who knows what I was waiting for. Instead, I end up marrying Cantinflas, short, clumsy, funny guy, but at least good in the sack; it's something. Life! This is my life, that's all there is! Are you getting married any time soon?

ROSALINDA: If you must know, I'm not lucky with men.

NORMA: Who the hell is? What I'm saying is sometimes you take what you can get. Sex is something, and that's what you did—

ROSALINDA: I'd call it romance.

NORMA: Romance with insertion thrown in. Sometimes, that's all you get from men. No shame in that, sweetie. My husband, he's a fine man, but I don't want him to talk, especially not politics. I just tell him, shut up already and throw me down on the bed, I'm your mistress, I'm your whore. Hey, it's OK. Role playing is allowed for Catholics.

ROSALINDA: It just doesn't seem dignified somehow.

NORMA: Sex is not about being dignified; it's about heat like, say, Deborah Kerr and Burt Lancaster in *From Here to Eternity*.

ROSALINDA: I thought that was romantic.

NORMA: That was lust!

ROSALINDA: One of the deadly sins—

NORMA: Sure, that's what I go to the movies for, to watch other people sin and go to hell. It just bothers me to see you like this, drinking your daily tea while shucking corn.

ROSALINDA: It's what you're doing, Norma.

NORMA: I'm helping you out! Look, you're young; you look good when you're not acting all prim and proper, which is half the time. You know, what about my brother?

ROSALINDA: Oh, no, don't, don't try that.

NORMA: He just got out of the army.

ROSALINDA: No, no—

NORMA: He'll take you to the movies. You sure like the movies.

ROSALINDA: And little Memo?

NORMA: I'll babysit. You'll go out with him?

ROSALINDA: I don't know if I should be going out with any man right now.

NORMA: Why not?

ROSALINDA: My mother said my purpose is to take care of my child from now on.

NORMA: That don't mean you can't find him a father, sweetie. Your parents couldn't possibly mean that just because of one sin you become a nun.

ROSALINDA: My parents believe I somehow . . . started it. He was a married man.

NORMA: And you get the blame, poor girl? Fuck them!

ROSALINDA: Sssssh! Please.

NORMA: He got something out of it, that married man. Why should you get all the blame?

ROSALINDA: He's the only man I'll ever love.

NORMA: Fuck that! My brother will take care of you real good!

ROSALINDA: You're done with your share of corn, aren't you?

NORMA: Yes, I am! You're not rejecting my beautiful brother, are you?

ROSALINDA: I'll go to the movies with him if you stop talking so much filth! I am trying to raise a son, and it's a vulgar world out there. I want my son to have polish, to have an education, and to have the means to see the world.

NORMA: So it's a date then.

ROSALINDA: No. Not yet.

NORMA: He'll come by for you on Friday night.

ROSALINDA: But—

NORMA: Wear something nice. He doesn't have to because his face inspires you to see him naked. Bye, bye.

NORMA exits. ROSALINDA transitions into the kitchen as she works on her corn pies.

ROSALINDA: . . . I've been selling my corn-meat pie for years now. My recipes are secret, although they're not mine, they're my grandma's. I'm saving up for a television set, and maybe then I'll stop going to the movies so much. TV is threatening the movies, and in a few years will probably completely take over our lives. But I'll never stop thinking of Cinerama and *Cleopatra*, *El Cid*, and all those other grand spectacles. I'll never abandon the big screen altogether because there's no other place to dream big. Television is fine for small dreams. Life fills out a bigger canvas, though; it practically demands a big screen.

ROCK HUDSON enters, surprising her.

ROCK: I agree with you entirely.

ROSALINDA: Why, Rock Hudson! Come on in. Kiss my hand.

ROCK: No, I'm the star. You kiss mine.

ROSALINDA: I'm the one who pays to see your pretty face. It's people like me who keep you in a Hollywood mansion entertaining all those beautiful ladies.

ROCK: You're really sure of yourself, aren't you?

ROSALINDA: Kiss it!

ROCK: It's full of corn!

ROSALINDA: It tastes good!

ROCK: All right, fine, to my biggest fan in Santiago, Chile. (*Kisses her hand.*) Delicious!

ROSALINDA: I wrote to you and you never answered back.

ROCK: My publicity department's a little slow. Please forgive.

ROSALINDA: Do you have any questions for me?

ROCK: I'm the star, I get to answer questions.

ROSALINDA: But don't you want to know about your fans? Isn't it about time we got interviewed?

ROCK: All right, who the heck are you, biggest fan?

ROSALINDA: Well, just a woman with too few options in life.

ROCK: Boring!

ROSALINDA: Not for lack of trying, really. I'm a mother now, but frankly, I'd rather be traveling the world. Maybe I'll become a singing nun who gets invited to sing for the Pope and for little children everywhere. Celibacy would do me good after what happened recently.

Rock Hudson (Adam Solon) and Rosalinda (Edith Donoghue-Chávez). *Photo: Jon Simpson*

ROCK: I know about heartbreak, trust me.

ROSALINDA: I want to abandon desire altogether.

ROCK: Me too.

ROSALINDA: I lust after life, not after men, per se.

ROCK: Yep.

ROSALINDA: Frankly, I find the sexual act perverse anyway. People make fools of themselves over it.

ROCK: I know all about that.

ROSALINDA: You get to make love to Doris Day and Liz Taylor.

ROCK: If only it were that simple.

ROSALINDA: They were both heartbroken when they found Lana Turner coming out of your mansion in the middle of the night.

ROCK: She and I just played poker.

ROSALINDA: She's too old for you, anyway. Kim Novak's more your type.

ROCK: Right as usual. You know everything about me; there's no privacy for us stars.

ROSALINDA: Our movie tickets pay for that lifestyle. Enjoy it!

ROCK: Don't you have better things to do? I mean, I love my fans, but shouldn't you get a life?

ROSALINDA: I'd love to have a business of my own, but—unlike Joan Crawford in *Mildred Pierce*—baking pies is something I do for extra money. What I really want is to run my own orphanage.

ROCK: I hate children.

ROSALINDA: No! When I get through with them, they're lovable; they're all singing and dancing. I was in a girls' school once because my mother had to work most of the day, so she put me under the care of sadistic nuns. I told myself one day I would take care of the little ones, and I would be a clown for them and make them smile. But one has to start small. That's why I may take that offer from the American preacher—

ROCK: What offer?

ROSALINDA: That's supposed to be a secret.

ROCK: I'll tell you my big secret if you tell me yours.

ROSALINDA: Nonsense, your life is an open book. Tall, handsome, and masculine!

ROCK: That's me.

GRANDMA: (*Offstage.*) Rosalinda, honey?

ROSALINDA: Ah, yes . . . in the kitchen!

ROCK exits. Enter ROSALINDA's mother, also called GRANDMA.

GRANDMA: Who were you talking to?

ROSALINDA: Reporters ask movie stars questions, so I figured why can't they ask average people about their lives. I mean what's so different about our lives? We live, we die, we have ambitions like everyone else. I just want to be ready for them in case they ask.

GRANDMA: You are my only daughter, Rosalinda. I don't want to lock you up, honey.

ROSALINDA: Well, your sons have no imagination. They drink, they womanize, they don't do anything else.

GRANDMA: They're normal. And don't call them "your sons." It's not as if your father was so special that you dare look down on your half-brothers.

ROSALINDA: My father was educated and theirs isn't.

GRANDMA: Well, that's none of your business, to compare like that. We have guests coming, and don't you treat them or your brothers or anybody else like peasants. Sometimes I wonder about you—

ROSALINDA: Wonder what?

GRANDMA: The things you say about people.

ROSALINDA: My hands are full of corn mush, Mother, it's not as if I'm afraid of hard work.

GRANDMA: It doesn't stop you from looking down on people, even in your own family.

ROSALINDA: I just get tired, Mother, tired of people who dream small!

GRANDMA: We're all in this together, the life the good Lord gave us.

ROSALINDA: Mother . . . there's this woman, she's a missionary from Bethesda, Maryland.

GRANDMA: Where?

ROSALINDA: That's in the United States, Mother.

GRANDMA: Oh, yes. And . . . ?

ROSALINDA: She's working on getting me papers to go work in the U.S.

GRANDMA: Why would you do that?

ROSALINDA: I want my son to aspire to greater things, and here you can only achieve such things if you're born rich. And besides, it's not just for my son.

GRANDMA: What do you mean? Everything you do must be for your son. You are a mother now.

ROSALINDA: I want to be the best mother possible, of course, but I want to experience a lot more myself.

GRANDMA: Is this about men? We've got men.

ROSALINDA: No, it's not about men. The one man I loved turned out to be married, and—

GRANDMA: The family curse, honey.

ROSALINDA: I saw him on the bus the other day.

GRANDMA: Stick your tongue out at him. That's what I did with your father.

ROSALINDA: He sees me with the boy and we don't even say hello. It's his own son. It's not right.

GRANDMA: I used to go buy milk at my father's own farm, and I didn't even know he was my father. But that's in the past. We're city people now, right?

ROSALINDA: Would you agree that a bit of travel would be good for me and the boy?

GRANDMA: This is about watching *Mildred Pierce* too many times.

ROSALINDA: Well, Mildred had the right idea; she built a pie empire for her daughter.

GRANDMA: It's just a movie, a fantasy, you fool! Life doesn't work that way, not even in the U.S. Most American mothers will spend their lives making cakes and pies for sale, but they won't get rich off that.

ROSALINDA: I can distinguish fantasy and reality just fine, but if it's possible to go work in the U.S., I will; that's no fantasy.

GRANDMA: I say there are some opportunities right here and now.

ROSALINDA: What?

NARRATOR: There was somebody waiting outside . . . somebody who'd come close to changing our lives.

ROSALINDA: (*To* GRANDMA.) Why didn't you tell me? You've had him waiting all this time?

GRANDMA: Yes, he can wait. He's talking to your brother. Soccer scores and things like that; who cares? I have guests to cook for.

ROSALINDA: I'll be ready in just a minute.

GRANDMA: What does Norma's brother want?

ROSALINDA: Oh, what do all men want? I want much more than they could ever give me in this neighborhood.

GRANDMA: I sense I'm losing my only daughter.

ROSALINDA: Miss me all you want, Mother, in anticipation of the great many things in store for me.

GRANDMA: Some lives don't have great things in store for them.

ROSALINDA: Well, mine does. So excuse me. (*Exits.*)

GRANDMA: God bless her soul and keep her safe from so many movies.

ROSALINDA goes to join VLADIMIR *at the other end of the stage.*

VLADIMIR: I bought the tickets. It's some Italian movie, fancy name.

ROSALINDA: *La Dolce Vita* maybe?

VLADIMIR: You've seen it, then.

ROSALINDA: I don't mind seeing it again. This dress here . . . I styled it after the one Anita Ekberg wore in that movie, but without so much cleavage, of course.

VLADIMIR: You make your own dresses, too.

ROSALINDA: And I knit and bake. My corn pie is a bestseller in the neighborhood.

VLADIMIR: My sister likes them, too.

ROSALINDA: What about you?

VLADIMIR: What?

ROSALINDA: You came here to size me up, right? To see how good I'd do around the house? I have a right to know about you. What makes you special?

VLADIMIR: Ah . . . I see. Like you're sizing me up, too.

ROSALINDA: Right. What are your talents?

VLADIMIR: Not in mixed company. (*Joke falls flat on her.*) Anyway . . . My sister says women look at men in the street just like men look at women. Sometimes they talk dirty about them, too.

ROSALINDA: We observe, yes, we just don't whistle or anything silly like that.

VLADIMIR: I think it's good.

ROSALINDA: You do?

VLADIMIR: I like it when they turn around and check me out.

ROSALINDA: Don't be vain.

VLADIMIR: No. Women have a right to look at me and I can turn around and say (*trying to sound Italian*), "Ciao, bella." As for my talents, well . . . let's start with this, not too many defects, see?

ROSALINDA: Really? You're almost perfect?

VLADIMIR: My personality, anyway. I'm really charming. I don't have much else, I admit, and I didn't finish school. But I want to own my own business, nothing fancy. I believe in an honest day's labor. I want a woman who'll agree with me about an honest day's labor, at least.

ROSALINDA: I agree with that, sure.

VLADIMIR: I want my own children.

ROSALINDA: I have a five-year-old already, you know.

VLADIMIR: Not a problem.

ROSALINDA: I—I might go to the U.S.

VLADIMIR: Ah . . . that might be a slight problem.

ROSALINDA: Have you ever considered going abroad yourself?

VLADIMIR: My entire family's here. I went away to the army and that was tough; I wanted to get right back. My mom makes me breakfast in bed. Not every day, mind you, but sometimes, and she only does it for me because I'm her favorite.

ROSALINDA: I'd have to be really in love to do that.

VLADIMIR: I'm willing to make breakfast in bed for somebody special. I don't want you to think I'm just some spoiled brat.

ROSALINDA: Well, I'm still considering a job abroad.

VLADIMIR: A woman all alone in the U.S. What would that be like?

ROSALINDA: I wouldn't be alone. I have a cousin in the D.C. area. It's called "Bethesda, Maryland." I hope I'm saying it right, and this missionary lady would take me as her children's nanny.

VLADIMIR: She belongs to one of those religions in which the priests marry.

ROSALINDA: An evangelist, yes.

VLADIMIR: Sounds like you've got it figured out. I won't waste my time then. (*Starts to leave.*)

ROSALINDA: Well . . . don't go.

VLADIMIR: Why? Why should I stay?

ROSALINDA: I don't know. Maybe a gentleman should work to change a lady's mind.

VLADIMIR: Like Rock Hudson in *A Touch of Mink.*

ROSALINDA: That was Cary Grant.

VLADIMIR: Oh.

ROSALINDA: But I think you meant Rock Hudson in *Pillow Talk.*

VLADIMIR: All right. Will this do any better?

VLADIMIR kisses her gently.

ROSALINDA: Yeah. Mom's looking.

VLADIMIR: Let her.

ROSALINDA: All right, let her.

They kiss again.

NARRATOR: Vladimir was named after Soviet revolutionary Vladimir Lenin by a socialist father, but he considered himself a moderate Christian Democrat. Mother did not leave for the U.S. quite just yet. Vladimir was a distinct temptation . . . who knows what life might have been like if she'd only . . . but let's not get ahead of ourselves. First, a few nights follow in which young people don't have to think so much about the future. . . .

VLADIMIR and ROSALINDA go dancing. The Ensemble can also be involved in a little dance with a mambo beat, let's say "Maracaibo Oriental" by

*Benny Moré and his orchestra. The dance ends in a tight embrace and, of
course, a kiss. Transition to the kitchen:* GRANDMA's *talking;* ROSALINDA
fills bowls to make her corn pie.

GRANDMA: If you don't marry him, I don't know what will happen to you.

ROSALINDA: Nothing personal, Mother, but this is a new generation.

GRANDMA: And what does that mean?

ROSALINDA: You grew up in a small town where girls were married off at 14.

GRANDMA: I was more civilized; I married at 16.

ROSALINDA: Exactly. Marriage is only one of the many options a woman should
have.

GRANDMA: I'm going to cry now.

ROSALINDA: You don't even think he's that special.

GRANDMA: He's not, but who marries men because they're special? Most of us
marry because we're afraid of death. Death and solitude, and how we'll be
judged by God if we don't marry early and multiply.

ROSALINDA: God is neither vindictive nor malicious.

GRANDMA: You young people are exposed to such horrible influences out there—
the Beatles, Elvis, the pill. . . .

ROSALINDA: Mother, I want to show you something.

GRANDMA: What?

ROSALINDA: This!

ROSALINDA *shows her the letter.*

GRANDMA: No, you read it to me. You know how the alphabet gets all tangled
up in my mind.

ROSALINDA: Mother, one day you'll learn to read.

GRANDMA: Don't treat me that way; just tell me what it says!

ROSALINDA: This is a letter from the U.S. consulate. My papers have been approved.

GRANDMA: Your papers?

ROSALINDA: Yes.

GRANDMA: So many other people apply to immigration and they get rejected.
Why you?

ROSALINDA: Mother—

GRANDMA: So many other people say, oh, one day we'll move, we'll go away,
do new things that nobody's done before, but it's all talk, everybody's got
plans, but you . . . you have to be different.

Starts to cry for real now.

ROSALINDA: Mom! Please! I haven't decided to accept yet.

GRANDMA: (*Crying appears to stop.*) Oh? Why? Why not?

ROSALINDA: I thought you didn't want me to leave. I'm your only daughter, right?

GRANDMA: What I want is not the point. What I don't want is for you to be one of those people who talks too much about the future, and never does it. I want you to stop talking, and . . . I will miss you, of course, and I'll cry later, all day, till I'm on my deathbed, but don't worry about me—and what about Vladimir?

ROSALINDA: I know. Him.

GRANDMA: He's been so helpful with your corn-meat pies, the way he's marketed them for you, helping you sell them to stores—

ROSALINDA: I know, he's been really great, and he kisses nicely in a cute, sloppy way, but what can I do?

GRANDMA: Tell that boy at once! And I won't be there when you do. I'm going to dig a hole and stick my head in it. I mean, I'm happy for you, but oh, shit, shit, shit!

Exits, crying.

NARRATOR: Vladimir joins her in style.

VLADIMIR: I brought you the finest wine.

ROSALINDA: A Pinot Noir from Colchagua?

VLADIMIR: My mom's favorite glasses—pure crystal. I brought them for you.

ROSALINDA: What a gentleman.

They drink and kiss lightly.

VLADIMIR: (*As if about to propose.*) Which brings me to the question . . .

ROSALINDA: You want to go see *Doctor Zhivago* with Omar Sharif and Julie Christie, don't you?

VLADIMIR: I wasn't going to ask that exactly, but, yes, that would be nice.

ROSALINDA: Norma and I already saw it, didn't she tell you? But I'll see it with you.

VLADIMIR: You don't mind seeing it again?

ROSALINDA: If I like a movie—

VLADIMIR: You really liked this *Doctor Chicago*?

ROSALINDA: Zhivago! I loved it, I am Lara!

VLADIMIR: Who?

ROSALINDA: The love of Dr. Zhivago's life. I am Lara. I couldn't be the sad wife played by Geraldine Chaplin. I don't see myself that way. I am the woman he wrote poems to, and then at the end of the movie she walks away while he's chasing after her. He has a heart attack, and she doesn't even notice. It's very tragic, but such is the poetry of their lives.

VLADIMIR: I see . . . So you are the woman who walks away?

ROSALINDA: Well . . . so to speak.

VLADIMIR: Is this your way of breaking up?

ROSALINDA: No! I didn't mean to—

VLADIMIR: You are using movies to break up? The same way you use movies to kiss? That's a strange talent—

ROSALINDA: I am not average, that's all.

VLADIMIR: You are the illegitimate daughter of some country lady, and your son is the illegitimate child of some horny teacher in the local school who's gotten other women pregnant.

She slaps him.

VLADIMIR: I'm such a jerk, I'm so sorry.

ROSALINDA: I don't want to be a simple person of any kind—

VLADIMIR: You'd rather be Lara, a mistress!

ROSALINDA: No, I meant I'd rather be the love of a poet's life; don't you understand? Look, you're a wonderful man—

VLADIMIR: But you don't love me, I've never heard you say it.

ROSALINDA: I've grown so fond of you.

VLADIMIR: Oh, great! We've been together almost an entire year. I've seen every single stupid Doris Day movie with you, and now you say you're just fond of me!

ROSALINDA: You will make a woman happy one day, the way you've made me—

VLADIMIR: What? But you won't—

ROSALINDA: Before you came along, I thought I was just meant to be a single mother, unnoticed by most men, something of a spinster already at twenty-four, but you made me feel wanted. You made me feel pretty. I thank you for that.

VLADIMIR: I've made you feel loved because it's true; it's what I feel! And you are pretty!

ROSALINDA: And I thank you—

VLADIMIR: Why is it that whenever I speak to you I feel like I'm at the end of some sad movie? Like there's fog on the runway and the plane is about to take off?

ROSALINDA: Because it is. I'm leaving for the U.S. by plane. My papers came through.

VLADIMIR: And when were you planning on telling me?

ROSALINDA: I'm telling you now. I've got to be on that plane in exactly three days.

VLADIMIR: Three days?

ROSALINDA: Yes. I'm sorry.

VLADIMIR: And now what? Will you be happy?

ROSALINDA: A line from *Now, Voyager*.

VLADIMIR: I don't live in your stupid movie land. Answer me.

ROSALINDA: Could we just smoke on it?

VLADIMIR: Smoke on it? Wait, don't tell me. *Now, Voyager* again?

ROSALINDA: I don't even smoke, but you do, and I figure if it helps you . . .

VLADIMIR: Thanks. I hope you'll remember this happiness.

ROSALINDA: I will. I'll take it with me wherever I go.

> *They do the cigarette bit from the end of* Now, Voyager.

VLADIMIR: Come here. This is the sweetest goodbye . . . to hold you like this. And I didn't mean it when I called you those names. I'm jealous, that's all. You have this other life, something I can't quite share, this movie world that's more alive in your imagination than anything else. I envy it, but I also admire it. I admire you and I'll miss you.

> *They kiss.*

NARRATOR: Fifteen years later, Reagan's running for president, Sally Field enjoys great acclaim for *Norma Rae*, and Blondie sings that "the tide is high and I'm moving on." A mysterious virus has begun its sinister path through the world, and we won't know until 1985 that it's killing our favorite movie star, Rock Hudson. After a brief stint in the Washington D.C. area, Rosalinda gets tired of working for evangelists who forbid their children to watch movies. We take off instead and drive across the country, just Rosalinda and me, and the car breaks down in New Mexico, which is what happened in *Alice Doesn't Live Here Anymore*. We continue on to California in a rental. Rosalinda now works for Mrs. Reinhold of Bel Air, a member of the Democratic Party who wants all her maids to call her Dorothea. But whatever you do, don't call Rosalinda a "domestic worker."

ROSALINDA: I don't do laundry.

DOROTHEA: I didn't mean to imply that—

ROSALINDA: You have two maids for that. I take care of the children.

DOROTHEA: I know that, but—

ROSALINDA: —I have an associate's degree in child care; I'm not one of those poor illegal alien ladies you pick up by the bus stop to work for you, Miss Dorothea—

DOROTHEA: Dorothea, just Dorothea.

ROSALINDA: Look, Dorothea. I want to make it perfectly clear that the upbringing of your children is something I take seriously. I have brought up a son, and he's at UCLA right now getting straight A's—

NARRATOR: (*From now on called* MEMO.) More or less.

ROSALINDA: —and I expect my work to mean something—

DOROTHEA: Of course it does. I just happen to think—

ROSALINDA: "The laundry lady is out sick, so why don't we ask Rosalinda to do it?" Is that what you thought?

DOROTHEA: I've asked my husband—

ROSALINDA: Doesn't matter! I take care of your two daughters who need me, that's my job—well, they need you, actually, but you are too busy campaigning for Jimmy Carter. The man's going to lose; get used to it.

DOROTHEA: Rosalinda!

ROSALINDA: I became a U.S. citizen last year, and the first thing they teach you in citizenship classes is—you don't do windows or laundry.

DOROTHEA: Who taught you—?

ROSALINDA: Let the laundry be dirty for a couple of days. Hire somebody else or do it yourself. I'm not the maid, and I'm not going to do the work that she does. Why? Because the children come first. That is in my contract, the good of the children who love you. They come first!

She gets a little tearful.

DOROTHEA: You're not gonna cry over that.

ROSALINDA: I sometimes think you should take them somewhere, to Disneyland perhaps. I don't think you understand—

DOROTHEA: I didn't ask for your evaluation of me as a mother.

ROSALINDA: I will give it anyway! I am a professional and it's what Maria Von Trapp would have done.

DOROTHEA: I don't believe this! Maria Von Trapp? A "no, thank you" would have done it.

ROSALINDA: My job is to make myself obsolete! I'm not going to cry about this— not anymore, no, no, I've said enough, thank you very much! I've got to—

DOROTHEA: Wait! Wait! Rosalinda . . . let me ask you in all seriousness . . . do you really think Jimmy Carter's going to lose?

ROSALINDA: I give up!

ROSALINDA runs out crying.

DOROTHEA: He's going to lose? No shit!

MEMO: That year, we befriended a neighbor, Armando, who also happened to be from Santiago, Chile. He had big plans of his own. I was of course living in my mother's tiny apartment, sleeping on her couch for the second year in a row while working toward a film degree at UCLA. There was no money to make film—video hadn't become accessible yet—and this neighbor thought he could help.

ARMANDO: Convince your mother to marry me.

MEMO: Right! As if I could convince my mother to do anything!

ARMANDO: But you—

MEMO: It's not up to me, Armando! She has her own ideas about everything, in case you haven't noticed.

ARMANDO: I'm making real money now.

MEMO: Good for you!

ARMANDO: When I stopped doing maintenance, I started contracting it.

MEMO: I don't care!

ARMANDO: I get a bunch of illegals who work for real cheap, and then I send them out. I speak English; the employers don't have to deal with them. Banks and other corporate buildings love the service, and they love me, too, of course. I mean look at me. If you need work, by the way—

MEMO: No, I got an opportunity grant at UCLA.

ARMANDO: Very impressive.

MEMO: It comes with loans attached. I'll have to pay those back, but not the grant.

ARMANDO: You don't need to, son.

MEMO: Armando, I'm not your son. You're barely a few years older than I am; that you're feeling older is another story. Or feeling jaded.

ARMANDO: You're lucky I'm a foreigner. I don't always understand the exact meaning of American words.

MEMO: Good.

ARMANDO: But this is where your mother comes in. She helps me get papers because I don't want to be an illegal who exploits other illegals all my life. Like an average American, I want to legally exploit illegals. You know, I left an entire monastery back home for this.

MEMO: A monastery? I didn't know this, I don't see you in a—

ARMANDO: I was celibate.

MEMO: No way, not you.

ARMANDO: I was going to be a monk, but no . . . something called me to these shores and said, you've got other, bigger things to do. So here I am, I contract illegals. It was either that or serve God the rest of my life. I couldn't do it. Face it, I couldn't withstand being alone with my hand.

MEMO: Does that count as a violation of celibacy?

ARMANDO: Technically, no, but it's a sin, and God knows.

MEMO: Yes, He does, doesn't He?

ARMANDO: He forgives the fact that I have babes now, more than one. You want to meet babes? They're Russian girls, Jewish. They fled persecution, they love their newly gained freedom, I have to service them all, man, and there's only so much juice down there!

MEMO: Eeeeuw!

ARMANDO: These girls like it loud, and in threesomes, man, I tell you! What's your favorite position?

MEMO: Ah . . . I'm just dating at my own pace.

ARMANDO: Men your age shouldn't be virgins.

MEMO: I . . . I had a beer at a party once and a shot of sambucca.

ARMANDO: And then what? Had a massive orgy?

MEMO: No. We played pin the tail on the donkey.

ARMANDO: It's a start. Have you named your genitals yet?

MEMO: I'm not required to, am I?

ARMANDO: Just don't use names of the saints. It's sacrilegious.

MEMO: Look, I–I just devote myself to my art.

ARMANDO: Don't be afraid to ask for help.

MEMO: I'm not.

ARMANDO: I started my business with the help of wealthy, lonely widows, if you get my drift.

MEMO: Wait, you were a gigolo?

ARMANDO: Not a gigolo, a gardener.

MEMO: Suspicious.

ARMANDO: Some of them developed affection toward me; that's not my fault. In this world, you've got to pay for that affection. They invested in my business. Trust me, kid, nobody makes it on minimum wage alone. I tell the Russians the same thing.

MEMO: If you got all these Russian "babes," why are you after my mother?

ARMANDO: I'll tell you why, son. Because she's a lady.

MEMO: OK, but a "lady" isn't just going to marry you to give you papers.

ARMANDO: That's why I need your help.

MEMO: No! No, don't get me inv—

ARMANDO: I'd like to invest in your future films.

MEMO: Really? But no, no, it's all right, no, thank you!

ARMANDO: It's not meant as a bribe. All right, it's a bribe, but it's on behalf of the arts. You artists need us. What type of movies are you going to make? Could I see a script? A thriller, or car chase, Romans in chariots—?

MEMO: Documentaries.

ARMANDO: Oh? Why?

MEMO: I want to capture the voices of modern immigrants on film.

ARMANDO: How is that going to make money in America?

MEMO: It won't, but there are millions of immigrants in the L.A. area.

ARMANDO: So?

MEMO: Not just Latin Americans, but as you know, Russian Jews, Armenians, Koreans—

ARMANDO: I get the point! But why documentaries, dammit?!?

MEMO: Because! Oh, my God, because!

ARMANDO: Because what?

MEMO: When I saw *The Sorrow and the Pity*—

ARMANDO: The what?

MEMO: People talking about what it was like to be under Nazi occupation—

ARMANDO: There are great action movies about that.

MEMO: But this was the real deal, Armando! Then, there was "The Battle of Chile" by Patricio Guzmán—

ARMANDO: Politics, boring!

MEMO: Yes, a three-hour film about the military coup in Chile. History caught on film in grainy black-and-white—and the cameraman gets shot while filming his own death, oh, my God!

ARMANDO: Don't have an orgasm over that!

MEMO: The point is—I don't see myself doing commercial films.

ARMANDO: Are you sure about that?

MEMO: I am.

ARMANDO: But I want to help. In fact, I have a little gift—

MEMO: Careful. Here she comes.

    ROSALINDA enters.

ROSALINDA: I can't believe it, for the second time, she asks me to do something I'm not supposed to do!

MEMO: The laundry again?

ROSALINDA: The dry cleaning! Can you imagine that? I lectured her.

MEMO: I'm sure you did, Mother. Bel Air hasn't seen the likes of you.

ROSALINDA: OK, so what's the little weasel doing in our apartment?

MEMO: Find out, Mother. I've got to go to school and pick up a friend. We're going to make a movie when we can afford it.

ARMANDO: Oh, I'd like to invest in motion pictures.

MEMO: OK, I've got to go. Good luck.

MEMO exits. ROSALINDA and ARMANDO are left alone.

ROSALINDA: The answer is no.

ARMANDO: How can you be so heartless? You have a son. You deserve so much more.

ROSALINDA: I do. I deserve a lot more.

ARMANDO: Did you come to the U.S. to live in solitude?

ROSALINDA: My business! I need to be alone now.

ARMANDO: That's precisely the problem.

ROSALINDA: Go!

ARMANDO: Trust me, I know all about solitude. It was a lonely monastery and I wasn't interested in the sexually ambiguous monks. I yearned for a lady. Audrey Hepburn, Doris Day—

ROSALINDA: Oh, those days of Hollywood glamour are over.

ARMANDO: Who says?

ROSALINDA: I do! Sally Field plays a simple worker in *Norma Rae* and Jane Fonda plays a loving housewife in *Coming Home* who has an affair with a Vietnam vet. The movies are about real people now; they're strong, harsh, and gritty. Life moves on, you know, and you should, too. All that fantasy and glamour, what good was it for? I am no longer Lara.

ARMANDO: Lara, Lara—let me see, yes, yes, I know. It's *Ben-Hur*.

ROSALINDA: No! You just don't know the movies! Out!

ARMANDO: Why can't you teach me?

ROSALINDA: Teach you?

ARMANDO: Yes, everything you know about the movies.

ROSALINDA: I don't want to dream any longer.

ARMANDO: So marry me.

ROSALINDA: It was nice going to the movies with you, but when you started talking about marriage—

ARMANDO: We don't have to see each other much, just learn enough so we can go to immigration, go through the interview, and I'd be an average husband—I'd cheat on you, of course.

ROSALINDA: Of course.

ARMANDO: I've got these Russian ba—

ROSALINDA: I know, in the Fairfax District, that's where they flock.

ARMANDO: Yes. So you wouldn't have to worry about me. It's not about love; it's about convenience. It's about what you can do for me, and what I could do for you.

ROSALINDA: I don't think this is fair.

ARMANDO: What's unfair? You help me get papers, and you can have anything I own, within reason, of course.

ROSALINDA: Go home now.

ARMANDO: Rosalinda, please . . .

ROSALINDA: Go home, Armando, go dream somewhere else.

ARMANDO: You'll do it, though, I know you will. You've been thinking about it, haven't you?

ROSALINDA: No!

ARMANDO: When I first brought it up, something lit up in those eyes—

ROSALINDA: I was shocked!

ARMANDO: Because deep down inside, it bothers you, doesn't it? Fifteen long years have gone by, and you still can't afford a home—

ROSALINDA: My problem, not yours!

Rosalinda (Edith Donoghue-Chávez) and Armando (David McCormick). *Photo: Jon Simpson*

ARMANDO: But it hurts, doesn't it? It hurts your pride to see some peasant like me make it on pure business instinct. I can handle employees, keep a payroll, balance checkbooks, and spend only when necessary. Somehow your money doesn't quite add up, does it?

ROSALINDA: I do honest work.

ARMANDO: Honest work doesn't pay for dreams bigger than life. It hurts—

ROSALINDA: No!

ARMANDO: It hurts that you can't give your son his own bedroom, that you can't afford L.A. rents, that he has to sleep on a couch. That he works as a busboy to work his way through school. And he can't even afford the film needed to complete his assignments.

ROSALINDA: We're trying—

ARMANDO: You've tried giving him everything, and yet something else is missing in this American lifestyle. It hurts that your father got sick and you couldn't afford to fly down to Santiago to spend time with him. It hurts taking the bus to go to work when you should be driving a car. It hurts to stand on Sunset Boulevard next to some illegal alien and a hooker waiting for that same bus. Hollywood's not quite the movie land you had in mind, admit it.

ROSALINDA: I—

ARMANDO: Anyway, I have a little surprise.

ROSALINDA: What?

ARMANDO: I had to hide it—it's a surprise . . . hold on.

He walks outside quickly and brings in a package.

ROSALINDA: What is that?

ARMANDO: It's a 16mm camera.

ROSALINDA: But . . .

ARMANDO: Don't worry, I found it used, on auction. This is for your son.

ROSALINDA: You're using him.

ARMANDO: Of course I am. I want him to be my son, I want to be a good father, which he's never had, and for you to be my wife.

ROSALINDA: I'd never marry for money.

ARMANDO: This isn't money; it's a camera. Take it. I am afraid he wouldn't accept it from me. It's not a real marriage anyway, and you're not being asked to provide all the—shall we say—obligations of a wife.

ROSALINDA: Go home now, and—no—he can't accept this camera.

ARMANDO: He's not going to make movies on some stupid 8mm camera without sound, come on. He needs this camera, and he needs the film that goes inside it. I can buy it. Let me help, Rosalinda.

ROSALINDA: We can't accept.

ARMANDO: A woman does not survive on pride alone.

ROSALINDA: Obviously I do! Take the camera, and go away, please!

ARMANDO: Let me—

ROSALINDA: No!

ARMANDO: If I even suspected for a minute that you could love me as a man, my proposition would be a little more romantic than this, but no, you're a cold woman. It's a pity somehow. Imagine me feeling something for you— imagine that! No, that would be wasted on you. This marriage would be just for convenience. You'll think about it, won't you? I'll have my lawyer draw up a prenup.

ROSALINDA: A what?

ARMANDO: A prenuptial agreement. It's the latest rage in California.

ROSALINDA: Good night now, Armando. Please go.

ARMANDO: Yes. Well, good night.

ARMANDO leaves. She's left alone.

ROSALINDA: Where have you gone, Rock Hudson?

Lights down.

NARRATOR: Mother could not possibly accept the gift. On that particular day, that is. But in the meantime a letter arrives, and with it, a surprise interrupts everyday life. . . .

Enter VLADIMIR reading and acting out his letter. GRANDMA is seen as a customer getting wine from VLADIMIR, then exiting.

VLADIMIR: "Dear Rosalinda, Your letter came back; I thought I'd lost you again until your mother explained you're in Hollywood. Well, that seems like the right place for you to be. My wife and I—we now have three children, two girls, one boy, and I own a wine shop not far from your old neighborhood. Vinos Finos de Vladimir, it's called. Wine is one of the essentials of this tough life. I sell it by the liter and I empty it into bottles, jars, even buckets. People buy it as if it were milk. Now, I can't say any of this to my wife, but sometimes, I wonder, I think about you and me . . . but no, there's no looking back. I took her to see *Saturday Night Fever,* and I imagined myself as John Travolta, and the young woman who wants to leave the neighborhood is definitely you. I cried, and my wife said, that's not a crying movie, you fool. She doesn't like movies much . . . She's become involved in politics, something about helping mothers of the missing, heavy stuff. Sometimes I think she'll get in trouble, but there's no escaping politics in this country, except perhaps when we go to the movies, which I still do by myself if necessary. Meanwhile, in case you don't know, Norma is out in Santa Barbara, California—"

ROSALINDA: What?

VLADIMIR: You got her letter, didn't you?

Enter NORMA, *exit* VLADIMIR.

ROSALINDA: Oh, my God, it's you!

NORMA: Don't I get a hug? Shit, you're cold. Come here!

NORMA *hugs her.* ROSALINDA *has trouble being warm and receptive.*

ROSALINDA: (*Not quite a compliment.*) Why, you haven't changed.

NORMA: I always looked old, you mean.

ROSALINDA: No, silly. So what brings you . . . ?

NORMA: My son-in-law.

ROSALINDA: Your son-in—?

NORMA: A lawyer, top of his class, nice American kid, Christian missionary, met my daughter when he went to work with the poor in Santiago. Well, he married her. He brought her over, and my daughter—God bless her soul— brought me and I get to see my grandchildren.

ROSALINDA: And you didn't warn me?

NORMA: Why? You didn't write back; you're an ingrate.

ROSALINDA: You must have written to the Maryland address. I wasn't trying to avoid you.

NORMA: It's fine, I know how you are.

ROSALINDA: No, you don't. You don't know me.

NORMA: Still testy after all these years! So . . . brought you some wine. I'm gonna have some of it, if you don't mind. Chilean, from Vladimir's shop.

ROSALINDA: Oh, yes, Vladimir.

NORMA: The guy you forgot to marry and fall in love with.

ROSALINDA: I didn't forget exactly—

NORMA: It's all in the past. (*She snaps her fingers.*) He forgot you like that!

ROSALINDA: Thanks. Well, I wasn't quite prepared for you.

NORMA: Yes, the apartment's a little messy—

ROSALINDA: I mean, psychologically, I'm not—

NORMA: I meant the apartment. People who are big dreamers rarely have time to straighten up. They're too busy thinking of all the wonderful things that lie ahead, you know. I'll help you clean up.

ROSALINDA: I can straighten up! My son just happens to live out here in the living room. We don't have another bedroom. I tried to give him mine, but he wouldn't take it. He insisted I should have it.

NORMA: Nice kid.

ROSALINDA: This is his mess then, not mine. Well . . . let me open that bottle, and . . .

NORMA: Look, you still go to the movies, don't you?

ROSALINDA: Of course.

NORMA: Movies have gotten nastier though, don't you think?

ROSALINDA: Why yes, like Bette Midler in *The Rose.* She gets to play this loud-mouthed, boozy bisexual woman, not exactly someone I can relate to. If you remember Doris Day in *Love Me or Leave Me,* there you have someone suffering in a very dignified manner.

NORMA: Her husband beat the shit out of her. How dignified is that?

ROSALINDA: He was the vulgar one, not her, not the heroine. Anyway, we have about fifteen years of movies to catch up on. Isn't that exciting?

NORMA: I knew there was a reason for looking you up! Serve me the wine already. I . . . I—I'm a merry widow, you know.

ROSALINDA: Oh. I'm sorry. (*She serves.*)

NORMA: Heart attack. Boozy old loser who sat around watching TV all day— his heart was bound to suffer. But it's been five years, so . . .

ROSALINDA: OK, be honest: your absolute favorite in the last fifteen years, something that knocked you off your feet, and you've seen it again and again.

NORMA: Why, no contest . . . Liza Minelli in *Cabaret.*

ROSALINDA: (*Disappointed.*) Oh.

NORMA: I know, too many bisexuals. It was about time movie musicals grew up, I say.

ROSALINDA: The choreography was watchable.

NORMA: What about you? Now that the movies are no longer glamorous, what on earth have you seen that you could possibly like?

ROSALINDA: Jane Fonda in *Julia.* The bond between women, see?

NORMA: I cried.

ROSALINDA: I did, too. I'm glad we can agree on that. Well. Thank you for coming.

NORMA: Could I stay?

ROSALINDA: What?

NORMA: I don't want to live in Santa Barbara. My daughter's got her own life, you know.

ROSALINDA: And you think I don't, Norma? I . . . I don't have space. My son sleeps in the foldout bed as it is.

NORMA: I don't mean here.

ROSALINDA: Oh. Where, then?

NORMA: I meant I could rent something nearby, or we could both move into a two-bedroom apartment. You work with Hollywood people. I'll work cleaning homes. I don't care as long as it's honest work.

ROSALINDA: I . . . I don't clean homes.

NORMA: Yes, I know. Your last letter made that clear, you got a degree, blah, blah, blah. But I'm a simple woman. I'm happy to be close to my daughter, but I don't have to see her all the time. I can stay here in Hollywood, and a simple job will help me make ends meet. I don't need much luxury. I just want someone to go to the movies with me, and I'm happy.

ROSALINDA: Well . . . there is an empty apartment upstairs, but . . .

NORMA: Fine, I've got some money for the down payment. I know how it works.

ROSALINDA: I don't know . . .

NORMA: All right . . . well, maybe coming here wasn't such a good idea.

ROSALINDA: You're always welcome, Norma, really.

NORMA: Look, I lived in Santiago. We got hit by a quake and a military coup around the same time. I can cope with disaster, I can even cope with lousy friendships.

NORMA exits.

ROSALINDA: You're welcome anytime. Really!

ROSALINDA looks guilty and sits down, feeling sorry for herself.

NARRATOR: I got Armando's camera, and thanked him for it! I began work on my first film—

ROSALINDA: What do you mean you want to interview me?

NARRATOR/MEMO: It's your chance to have your say.

ROSALINDA: I'm a quiet, modest woman.

MEMO: Yeah, right. Look, my documentary will be about immigrant women who work for Hollywood people.

ROSALINDA: I don't want to be compared to—

MEMO: Mother, I need an "A" in this class. I want you to get me the names of all the Hollywood maids—

ROSALINDA: I will not be compared to untrained labor. I have an associate's degree in child care.

MEMO: I know, I know! But everyone has a take—

ROSALINDA: A take?

MEMO: The women you dismiss as "maids." Surely they see themselves in some other light, as well. They dream of becoming princesses—

ROSALINDA: Don't be stupid; they're maids. They come from savage, rural low-class backgrounds.

MEMO: I want to interview them anyway—

ROSALINDA: You're filming. You're pushing that button without my permission.

MEMO: I was testing! Will you help me please?

ROSALINDA: I don't want the world to see me like this.

MEMO: I'll make sure I put a subtitle that says, "Rosalinda, not a maid."

ROSALINDA: You'll have to call me "a childhood engineer."

MEMO: Of course, anything.

ROSALINDA: Turn it on. No, wait, makeup. I must have—

MEMO: No, no makeup.

ROSALINDA: I feel all plain and raw.

MEMO: My documentary must be plain and raw, Mother.

ROSALINDA: Well, a little powder at least!

MEMO: Mother! Don't ruin it. There must be no glamour in this.

ROSALINDA: I don't want to look plain, that's all. Be patient. (*She powders her nose a bit.*) This is as good as it's going to get. God could have helped me more around the face, but he didn't.

MEMO: Don't say that, Mother, you are bea—

ROSALINDA: I'm not fishing for compliments. Start filming now! OK, first . . . my mother is dying!

MEMO: What?

GRANDMA *enters in her own space as a memory or a ghost.*

GRANDMA: She should have married Vladimir. He looked good in his soccer shorts.

ROSALINDA: I couldn't tell you. I was trying to protect you.

MEMO: I'm not a child.

ROSALINDA: She's been diagnosed with ovarian cancer. Keep filming! I can't afford to just fly back home and spend time with her. Just like when your grandfather got sick, I couldn't be there by his side. Stop filming.

MEMO: This isn't how I want my interviews—

ROSALINDA: Listen to me. I should have married . . .

GRANDMA: Vladimir! He's such a dork, poor thing, but he's popular. He flirts with all the ladies in his liquor store. No wonder the business is doing so well. I will miss those things in my neighborhood. I'll miss the long procession toward the church for the ascension of the Virgin Mary into heaven. I will miss my children. I have four sons who dedicate themselves to soccer, I think, and I have a daughter in Hollywood, California. She will star in her own movies one of these days. (*Exits.*)

MEMO: I'm sorry to hear it, Ma.

ROSALINDA: As for Vladimir, sometimes I just want to call him and tell him, "I'll send you money for you to come visit me," and while he's here, I make him stay and leave his wife, but it's an adulterous thought and I hate myself for it.

MEMO: My documentary is not about adultery.

ROSALINDA: Then there's a real reason we left the DC area.

MEMO: To be closer to Hollywood.

ROSALINDA: I had an affair with the janitor.

MEMO: I don't need to know this.

ROSALINDA: Yes, Melvin, the black janitor! He was married, of course. I seem to gravitate toward them, don't I? His wife came to the door—you were away at camp with the Boy Scouts—and she asked me to leave town. Can you imagine that? The humiliation! To have some janitor's wife telling you in so many words to leave town as if you were some prostitute! And I wasn't even thinking of marrying him. I mean—I mean—he—

MEMO: He was black, so what?

ROSALINDA: Well . . . I had no problem having sex with him, but apparently marrying a black man was more difficult for me. Heaven help me, how can I even admit to such a thing? What type of monster am I?

MEMO: I'm trying to make a simple documentary.

ROSALINDA: I've kept things from you. Deep down inside, you gravitated toward the documentary to see how much truth you'd get out of me.

MEMO: Too much, apparently.

ROSALINDA: I need to give you a real home now. The gears are in motion.

MEMO: Mother, no, you're not thinking what I think . . .

ARMANDO enters.

MEMO: What is he doing here?

ARMANDO: That's what I want to know, too. She hadn't called in weeks until today.

MEMO: You called him?

ROSALINDA: You still got those papers lying around?

MEMO: Mother!

ARMANDO: Don't you "mother" her now. What? What are you saying, Rosalinda?

ROSALINDA: Well . . . I need to know what the prenup looks like.

ARMANDO: Trust me, it looks good!

MEMO: Mom . . .

ROSALINDA: That's all I need to know, Armando. Come here!

ARMANDO rushes toward her, lifts her, and the two hug while MEMO just exits in disgust.

MEMO/NARRATOR: Norma and I were the only witnesses to the one big disaster of that day—the first one, I should say, the big one and the tsunami all rolled into one. Yet, somehow it all seemed sweet and harmless enough. Armando would get his papers and Mother would get a home. A house! In Los Angeles! In North Hollywood, California.

ARMANDO lifts a glass of champagne. NORMA joins in along with MEMO as a witness. A FEMALE PRIEST, played by same actress who played DOR-OTHEA, presides over them.

PRIEST: I declare you husband and wife. You may kiss the bride.

ROSALINDA shows discomfort at the idea of having to kiss her younger husband, but then he does it, willingly, surprising her, surprising MEMO, who has to watch, and befuddling the priest, who doesn't quite under-stand what's going on. Lights down.

Act Two

SCENE 1

Enter the NARRATOR. He shows us around the house. It's not a realistic set. One can't expect a fully constructed home, but at least the furniture makes it clear that the family has moved into a house. They look more prosperous, and the lighting is richer. For reasons that will become clear later, ARMANDO plays a ghostly presence in some of these early scenes of Act Two, commenting within his own area until he officially enters. His space could be defined as "a bar where drunks talk to themselves out loud"; however, it's not a literal space, but a metaphysical one.

MEMO: And thus it came to be that this family moved into a home in North Hollywood, an actual house with bedrooms and furniture, a couple of cars, and of course, a mother and a father.

ARMANDO: I always wanted a son.

ROSALINDA: I told Dorothea to introduce you to Robert Redford, but it hasn't happened yet.

MEMO: Mother, I'll meet Robert Redford when the time comes.

ROSALINDA: Your film should have been shown at Sundance.

MEMO: I'm still a student. I got an A.

ROSALINDA: You need to do better than that.

MEMO: Better than the top grade?

ARMANDO: To her I'm just a ghost passing by. Might as well get used to it.

ROSALINDA: People in Hollywood don't ask for transcripts. It's all about who you know.

MEMO: I know that. Right now, I'm in school and I'm learning new things.

ROSALINDA: Too much schooling, I'm sorry. But, fine, the fact that you finished a short film and impressed your professors, that's certainly a lot more than any peasants in our family ever did.

MEMO: I wish you wouldn't talk about our family that way.

ROSALINDA: They are who they are, and I'm just trying to help you with my Hollywood contacts.

MEMO: Mother—

ROSALINDA: —what matters most is that you're happy doing what you want to do, my darling, precious sweetie.

MEMO: You're being cooperative, noncombative, and cheerful all of a sudden— what on earth is wrong?

ROSALINDA: Nothing, I just like my home.

ARMANDO: It's actually my home!

MEMO: As long as you're happy.

ROSALINDA: You don't sound convincing.

MEMO: I won't get into it right now.

ROSALINDA: I'm glad. Let us enjoy the best home that marriage to that awful man can buy.

ARMANDO: I've been nothing but kind to her, but my friends warned me, she is a lady, "not like the Hollywood trash you pick up on streets." She's out of my league.

MEMO: Well, for someone who hates her husband, you're sure looking good these days.

ROSALINDA: I needed to fit into new outfits.

MEMO: And you do.

ROSALINDA: I've been dieting. We're going to the INS today.

MEMO: For the papers—finally?

ROSALINDA: Almost. It's the last interview. I must convince them that this man, though ten years younger, is my husband.

MEMO: Well, you coulda fooled me.

ROSALINDA: Exactly. I'm all about appearances right now.

MEMO: You're the expert.

ROSALINDA: (*Suspicious.*) What do you mean by that?

MEMO: Nothing.

   ARMANDO *enters. He's been drinking.*

ARMANDO: Hello . . . all right, no lecturing.

ROSALINDA: No, no, you couldn't have, Armando!

MEMO: Don't you have an important appoint—?

ARMANDO: I know! I just had lunch—

ROSALINDA: You had *her* for lunch, that woman, that Russian, Anatovska, whatever her name is.

ARMANDO: I'm not about to talk about my private life.

ROSALINDA: Not to your wife, no. I'm not involved in it.

ARMANDO: Rosalinda . . . lay off!

ROSALINDA: If you're going to defraud the U.S. government, the least you could do is be prepared.

ARMANDO: I work, I pay the bills. I'll do this my way.

MEMO: Nobody's questioning your ability to pay the bills, Armando.

ARMANDO: You people are not satisfied ever.

MEMO: Don't include me in this argument.

ROSALINDA: But it's true about me.

MEMO: Let's not make it worse—

ARMANDO: I've only had three drinks. And a line of coke.

ROSALINDA: Coke?

ARMANDO: Yeah, as in cocaine. The recreational drug for people who matter.

ROSALINDA: Great! Now my age really begins to show because I'm feeling like a mother here! I can't help it; you're a child!

ARMANDO: Memo, my son—

MEMO: Stop it! Could we just get this over with? And the two of you can then go your separate ways. You to your way of life, Mother to hers.

ARMANDO: You hear that, Rosita Lindita, we have different ways of life!

ROSALINDA: That's right, you're immoral, and you bask in the glory of it.

MEMO: Stop this! Please! Just . . . just don't blow it.

ARMANDO: We have an entire way of life at stake, huh? One that I finance, one that I hope one day the two of you will honor!

ROSALINDA: We know the situation; we just don't have to honor *you!*

MEMO: The less we talk about it, the better.

ARMANDO: Before you go, son, here . . .

He hands MEMO *car keys.*

MEMO: Cool!

ARMANDO: I thought I'd celebrate with a new little Mercedes.

MEMO: What?

ROSALINDA: We can't afford a Mer—

ARMANDO: It's pre-owned, all right? But it looks new. An old movie star died and someone had to get rid of it quick. Why don't you go ride it, m'ijo?

ROSALINDA: Memo, don't you dare!

MEMO: Just a little ride.

MEMO *exits, looking mesmerized, holding the keys.*

ARMANDO: Did you notice the look on his face?

ROSALINDA: You're spending too much money and I don't appreciate you turning my son against me.

ARMANDO: I'm spending money on both of you; somebody should feel grateful.

ROSALINDA: I just wanted a home.

ARMANDO: Is that all? In the most expensive real estate in the country.

ROSALINDA: You knew quite well this was the most important day of your stupid illegal immigrant life, and you purposely—

ARMANDO: I didn't purposely do anything. I needed to get laid, that's all. I don't really have a wife, remember?

ROSALINDA: Not according to what you have to tell the INS.

ARMANDO: Except, except that I look at you and I have to wonder . . .

ROSALINDA: Could we not . . . ?

ARMANDO: . . . you've thought about it, haven't you?

ROSALINDA: Thought what?

ARMANDO: That you're incredibly fascinated by me.

ROSALINDA: Don't flatter yourself.

ARMANDO: What I do with my many, many muchachas—that really fascinates you.

ROSALINDA: Go back to the monastery, young man.

ARMANDO: They tried, those monks, they tried very hard to get the lust out of my system.

ROSALINDA: They obviously failed.

ARMANDO: What about you, Rosalinda? What have they done to you that you can't be honest with yourself about what you want and what you need?

ROSALINDA: I am just a decent, average woman.

ARMANDO: You're just as willing to defraud the government!

ROSALINDA: I'm trying to give my son a home!

ARMANDO: And it hasn't even crossed your mind that your young, hung husband—?

ROSALINDA: Of course not.

ARMANDO: Look, I've decided I'm not going to lie to the INS.

ROSALINDA: You're going to give us away, then?

ARMANDO: No, we're going to consummate this marriage, then it won't be a lie.

ROSALINDA: What? You propose to do that now in the next five minutes?

ARMANDO: I can be quick.

ROSALINDA: Sober up!

> *ARMANDO kisses her. ROSALINDA struggles, but ARMANDO is strong and kisses her again. ROSALINDA pushes him away. ARMANDO insists and comes at her with even more ferocity. He's touching her and she's barely resisting until she slaps him. MEMO comes running.*

MEMO: What's going on?

ARMANDO: I'm kissing my wife!

MEMO: Leave her alone!

ARMANDO: You stay away from me, kid.

MEMO: I mean it!

ROSALINDA: Stop it, the two of you! I'm not giving back the house no matter what happens!

This announcement stops MEMO *and* ARMANDO *cold.*

ROSALINDA: We're going to the INS to get your stupid papers. After that, you're leaving this house! And if you touch me again, I will castrate you myself! . . . (*Smiling.*) OK, let's not be late.

She exits. The two men are left staring at her in great amazement.

MEMO: (*As* NARRATOR.) An officer of the INS took one look at them, the nagging wife straightening out her husband's hair and decided—these people couldn't possibly be faking marriage. He approved their papers without a formal interview. Funny what good actors we had become in Hollywood.

Exits.

SCENE 2

NORMA and ROSALINDA shuck corn as they might have done twenty years earlier, but this time, it's clear ROSALINDA is overdressed, prosperous, and unhappy. ARMANDO's back in his space.

NORMA: You have this young husband and yet you won't take advantage of him.

ROSALINDA: What goes on between two people is private.

ARMANDO: I undress myself in front of her every day.

ROSALINDA: That man's an exhibitionist.

ARMANDO: I love watching her reaction.

NORMA: You guys finally did it, didn't you?

ROSALINDA: Look—

NORMA: Right after the INS interview, the two of you went off somewhere—

ROSALINDA: To a movie, *On Golden Pond.*

NORMA: Don't change the subject. What's he like, you know . . . ?

ARMANDO: I'm a real man down there.

ROSALINDA: Don't be ridiculous. What did you think about Katherine Hepburn, huh?

NORMA: Send the bitch to a nursing home! What do I care?

ROSALINDA: She gets to win a fourth Oscar after all these years.

NORMA: I don't care. And stop keeping secrets.

ROSALINDA: It's a world of dangerous enemies. I learned it from the movies.

NORMA: You learned it from Ronald Reagan, and he's paranoid.

ARMANDO: I want my wife and she wants me. Why should we hate each other over that?

NORMA: Why are we doing this? I don't even like corn.

ROSALINDA: I want to cook today, that's all, for my little Memo.

ARMANDO: Everything's for her little Memo!

NORMA: He's going to San Diego—you need time alone with your husband.

ROSALINDA: He's got his whores. Let them cook for him.

NORMA: You're jealous.

ROSALINDA: I said I—

NORMA: Let me give you some advi—

ROSALINDA: Shut up, Norma! Don't ridicule me! I know what I feel! I know what I want and don't want!

NORMA: But you've been denying yourself—

ROSALINDA: I deny him!

ARMANDO: Passion ferments in the blood like booze itself, and it spreads through all our organs until too much of it kills you. Our love is an indulgence.

NORMA: The man actually loves you.

ROSALINDA: Don't be absurd.

NORMA: It's his one redeeming quality.

ARMANDO: Save me from this love, but don't leave me completely without it.

NORMA: He has found you, the most difficult woman ever, and he's willing to put up a good fight for you. He's dying to earn your respect but—like most men—he only knows how to make you jealous. Look, I give you permission to enjoy your husband.

ARMANDO: I want my seed swimming inside her.

ROSALINDA: We'll get divorced and that'll be the end of it. I get to keep the home, of course. That's part of the prenup along with other stipulations.

NORMA: What else is in that stupid prenup?

ROSALINDA: It's not for me, mind you; it's all for my son.

ARMANDO: What about our children?

NORMA: This marriage is for you, too!

ROSALINDA: What does—?

NORMA: Make love to him!

ARMANDO: Make love to me! Somebody!

ROSALINDA: Enough!

NORMA: Touch your husband, kiss him all over, fuck his brains out!

ARMANDO: Fuck my brains out!

ROSALINDA: Norma! Please! Oh, oh, oh!

ROSALINDA runs inside crying.

NORMA: OK. Just kiss him. Lightly. On the lips. Rosalinda? Don't be like this. Bitch!

ARMANDO: Bitch! If I can't get a woman tonight, I'll go fuck a fairy!

Exits. MEMO walks in, in a rush.

MEMO: Hi.

NORMA: I thought you'd gone to San Diego.

MEMO: On my way. I had to go buy some camping equipment. I'm getting my camera, then gotta go pick up some friends—

NORMA: How nice. A girlfriend?

MEMO: More than one.

NORMA: Like father like son?

MEMO: No, nothing like that. I mean—we're all colleagues—

NORMA: No need to explain to an old lady. Give me details later after it happens. That's how I like my gossip.

MEMO: OK. Where's Mom?

NORMA: In there, feeling sorry for herself.

MEMO: Sounds like Mom. Well, I hope she'll be all right—

NORMA: You go and do what you do best.

MEMO: I'll get to interview a bunch of border patrolmen and women, and a coyote—

NORMA: A what?

MEMO: They're the ones who smuggle people.

NORMA: Oh. See how little I know, such a pea brain!

MEMO: You know, you haven't answered my call for an interview.

NORMA: Me? I'm just a simple woman.

MEMO: You're not the quiet type, Norma.

NORMA: Nothing I say matters, really. I just come by and listen to your mother, that's my purpose in life.

MEMO: False modesty, Norma.

NORMA: No, I'm glad to be her friend. She doesn't have many, you realize. She turns people off, the poor thing. You're her only real purpose in life, you know.

MEMO: Well, she's a married woman now.

NORMA: Well, she seriously needs to screw her husband.

MEMO: (*Laughing.*) Ah, Norma, we can always count on you to put things in perspective. That's why you owe my camera some face-to-face.

NORMA: Look, I'm shy, dammit!

MEMO: I doubt that somehow.

NORMA: All right, then I'm afraid of being in front of a camera.

MEMO: You'll get over it very quickly.

NORMA: But I haven't done anything special.

MEMO: Don't buy into that big Hollywood lie that only pretty people matter.

NORMA: Are you calling me ugly?

MEMO: No, I'm saying most of us are not movie stars and we have stories worth telling anyway.

NORMA: I even immigrated legally! No crossing the desert in the middle of the summer, no dangerous fights with smugglers and drug dealing. How boring does an immigrant get?

MEMO: I think you're quite amusing, Norma.

NORMA: I should not be seen on the big screen.

MEMO: All right, fine, I'm outa here! And tell me why she won't let me drive that Mercedes.

NORMA: Mother knows best.

MEMO: I certainly hope so. What a family!

He exits.

NORMA: All right, are you coming out here? I'm gonna stay out here until you come to your senses! (*Beat.*) Hey, Rock Hudson? You really talk to her? Rock? I'll talk to you. Rock? Rock? (*No answer from Rock.*) Well, the hell with you, maricón!

Lights out.

SCENE 3

Later that night, 1:00 a.m. ARMANDO is sleeping on the couch. MEMO sneaks in again, and on his way out is carrying a big box. ARMANDO catches him.

ARMANDO: Hey, where are you going?

MEMO: Ah . . . just to San Diego.

ARMANDO: I thought you already left for San—what's in those boxes?

MEMO: None of your business. Where's Mom?

ARMANDO: Locked in her room, talking to Cary Grant.

MEMO: No, Rock Hudson.

ARMANDO: Whatever. Are you—are you moving out?

MEMO: Ah, what?

ARMANDO: And you weren't going to tell us, were you?

MEMO: I'm a grown-up, you know.

ARMANDO: Then announce it; be a man about it.

MEMO: That's hard.

ARMANDO: Being a man?

MEMO: No, announcing things to Mother. Look, I'll still be in town, closer to the beach. San Diego was just an excuse.

ARMANDO: But why are you—?

MEMO: I don't want to live among immigrants anymore!

ARMANDO: What about the documentary?

MEMO: You encouraged me to do something commercial. I'm going for teenage mutants and lots of chases with flying saucers.

ARMANDO: You need money?

MEMO: Yes, but not from you.

ARMANDO: You need it. Take my money.

MEMO: Look, I know you're deluded enough to think this might be a real marriage, but I'm not your stepson. You don't have to feel obliged to give me anything, certainly not fatherly affection, yuck!

ARMANDO: But I want to help.

MEMO: Just . . . just be kind to my mother.

ARMANDO: I'm trying!

MEMO: Be patient. I suspect that deep down inside she likes *something* about you, something deeper than sex.

ARMANDO: I'm not just about sex, you know. God knows I can be, but with her . . . how would you like a little sister?

MEMO: They've made great advances in artificial insemination.

ARMANDO: No! I mean it, Memo, I want you to have brothers and sisters—

MEMO: We're in the plurals now?

ARMANDO: Help me reach her . . . I think I love her.

MEMO: I'll let the two of you play out your Spanish soap opera. I'm going prime time, baby. Great things are in store for me, just not here.

ARMANDO: I'll miss you.

MEMO: Don't say that.

ARMANDO: I'm your stepfather whether you like it or not! I have feelings! I'm not cold like you Hollywood people! I think of you as my son.

MEMO: This isn't the family life I envisioned for myself when I saw *Life with Father* starring William Powell! And please, just for Mother's sake, stay away from drugs and from the dangerous people who sell them.

ARMANDO: That's just an occasional thing. Please, just take my money.

MEMO: Oh, all right. Goodbye, stepdaddy. I'm sorry. (*Exits.*)

ARMANDO: Goodbye, son. (*Beat.*) Rosalinda, come on out here! Be my wife! That's it, I'm outa here. I'll do a three-way, a multiple-way with blonde Russian Jews on coke, all in one bed, one big fuck-fest for me, you hear, all for me, because I don't spend time alone. Unlike you, I refuse to be alone!

He exits.

SCENE 4

Three days later, around 11:00 p.m. ROSALINDA *paces around the room by herself. She picks up the phone and dials.*

ROSALINDA: Hello . . . pick up, pick up, pick up. Hello— You said you were coming back to pick up what's left of your things, Armando. That was three days ago. If you don't come by midnight, I'll throw them out the window. They'll be lying on the curbside and the bums in the street will get them, including your tank top, which you shouldn't wear in public anymore. You're getting pudgy; the love handles are beginning to show! It's 11:02 right now. You've got 58 long minutes and . . .

She hangs up and looks desperate. She pours herself some wine.

ROSALINDA: OK, fifty-seven minutes now. And then it's over. Over.

We hear a man's voice.

VOICE: Hello out there . . .

ROSALINDA: Armando?

Enter ROCK HUDSON.

ROCK: No, Doris, it is I.

ROSALINDA: Doris? No, I'm Rosalinda, remember?

ROCK: Oh, yes, the lady from Santiago.

ROSALINDA: No longer in Santiago. I'm right down the hill from where you live, but no, I get no visits.

ROCK: I'm here now; talk to me. Oh, and let me—of course—kiss that hand, I know how much you appreciate that, sweet, sweet lady. What are you thinking?

ROSALINDA: Frankly, I wasn't thinking about you, Rock, I'm sorry, not today anyway.

ROCK: My heart is broken.

ROSALINDA: Don't be silly.

ROCK: Have I lost the touch, the flair? The savoir faire? I was just a simple high school football player from Winnetka, Illinois. Gallant manners came later, part of the process of refinement. I've learned to sell this illusion of Rock Hudson. My real name was—

ROSALINDA: I don't want to know. Keep the illusion. I have other things to think about tonight.

ROCK: What's on your mind, then? How could it have strayed away from me?

ROSALINDA: How could I tell people what I really feel?

ROCK: You don't—I mean if you're not comfortable. Hide, if you must. It works for me.

ROSALINDA: But that's a double life.

ROCK: You can live with it and still thrive, and at the end of the day, at the end of the road, let them figure out what it all means. You gave it your best shot. You provided them with a certain veneer, a certain flair, something they liked to watch, but that's all you owe them. In your privacy, however, you must still strive for some form of truth.

ROSALINDA: Truth, yet hidden from view. That means I will never express what I feel, not to him.

ROCK: Then tell me.

ROSALINDA: Why should my feelings matter to you?

ROCK: I know, I'm a megastar, aren't I? Just try me.

ROSALINDA: He's my husband. Am I supposed to feel something for him?

ROCK: Some women actually love their husbands. I've met one or two. Is it the passion? The sex?

ROSALINDA: Sometimes I wish I could just tell him, "Fuck me and go home."

ROCK: Rosalinda! That's not very romantic.

ROSALINDA: No. And he lives right here, so I can't send him "home." But I'm having him move out, maybe then we'll finally have a sex life; separation worked for Kate Hepburn and Spencer Tracy. With some men, you have to use up their manly energy and then kick them out of bed.

ROCK: (*Sighing.*) I know the feeling.

ROSALINDA: Know what?

ROCK: I could never master the trick myself. Maybe I don't have the answers for you. I should leave now.

ROSALINDA: Wait.

ROCK: I mean it, Rosalinda. I've begun to feel some distance . . .

ROSALINDA: Why?

ROCK: A man has finally come between us.

ROSALINDA: You think so?

ROCK: And I'm happy for you; I just wish you owned up to your feelings. It's all right to feel passion for a man even if he's not a 100 percent right for you, even if he's a bit of a bad boy. We're all sinners. So, my dear . . . you won't be seeing me again.

ROSALINDA: What?

ROCK: My time is running out, in many more ways than one.

ROSALINDA: Why do you say that?

ROCK: I haven't been feeling like myself recently—

ROSALINDA: No, let that boy from Winnetka, Illinois, fade away to age and illness. But Rock Hudson will always remain that beautiful gentleman who inspired me to dream in a shabby, rundown theater in Santiago.

ROCK: I'll remember that. There's no one else like you—you, my biggest fan.

ROSALINDA: (*As he retreats.*) Rock? Rock?

The phone rings with a deafening sound. Lights change. ROCK exits. ROSALINDA reaches for it.

ROSALINDA: Hello . . . Memo, darling . . . it's OK. Yes. I'll be OK by myself. You enjoy that party, go out with your friends and be young. Watch the drinking, though. No, he was supposed to come by, and he hasn't, you know, not yet. Listen, I'm sorry to keep you, I needed to tell you . . . What you should know is . . . there are moments. Yes, moments when I can think beyond Armando's tricks, and I can think of him differently . . . Not that I forgive what he does! The way he exploits immigrants, his own kind!— But honestly now, sometimes, I feel that, yes, I am his wife—I can have feelings for such a man, and they're not innocent little feelings. I have managed to marry a man I actually feel something for! Marriage wasn't supposed to be like this! This much emotion, this much unsettling lust for his passion and his body, and, yes, I am going to say it finally, if he ever gets here tonight. I am his wife, and the feds can rest assured, our marriage is not a lie! My entire life is *not* a lie! I lust after him! Does that mean I love him, too? Honey? Honey, wake up! No, I was just saying, never mind, such silly things I say! Yes, you've had a bit too many, I'm glad you're not driving. Just stay there at your friend's and take care of yourself . . . No, I was just babbling on like a fool—I've gotta go. Bye, bye, baby.

She hangs up, looking relieved somehow. She goes to get another bottle of wine. She lights candles. She straightens her hair. She hears a noise. There's a knock. She approaches the door.

ROSALINDA: Armando? Did you lose your key?

POLICEMAN'S VOICE: Ma'am . . . are you the wife . . . ?

ROSALINDA: Yes, officer, I am the wife around here.

POLICEMAN'S VOICE: Well, ma'am. It's about your husband.

Lights down on main stage. Lights on ARMANDO'*s space as we proceed to a transition.*
    He exits. Lights down.
    In the transition, the women change quickly to black clothing. Organ sounds, funerary music is heard.

SCENE 5

A few days later in the living room.

NORMA: *Missing* with Jack Lemmon is coming out, and it'll finally tell the story of what happened back in Chile, but the State Department's threatening to sue the filmmaker.

ROSALINDA: It's probably Marxist propaganda anyway.

NORMA: The truth hurts.

ROSALINDA: Hollywood people! I'd rather go see Julie Andrews play a drag queen anyway.

NORMA: You won't like it. Gender bending, you don't really approve of that.

ROSALINDA: I had a good talk with Rock. I'm a little more tolerant now.

MEMO enters.

MEMO: All right, I took care of it.

ROSALINDA: I don't really approve of cremation, but—

MEMO: It's the only way you'll be able to take the ashes back to Chile.

NORMA: But we're traditional about that, you know, the need to see the body—

MEMO: No, the cops warned us that we shouldn't see the body. Bad shape.

ROSALINDA: Fine! Look, I got a call. Some family member's flying in today.

MEMO: Who?

ROSALINDA: Ah—a cousin or something. She'll take the ashes back to Chile.

NORMA: But don't you think you should do that?

ROSALINDA: It's best that we put this entire episode behind us. Let his "cousin" or whatever she is take care of it.

MEMO: You're holding up well.

ROSALINDA: That's what I do always. I hold up well.

MEMO: Could we talk?

ROSALINDA: Anything, darling. What's on your mind?

MEMO: We need to make some decisions.

ROSALINDA: I trust you to make the right ones.

MEMO: No, you don't. You know quite well you're way too opinionated, so let's get it done now, shall we? I'd like to sell the Mercedes.

ROSALINDA: If it makes you happy.

MEMO: That's what I mean. What do you really think, Mother? Please just get to it.

NORMA: You should sell it and buy something less flashy.

ROSALINDA: Keep it, then!

MEMO: He was killed in that car, Mother, and you didn't want to drive it to begin with.

ROSALINDA: You should use it.

MEMO: Why?

ROSALINDA: To drive to business meetings, for instance.

MEMO: Mother . . .

NORMA: That car is cursed. I wouldn't want my son—

ROSALINDA: The Mercedes will help you get a look, or get a job at least. A real job.

NORMA: I don't see how you could avoid seeing this dead man's face everywhere you go with that thing.

MEMO: We'll trade it in for a pickup truck or something.

ROSALINDA: My son is not a pickup-truck-type of guy.

MEMO: Well, it could hold film equipment—see? That's practical. Which brings us to the actual business.

ROSALINDA: You'll run Armando's business, of course.

MEMO: I'm a filmmaker, Mother. I don't want to run a cleaning service.

NORMA: He's right. I don't see him running a business like that.

ROSALINDA: I was hoping you'd be man enough to do it by yourself.

MEMO: See that, Norma? My manhood is being questioned now!

ROSALINDA: If that's what it takes to make you think seriously about your future!

NORMA: Rosalinda, shut the fuck up. Just sell the business. Money was Armando's downfall.

ROSALINDA: Money makes film school possible.

MEMO: Money had him killed.

ROSALINDA: No, hoodlums killed him!

MEMO: Those stupid teenagers wouldn't have beaten his brains out if they hadn't wanted the car and what it represented.

NORMA: They just needed a car to flee from their crimes.

MEMO: They targeted him. It was a hate crime.

ROSALINDA: A murder is always a hate crime!

MEMO: No, they saw success and they also saw an immigrant, and they wondered, how does some foreigner get more money than we do?

ROSALINDA: If you're not going to take responsibility, then I will.

MEMO: There we go! We finally get to the point where we should have started this talk to begin with.

ROSALINDA: And you will be there for the ride because you won't stop taking my money like a true hippie. Nancy Reagan has the same problem with her children.

MEMO: Then I will have to make it without you, Mother.

ROSALINDA: I'd like to see that.

MEMO: Not everyone wants to sell themselves, Mother!

ROSALINDA slaps him.

NORMA: That's enough. Memo, you should never speak to your mother that way, even if she's wrong most of the time.

ROSALINDA: (*To* MEMO.) I married a man for you!

MEMO: I didn't ask you to!

NORMA: You had feelings for him, Rosalinda, admit it!

ROSALINDA picks up her handbag and car keys.

NORMA: OK. Where are you going?

ROSALINDA: Julie Andrews stars in *Victor/Victoria*, and I'm not about to miss that.

She starts to walk out, leaving NORMA and MEMO looking on, aghast. ROSALINDA stops. By the door stands HELENA, a woman in her early thirties.

HELENA: Hello . . . is this . . . ?

ROSALINDA: Yes, it is.

NORMA: You're from Chile?

HELENA: Yes. You can tell?

NORMA: That scarf—I bought one of those in Santiago. At the Plaza de Armas.

HELENA: That's right.

MEMO: You must be Armando's relative.

HELENA: Ah, yes. May I?

ROSALINDA: Come on in, please. Sit down. Make room, Memo.

HELENA: Which one of you is la Señora Rosalinda?

NORMA: Coffee?

HELENA: Yes, thank you.

ROSALINDA: I'm Rosalinda. Nice to meet you.

HELENA: If you were on your way out—?

ROSALINDA: It's all right. I wanted to avoid these two, but I can't. Story of my life. Try to ignore them; they're irrelevant.

NORMA: You're cruel and pathetic.

MEMO: But we love you anyway!

ROSALINDA: Shut up, both of you! (*Smiles at* HELENA.) So . . .

HELENA: Well . . . it's a nice home. But so much of this city looks incredible . . . I am overwhelmed.

MEMO: When did you fly in?

HELENA: Last night. I'm staying with friends in the San Francisco Valley.

ROSALINDA: San Fernando. We live in the San Fernando Valley, too, right here. This area's called North Hollywood.

HELENA: Oh, yes, I'm sorry.

NORMA: First time?

HELENA: First time outside of Chile altogether. If I could stay, I would.

ROSALINDA: Let's not get too far ahead of ourselves.

HELENA: Sorry.

ROSALINDA: Tomorrow's the ceremony, and you're invited, of course.

HELENA: Will there be a viewing?

ROSALINDA: No, he's being cremated.

HELENA: Oh. I see. Well, we should talk alone.

NORMA: Why?

HELENA: (*To* ROSALINDA.) I mean . . . it's between you and me, isn't it?

NORMA: Didn't you just come here to pick up the ashes?

HELENA: I didn't even know about any ashes, but I can if you want me to.

MEMO: Aren't you a cousin?

HELENA: No. I'm Armando's wife. (*Pause.*) Didn't you know?

MEMO: No.

NORMA: Fuck, no!

ROSALINDA: I did.

MEMO: Mother!

NORMA: You didn't say anything, Rosali—

ROSALINDA: I know.

HELENA: So . . . can't we talk alone?

ROSALINDA: Like I said, it's hard to get rid of these two peasants. Ignore them, go on.

HELENA: I don't know all the laws in this country, but I am entitled to some . . . compensation. I have our marriage certificate.

MEMO: Damn, that would mean that . . .

NORMA: How can some marriage certificate from a faraway country count for anything here?

HELENA: I am a little lost just by walking the streets . . . but my cousin . . . he had me talk to a lawyer in Chile, one of those who volunteers for the poor.

ROSALINDA: How quaint!

HELENA: He helped collect the money for me to buy a ticket to fly out here. He said there's no bigamy law in the U.S., and that the first marriage is the only valid one.

ROSALINDA: Really? Is that so?

HELENA: Well, yes. And the coffee's cold! But . . . I have a son by him, twelve years old. Armando owes us support. My friends here in L.A. are telling me I should get an American lawyer who knows the law in California and I told them I don't want to do that.

ROSALINDA: You don't?

HELENA: Yours is a marriage, too, and I'm sure you—you loved him, and it's not your fault he lied to you. My friends say we could claim your marriage to him was false, that he married you for papers. I mean, you're an older woman— it's what they said. I mean, they said I could make a claim that his entire property belongs to me, his first and real wife. I really hope we don't have to go through all that, but it's important that we talk this out, you know.

MEMO: The marriage certificate looks real enough.

NORMA: We're fucked.

HELENA: I'm sorry—

ROSALINDA: Don't worry so much about us, Helena. We won't have to go through all that.

HELENA: Really?

ROSALINDA: Yes, because I have a lawyer who *does not* volunteer for the poor. He gets paid, big time.

Memo: Mother, could we not—?

ROSALINDA: Please, I'm prepared.

HELENA: Good, then we can talk.

ROSALINDA: First of all, I got the truth out of him very early on in this marriage. I needed to know everything, and I needed to know what on earth could possibly affect my well-being and that of my son.

HELENA: And I'm doing the same with mine, that's all.

ROSALINDA: Except you left a few details unfinished.

HELENA: Excuse me?

ROSALINDA: A few letters carelessly sent to the wrong people.

HELENA: I don't understand.

ROSALINDA: Armando knew you'd come sooner or later. You met him when he'd just left the monastery. He was in need of women, and you were clearly the most insistent one, the one who got pregnant. He went ahead and married you, still enough of a Catholic boy to trade celibacy for monogamy. He, however, found copies of your love letters written to several other boyfriends. And their replies. You had a penchant for repressed celibate boys from fairly well-off backgrounds.

HELENA: Wait a second. Armando was my husband, and he abandoned us. I'm the victim here.

ROSALINDA: He felt betrayed, of course, because when he read your letters, he didn't believe any longer he'd left you pregnant.

HELENA: Why, he never mentioned—

ROSALINDA: The dates coincide with your pregnancy. Any of these other men could have knocked you up. My goodness, so many lovers. How greedy! He made copies of these letters as evidence. He thought it best to leave the country as soon as he could, and he did. It took you years to track him down to L.A. He knew you'd want to.

HELENA: I admit I was born poor and that I needed a man to take care of me at the time.

ROSALINDA: You don't deny having other boyfriends.

HELENA: Armando reserved the right to have all the women he wanted, but a woman is suddenly a whore—

ROSALINDA: You said it!

HELENA: He was not faithful to me, either! I can prove that, too. And what about you, Rosalinda?

ROSALINDA: What about me, dear?

HELENA: My friends tell me that he rented an apartment and that he stayed there most of the time—

ROSALINDA: He had mistresses; I don't deny that. But the will was specifically drawn up to benefit me. I made certain of it.

HELENA: I'm sorry, but my friends even doubt your marriage was even consummated.

ROSALINDA: And how will you prove that?

HELENA: He liked young women, young! Especially Russian girls from the Fairmont District.

ROSALINDA: Fairfax!

HELENA: Fine, Fairfax! He told them you were planning to divorce as soon the papers came through. This is what I've found out, and I am his wife. I have the truth on my side. I think you are false and you've cheated the United States of America with a phony marriage. I'm sure the government won't take kindly to that when they consider how to split up the property.

ROSALINDA: You might be entitled to one thing.

HELENA: I'm not making any deals with you, I'm just here to—.

ROSALINDA: I recognize the power of a marriage certificate, if only for sentimental reasons. I know what it might mean to you and to your son. I also know all about poor people. They have a thing about other people's money; they ask for it all the time—

HELENA: When we're entitled to it!

ROSALINDA: I don't blame you for trying, dear. So tell you what, I'm willing to let go of that Mercedes Benz.

MEMO: Mother—

ROSALINDA: Take it! You could sell it, do with it what you will. It's more than you'll get, really. And I'll get the satisfaction of knowing you'll be taking care of his son, if by any chance he is his son.

HELENA: I don't think you have the upper hand here. I can prove that son is his.

ROSALINDA: We're even, then. A paternity test can be run on mine.

HELENA: (*Meaning MEMO.*) He's a stepson.

ROSALINDA: Not him . . . I'm carrying his latest child.

NORMA AND MEMO: What?

HELENA: Even they're surprised.

ROSALINDA: It's news to me, too . . . I'm pregnant.

NORMA: No shit!

ROSALINDA: He did want me after all. I also have a copy of the will that leaves everything to me—well, except for a part of the life insurance generously left to his stepson.

MEMO: Righteous.

ROSALINDA: Armando was entitled to leave his property to whomever he wanted. You can, of course, go through years of litigation, which will be very costly, definitely more expensive than the Mercedes Benz I'm willing to endow to you, as a parting gift. It's my one and only offer. What's it going to be?

HELENA: What? I . . . I . . .

ROSALINDA: Say it!

HELENA: I . . . I'll take cash!

ROSALINDA: Good choice!

HELENA: I wouldn't know how to sell a car around here, it's so frightful this city, this country—

ROSALINDA: Oh, yes, be afraid of *me*!

HELENA: My mother put me up to this, really, I just—

ROSALINDA: The car was worth $10,000.

HELENA: How much is that in—

ROSALINDA: That's plenty of money for a peasant like you, a small fortune really. Don't even think about getting more.

HELENA: Just put what you think is fair in an envelope—and, and I'm not a puss—peasant! I live in Santiago, and my priest is teaching me about the Vatican and Michelangelo, real high-class stuff. These earrings were gifts from a French hypnotist. He goes around the world hypnotizing women—not just women, of course, but the public, and he taught me about the world, and the only reason he left me is because his work requires travel, but thanks to him and my wonderful priest, I learned to read, and I now enjoy translations of Agatha Christie and Jacqueline Susann. I've got culture in me, and—oh, forget it! You're all a bunch of Hollywood help! That's what you are! (*She exits, crying.*)

NORMA: Rosalinda . . . that was so . . .

MEMO: So Joan Crawford.

ROSALINDA: Well, I didn't lie. Armando was my husband. That I allowed him to come near me . . . once! (*to* NORMA) yes, after the INS interview, Miss Busybody, that was my prerogative. Well, forget *Victor/Victoria*, I'm in the mood for *Scarface*.

Lights down.

Transition to the ceremony. ROSALINDA *picks up the urn, touches it, and then hands it over to* HELENA—*along with an envelope full of cash.* HELENA *exits with them.*

> ARMANDO *is back in his space.* ROSALINDA *joins him in a hotel bar in the afternoon.* MEMO *as* NARRATOR *reveals to the audience:*

MEMO: The viewer will forgive a much delayed scene. A few months earlier.

ARMANDO: Sit down, we're having a drink.

ROSALINDA: I just want to go home and watch *The Thorn Birds.*

ARMANDO: We're celebrating. Tequila shots! Double!

ROSALINDA: You got your papers; aren't you satisfied?

ARMANDO: Yes, I always get what I want! And it's not the only thing I want.

ROSALINDA: I'm warning you! I am Catholic and I—

ARMANDO: Drink up.

ROSALINDA: I don't dare "imbibe" in the middle of the afternoon.

ARMANDO: This hotel's got a great bar, don't you think?

ROSALINDA: No, we'll save money for Memo's film supplies. And I usually make dinner for him on Tuesday nights. He likes grilled salmon with baked potatoes (*as* ARMANDO *touches her somewhere intimate*), you know these baby potatoes—

ARMANDO: Let the brat get takeout, sweetheart.

ROSALINDA: Oh! Why? Why are you doing this?

ARMANDO: Because I want to work your body over, something I learned after the monastery, the female orgasm, man, what a discovery! You're America and I'm Columbus, exploring your continental ridge, learning how it functions, stimulating it, making it explode. Implode! I'm at the service of your clit.

ROSALINDA: OK, thank you.

ARMANDO: Save your thanks for the aftermath.

ROSALINDA: For once in your life, a woman will walk away now. The answer, Armando, is . . . (*She downs her shot and there's a second of hesitation, in which the answer could easily be yes; instead she says*) No! Come pick up your things and go. You're out of my life!

ARMANDO: Rosalinda . . .

ROSALINDA: NO! NO! NO!

MEMO/NARRATOR: They checked into the hotel a few seconds later.

> *Montage of some 80s films, starting with* Scarface, Victor/Victoria, Missing, Tootsie, Yentl, Black Widow, *and, of course,* Mommie Dearest *with its classic line, "Don't fuck with me, fellas." There's also Gena Rowlands protecting a boy in the original* Gloria, *and Sigourney Weaver protecting a little girl from the monster mother in* Alien. *In the background, a child is born. We see a silhouette of* DOCTOR *and* NURSE *birthing a child, handing him over to* MOTHER.

SCENE 6

> VLADIMIR *enters composing one of his letters. In the background,* PRO-TESTERS, *played by the* ENSEMBLE, *carry anti-Pinochet placards.*

VLADIMIR: Dear Rosalinda: I own ten liquor stores throughout Santiago. As you can imagine, my time is all consumed by business. My wife spends hers protesting against the dictator. Pinochet's secret police have come into our house looking for evidence of "terrorist activities." I have to tell them I'm a respected businessman; we're not terrorists just because my wife campaigns for human rights. A couple of kickbacks and I take care of them. We've been lucky, really. Activists have disappeared, their bodies found by the road, throats slit. Some bodies are never found at all. Still, I have managed to keep it together for the sake of the kids. I've heard your son is making movies . . . somehow, that seems to make sense. I've always felt that I lost you, Rosalinda, at the movies and maybe *to* the movies.

SCENE 7

> *At a restaurant in Santa Monica, overlooking the beach.* MEMO *is doing lunch with a Hollywood woman.* ROSALINDA *enters.*

MEMO: You came!

WOMAN: So this is your mom. ¡Mucho gusto!

ROSALINDA: (*Not in the mood.*) I speak English.

WOMAN: Ah, OK. I was just leaving.

MEMO: You don't have to—

WOMAN: It's OK. I've got a full day ahead—

MEMO: Mary Ann works for ICM.

WOMAN: An agent in training, but that's just a formality, really. (*To* MEMO.) Anyway, Phil wants us by the dock at 7 sharp—drinks and appetizers on the boat—oh, and one of Sophia Loren's hunky sons is joining us. We'll go off to Catalina Island, to Avalon, I think—

MEMO: Cool, that's hot.

WOMAN: Uh-huh— and then we'll have a lobster dinner, and more drinks and stimulating conversation till late night. Wear something stylish, if you don't mind, but coastal and comfy. Anyway, so nice to meet you, Mrs., ah—

ROSALINDA: Rosalinda.

WOMAN: Yes, Rosalinda. You have quite a talented son there. (*To* MEMO.) And we'd really like that rewrite by next week, if you don't mind.

MEMO: I'll send my courier.

WOMAN: Fabulous. Bye. (*Exits.*)

ROSALINDA: (*Mocking him.*) "Cool, that's hot?" "I'll send my courier?"

MEMO: You have to learn the lingo, Mother.

ROSALINDA: Shouldn't you be shopping in Beverly Hills for something more "coastal and comfy"?

MEMO: After lunch, you can come with. Anyway, you should try the crab cakes here, and the mimosa comes in a birdbath.

ROSALINDA: Is this why you brought me out here? To show off the mimosa?

MEMO: No, I just haven't seen you recently, Mommie dearest.

ROSALINDA: Your stepfather left you money for you to use wisely—

MEMO: I'm trying to network—

ROSALINDA: To party! To waste money on expensive clothes and—

MEMO: To meet people in this business.

ROSALINDA: And to drink from birdbaths, apparently? Drugs maybe?

MEMO: No! No drugs!

ROSALINDA: What ever happened to the documentary?

MEMO: It hasn't gone anywhere, obviously.

ROSALINDA: I'm the one who made Armando name you as one of the beneficiaries for the life insurance.

MEMO: Who's sorry now, baby cakes?

ROSALINDA: I didn't think he'd die this young.

MEMO: Besides, he's the one who encouraged me to work on a more commercial type of film—action, chase, criminals fleeing from the law, with helicopters filming the escape.

ROSALINDA: But what about the documentary?

MEMO: You never liked my docum—

ROSALINDA: No, but it was more you, idealistic and hopeless. I don't like this new commercial Memo. Even your clothes are all wrong. You were more like a bohemian, a hippie—

MEMO: And you don't like those kinds of people.

ROSALINDA: No, but it was you, my son. I could get used to the idea that your ambitions were limited, independent, not likely to go anywhere.

MEMO: But thanks to this money, I can work on improving myself. For instance, I hired a professional screenwriter to polish the dialogue in my action-chase adventure screenplay.

ROSALINDA: Use the money to finish the documentary!

MEMO: Mother, it's already been rejected at Sundance and everywhere else I've sent it to, no matter who I've slept with!

ROSALINDA: You mean you're not "innocent" any longer? Oh!

MEMO: You're not going to cry about that, are you?

ROSALINDA: Yes, I am.

MEMO: Mother, I'm a grown-up.

ROSALINDA: I know that! I just always saw you as this nice, asexual type of boy.

MEMO: I desperately need to work on my image.

ROSALINDA: What can I do to—?

MEMO: To do what? Restore my virginity?

ROSALINDA: No. I mean about the documentary, Sundance—

MEMO: Nothing! You can't be involved! You need to let me do things my way, and if I make mistakes, then they're my own, not yours. You have Armando's son to spoil now, and you were left fairly well off thanks to the excellent job you did impersonating Attila the Hun. You own your day care center now like you always wanted. We're all doing quite well, thanks to you, so let's just leave it at that, Mother, please. You really have done enough. Really!

ROSALINDA: I am losing you.

MEMO: Mother . . . it's normal for a twenty-three-year-old to be on his own.

ROSALINDA: After you finish this action chase thing, whatever it is, promise me you'll try again to finish the documentary.

MEMO: I can't promise that.

ROSALINDA: Look, Memo! Get debauchery out of your system, even if it breaks my heart to think of you as a sexually active person, but that's my problem, not yours! Meanwhile, you were meant to chronicle the lives of the immigrants! Somebody's got to do it! Fuck action-adventure! Fuck the entire system of Hollywood trash scumbag cinema, and take your work seriously for once because that's what my son was meant to do! (*Shocked at her own language, she runs off.*) Oh! Such language! I'm not myself any longer, not myself at all, damn it! (*Exits.*)

MEMO: Well . . . thank you for sharing!

Lights down.

SCENE 8

At the home in North Hollywood. NORMA *and* ROSALINDA *are shucking corn as they might have done years earlier.*

NORMA: I'm dying.

ROSALINDA: You've been saying that since you turned fifty.

NORMA: Too many aches all over.

ROSALINDA: Go to the doctor and stop talking about it.

NORMA: I don't go to doctors. I don't believe in them. I want you to take me back to Chile and spread my ashes all over the Pacific.

ROSALINDA: I saw Debbie Reynolds on TV—

NORMA: So?

ROSALINDA: She's who-knows-how-old, and she's still doing shows in Las Vegas. What does she know that you don't?

NORMA: Both my parents died of cancer in their fifties. The curse is on me.

ROSALINDA: First, let's go to Las Vegas and see Debbie Reynolds before you die.

NORMA: OK, let's.

ROSALINDA: That was easy.

NORMA: In exchange, there's Vladimir.

ROSALINDA: Vladimir?

NORMA: His wife left him.

ROSALINDA: This is why you're dying, Norma, so that I can go back to Chile to see your brother again? Vladimir with a pot belly?

NORMA: Not true, he still plays soccer. He's in shape.

ROSALINDA: I don't live in the past.

NORMA: You're still watching *The Sound of Music*. Let's just go see *Fatal Attraction* again.

ROSALINDA: Once was enough! That movie's an insult to all the women who've ever been in love with married men. I gave birth to my son without having to harass the father. That man died, by the way—

NORMA: He did?

ROSALINDA: Yeah, so did the black janitor in Maryland.

NORMA: And Armando. You're a black widow.

ROSALINDA: No, a femme fatale. And then there's Rock Hudson.

NORMA: He wasn't a real man.

ROSALINDA: That's rude!

NORMA: I don't mean because he was, you know, but because he was a fantasy.

ROSALINDA: I met him once.

NORMA: In your dreams!

ROSALINDA: Briefly, but I did. The agency sent me to interview with him and I told him I was the best nanny ever. It turned out he didn't have any children.

NORMA: Duh!

ROSALINDA: I didn't know. I didn't realize. It explained a lot of things. He only needed maids, and as you know—

NORMA: I know.

ROSALINDA: He wasn't looking very good. And only a few months later, I heard it on the news.

ROCK enters.

ROCK: I want to thank the American people for all their support. I, of course, cannot rejoice at the news that I have AIDS, but if it helps the public become aware of this disease, then I am glad I've told the truth about it. I've had a good life, a great career, and great friends who've been by my side, like Doris and Liz, and my only regret is that I won't see any more of them in this life. Otherwise, no regrets. (*Exits.*)

NORMA: Imagine, you could have been by his side. He probably could have used someone like you.

ROSALINDA: But like he said, no regrets. I was still his fan till the bitter end. Goodbye, Rock Hudson.

Lights down.

SCENE 9

NORMA on her deathbed in a hospital, a year or so later. ROSALINDA is by her bedside.

NORMA: You have to go shout at the nurses.

ROSALINDA: Why? What's happening?

NORMA: I don't know. It's something you would do, like Shirley MacLaine in *Terms of Endearment.* "My daughter needs her shot—now!"

ROSALINDA: You've had your shot.

NORMA: I know! But it's something you would do.

ROSALINDA: Well, if I can shout at them for any other reason, I will, OK?

NORMA: OK. You do that. You didn't believe me. I told you I was dying.

ROSALINDA: Well, why should I have believed you? We're still young.

NORMA: Not in my family. This is the lifespan that's normal for us.

ROSALINDA: I know. You rest, OK? Memo called and said he has some surprises.

NORMA: More than one, huh?

ROSALINDA: That's what he said.

MEMO enters.

MEMO: Aunt Norma . . . you're looking well today.

NORMA: He calls me "Aunt" Norma now.

ROSALINDA: To me, you're a sister.

NORMA: A sister-in-law, that's what I wanted to be. And no, I'm not looking better, you fool.

MEMO: You're not as pale as you were a few days ago.

NORMA: It's illusion, I'm not doing better; I'm feeling no pain. The medicine is very strong, keeps me from feeling, but at least it doesn't hurt. You have some news, right?

MEMO: Well, Norma, it's not a surprise to you . . . but for Mom here . . .

ROSALINDA: What?

MEMO: We have a special guest.

> VLADIMIR *walks in.*

VLADIMIR: Hello . . .

NORMA: He made it!

ROSALINDA: My God!

NORMA: I told you he still looked good.

VLADIMIR: Norma! I'm glad, Norma, I'm glad you're still, well, here. I didn't know what to expect—

NORMA: I'm not dead yet!

VLADIMIR: Same old Norma. And you, Rosalinda . . .

ROSALINDA: Yes, I'm still here. So how did you . . . ?

VLADIMIR: I can afford it now.

NORMA: Things are looking up.

VLADIMIR: Rosalinda . . . don't mind Norma.

NORMA: So, while he's in L.A. waiting for me to die, why don't the two of you go to—the movies!

ROSALINDA: Norma!

VLADIMIR: After all these years, Rosalinda, do you still want to go to the movies with me?

ROSALINDA: Well, *Baby Boom* features Diane Keaton playing a corporate executive who's forced into taking care of a baby.

NORMA: That's nice. A feel-good comedy.

VLADIMIR: Taking care of babies has been good to you, I hear.

MEMO: Well . . . I have to go now, but—

NORMA: You said you had another surprise.

MEMO: Is this the right m—?

NORMA: This is the perfect moment and I'm pressed for time! So hurry up!

MEMO: OK. Well, it looks like I got my documentary into Sundance.

ROSALINDA: What? Really?

VLADIMIR: What is that?

NORMA: Sounds great, whatever it is!

MEMO: It's a festival. It's run by Robert Redford.

NORMA: He was so good-looking. I chose him for my night fantasy whenever I needed to finish myself off.

ROSALINDA: Norma!

VLADIMIR: Yes, Norma!

NORMA: What? God gave us hands! My only regret is that I never did an interview.

MEMO: Well, it's not too late. I've got my camera outside and you're looking great. I don't need days, just a couple of hours.

ROSALINDA: That's a great idea.

NORMA: No, I couldn't!

ROSALINDA: Norma, you will finally get your say.

NORMA: I don't know. Movie stars need their makeup artists.

ROSALINDA: I'll do your makeup, don't worry.

NORMA: I must look like shit.

VLADIMIR: Rosalinda will fix you up.

MEMO: So, for real? I get one final shot?

ROSALINDA: He's been re-editing the old interviews forever, even I'm in one of them.

VLADIMIR: You're the star, Rosalinda.

ROSALINDA: Yes, I am.

NORMA: So there's still room for one more? You're serious about this?

MEMO: If you are.

NORMA: All right, but I get to approve the final cut—if God allows, that is.

MEMO: Whatever you want. I'll go get the camera. Thank you, Aunt Norma.

> MEMO *exits.*

ROSALINDA: I don't believe it, Norma. You've made me so happy!

NORMA: Why are you so happy at my deathbed?

ROSALINDA: We get to help the boy. What are you going to say in your interview?

NORMA: Let's see. I'm going to tell the world that I had a friend once—

ROSALINDA: A what?

NORMA: A friend who sacrificed for her son, immigrated for her son, married a man for her son, and worried and worried about him until she even stuck her nose in his business.

ROSALINDA: Stuck her nose?

NORMA: Ah, let's see, she got her friend Dorothea to get in touch with people at that Sun-Dancer thing.

ROSALINDA: Sundance. That was to make sure the right people got to see the documentary, really, just a couple of phone calls.

VLADIMIR: Just don't tell him. A man has his pride.

ROSALINDA: The film made it on its own merits, really. I just thought, use the people you know.

NORMA: The point is now that he's doing well, maybe it's time for my friend to finally get her own life.

ROSALINDA: I have a second child now.

NORMA: Fine! Love your little Tito, but without your usual tricks! You're only in your mid-forties, you own a successful day care center, you can even afford your own nanny now. Enjoy yourself. Besides, Vladimir's here.

ROSALINDA: There was no need to stage this reunion, really.

NORMA: I will say it to the camera. Let this woman take pleasure in this world! God allows it! Life can be as light and breezy as . . . as a romantic comedy.

ROSALINDA: With Irene Dunne.

NORMA: With Molly Ringwald! *Pretty in Pink*! Get up to date, girl! Vladimir, help this woman, please!

ROSALINDA: Does it matter now? We'll both have interviews in Memo's documentary. Yes, you and I, women who only went to the movies once, now will get to be *in them.*

VLADIMIR: Stars on the big screen, the two of you!

VLADIMIR kisses her on the lips very spontaneously.

ROSALINDA: What was that?

VLADIMIR: I'm just happy all of a sudden. Don't let us ask for the moon.

ROSALINDA: You hear that, Norma? He's quoting from . . .

ROSALINDA AND NORMA: *Now, Voyager!*

NORMA: Yes! Now I can die in peace in a hospital in Hollywood.

VLADIMIR: (*As he pulls out a pack of cigarettes.*) Sorry to violate hospital rules, but . . .

ROSALINDA: Ah, yes. Let's just have a cigarette on it.

He lights a cigarette and hands it to her à la Paul Henreid in Now, Voyager.

VLADIMIR: We don't have the moon.

ROSALINDA: But we shall always have the movies.

Lights down. **End of play.**

VAQUEEROS

AN ETHNODRAMA

CARLOS-MANUEL

About the Play

t took the author of *Vaqueeros* just six months to write this play. However, gathering all the information, managing interviews and conversations, and getting legal permissions to get the work done took the author close to two years of work. And even after that the author continued to follow up with some of the people he interviewed.

The reason is simple: the play is based on separate interviews with twenty-three different men who met the author at various times and locations to talk about one single subject—sexual practices. Aside from the interviews, the author spent time researching information, gathering data, and reviewing and updating his findings as time went on.

This kind of work has been done before, but there is not a lot of it when it comes to Latinos and sexuality, nor is it usually presented dramatically while still being informational and educational.

In his book *Ethnodrama*, professor John Saldaña of Arizona State University defines an ethnodrama as follows:

> An ethnodrama consists of dramatized, significant selections of narrative collected through interviews, participant observation field notes, journal entries, and/or print and media artifacts such as diaries, television broadcasts, newspaper articles, and court proceedings. Simply put, this is dramatizing the data.

With this in mind, *Vaqueeros* becomes an ethnodrama in which Latino culture and Latino sexuality are presented from a male perspective, and an attempt is made to break the stereotypes of "machismo" and, at the same time, to define what "gay" means in different cultural settings.

Vaqueeros was written with the purpose of answering one question: If men have sex with other men, are they gay and do they need to come out? As the characters reveal themselves to the audience and illuminate different definitions of what "gay" means in different cultural settings, the original question starts to vanish and a more nuanced conclusion begins to appear: we are all different and we all do different things for different reasons, so let it be.

Aside from the amusing moments the author sets up between two characters, Carlos and Juan, who seem to be both as different and as similar as possible, he creates a work in which actors are able to "play" with fantasy, reality, and time. By breaking the fourth wall, stepping in and out of character, introducing themselves as actors, and placing the interviewees among the audience (drawing upon its empathy), the author presents a world where the audience is constantly aware that what they are watching is a play. Even though it might be funny, sad, and/or horrifying, the fact of the matter is that the people presented on the stage are living, breathing human beings who move among us every day and who could be sitting next to you.

The author's approach to the play uses a specific style introduced by Bertolt Brecht in the 1900s: always making sure the audience understands they are watching a play and that emotions, although important, are secondary to the play's message. Such an approach has been used with great effect by many American playwrights, most notably Moisés Kauffman.

If the author of *Vaqueeros* were to be asked if the purpose of the play is to shock you, inform you, entertain you, involve you emotionally, or make you aware, the author most likely would answer "yes and no" to every single aspect. He wrote the play as a means to understand a certain group of Latino men in relation to their sexual practices. The author hopes to inform you and make you aware and also to entertain you and get you emotionally involved in the work without losing the message. Only the audience may judge whether he is successful.

About the Author

arlos-Manuel is currently the director of the Theatre Program and an assistant professor at Bellarmine University. He holds an MFA in playwriting from Arizona State University, an MA in directing from the University of New Mexico, and a BA from Santa Clara University. He is also a member of the Theatre Communications Group and the Dramatists Guild of America.

As a playwright, his work focuses on the US Latino experience and on social justice issues. Carlos-Manuel has penned numerous ten-minute, one-act, and children's plays, as well as one-man shows and full-length plays. These include *La Vida Loca, Vaqueeros, Lloronas, Novela, That's Life, Postcards from la Raza, Midnights, Henny Penny, Esno White, Games People Play, Birthday, Carlos-Manuel's F.A.T., Frida Kahlo: A Portrait*, and his most recent one-man show, *Macho Secrets with Tequila*.

Aside from performing, directing, and playwriting, Carlos-Manuel is the creator and producer of "Teatro Latino Conversations," a monthly podcast dedicated to Latino theater artists from across the nation whose goal is to create a digital archive for and about US Latino theater. He has also published several short stories and interviews about playwriting. Other publications include the children's play *Esno White*, which appeared in an anthology of contemporary works titled *Readings in the Lively Dramatic Arts*; *La Vida Loca: An apolitical in-your-face odyssey of a Mexican immigrant*; and the play *Creation*, published in *Ariel*, a literary magazine at Bellarmine University. He has three forthcoming publications: the play *Lloronas*, which will be in an anthology titled *Staging Heritage on Stage*, and both his one-man show *La Vida Loca* and a personal essay titled "Immigrant, Maricón, and Mexican. Any Questions?" in the anthology *Queer in Aztlan: Male Recollections of Consciousness and Coming Out*.

For information about Carlos-Manuel's performances, please visit his website: www.carlosmanuel.com or e-mail him at hola@carlosmanuel.com.

CHARACTERS

The play is written for six male actors. The roles are broken down as follows:

ACTOR 1: Carlos

ACTOR 2: Narrator 1, Stranger 1, Compadre 1, Mauricio, Older Brother, and Óscar.

ACTOR 3: Narrator 2, Stranger 2, Compadre 2, Tony, Father, and Ángel.

ACTOR 4: Dr. Sandoval, Sal, Pedro, Cousin, Rogelio, and Javier

ACTOR 5: Club Owner, Juan, Fernando, Víctor, and Daniel

ACTOR 6: Enrique, Cristóbal, Compadre 3, Gustavo, Luis, and Temo

TIME AND PLACE

Phoenix, Arizona, and surrounding areas. The present.

SET

An open stage where, if scenery is needed, it is left to the director's discretion and the designer's imagination.

LIGHTS AND SOUND

The play has no blackouts except on page 202. However, transition lights, music, and sound effects are essential for a successful production. Transition means a lighting change to indicate a different location. Characters can move from one location to the next as they talk.

A phone rings.

DANIEL: Hello!

CARLOS: Hola, Daniel, habla Carlos.

DANIEL: Hey, man! What's up?

CARLOS: Not much. I'm just, um . . . You know how I've been talking about a special school project . . .

DANIEL: What project?

CARLOS: You know, the one about Latino gay men in the closet.

DANIEL: Oh, yeah. I kinda remember you said something about that.

CARLOS: Yeah, well . . . I was wondering if you could help me.

DANIEL: Me? What do you mean?

CARLOS: I was thinking that perhaps you know a few people who . . .

DANIEL: Me? Ah, no. I don't know anyone like that.

CARLOS: Oh.

DANIEL: I mean. Why are you asking me?

CARLOS: Well . . . you, ah . . .

DANIEL: What? Me, what?

CARLOS: Well, you, um . . . The project has to do with men who have sex with men, and some of them are vaqueros, so . . .

DANIEL: So you think because I'm sort of a vaquero, listen to banda music, and stuff like that I . . .

CARLOS: Yeah. You know a lot of vaqueros. It's your circle. I thought you might know some of them who fit the profile.

DANIEL: No. I don't.

CARLOS: Oh. I thought you would . . .

DANIEL: Carlos . . . I'm just curious.

CARLOS: Yeah?

DANIEL: Why are you asking me?

CARLOS: Ah . . . well . . . you're a vaquero.

DANIEL: I know that. But why are you asking me?

CARLOS: I told you. You're a vaquero and you . . .

DANIEL: Cut the bullshit, Carlos.

CARLOS: Well . . . OK. I just think that . . . maybe . . . you fit the profile.

DANIEL: What do you mean?

CARLOS: You know what I mean.

DANIEL: No. No, I don't. What do you mean?

CARLOS: Well . . . um . . . you and I had talked about this kind of stuff before . . . and . . . um . . . and you have a very close friend who . . . um . . .

DANIEL: I'm not gay.

CARLOS: I didn't say you were.

DANIEL: But you're insinuating it.

CARLOS: No. What I'm trying to say is . . .

DANIEL: I know what you're trying to say, Carlos. I know exactly what you're trying to say.

CARLOS: Hello? Hello? Daniel? Shit!

Transition.

CARLOS: (*Reading to the audience.*) "None of us wants to be a fraud or to live a lie; none of us wants to be a sham, a phony. But the fears that we experience and the risks that honest self-communication would involve seem so intense to us that seeking refuge in our roles, masks, and games becomes an almost natural reflex action." From the book *Why Am I Afraid to Tell You Who I Am?* by Father Joseph Powell, S. J.

NARRATOR 1: The material used in this play comes from several different interviews compiled by Carlos, the author of this play.

NARRATOR 2: If other sources are used, they will be cited accordingly.

NARRATOR 1: If the stories, situations, or characters in this play reflect anything or anyone you might know, you might have heard of, or you might have lived with, the author assures you, it's purely coincidental. (*To* CARLOS.) Really?

CARLOS: Yes!

NARRATOR 2: The interviews were done in English, Spanish, or both languages. They have been translated accordingly.

NARRATOR 1: And because the interviews were done with people living today, perhaps with a person that might be seated next to you, all names have been changed to protect the innocent.

NARRATOR 2: In short, the views and opinions expressed in this play are those of the individual speakers and do not necessarily represent the views and opinions of this theater company, the producers, the playwright, the director, the actors, the technical crew, or any respective affiliate or employee.

ACTOR 4: According to Wikipedia, the free online encyclopedia, homosexuality "refers to sexual and romantic attraction between individuals of the same sex."

ACTOR 5: The *Webster's Collegiate Dictionary* defines homosexuality as the "erotic activity with another of the same sex."

ACTOR 6: The *Encyclopedia Britannica* describes homosexuality as "sexual interest in and attraction to members of one's own sex."

ACTOR 5: The current use of the term "homosexuality" has its roots in nineteenth-century Germany.

ACTOR 6: In the US, today's definition and understanding of the term "homosexuality" is highly influenced by very strong Western European views.

Transition.

CARLOS: Finally. I was about to leave.

JUAN: I'm only a couple of minutes late.

CARLOS: Fifteen minutes late, Juan. Not a couple of minutes late, but fifteen.

JUAN: I needed my time to look desirable.

CARLOS: We're just having lunch.

JUAN: The man of my dreams could be around here somewhere, and he might not be able to see me because I look like you.

CARLOS: Whatever.

JUAN: So, Papi, what's new in the wonderful world of graduate school?

CARLOS: I'm about to start my research project.

JUAN: Oh, yeah. That.

CARLOS: That? I'll have you know the research is very important.

JUAN: If you say so.

CARLOS: Juan, doesn't it intrigue you there are many Latino men out there who are having sex with other men and they say nothing about it?

JUAN: No.

CARLOS: Oh, come on, Juan. When we go out to Karamba Club, and you see those Mexican vaqueros, wearing their cowboy boots, tight jeans, and their cowboy hats, driving those huge trucks, and listening to ranchera and banda music very loud, looking very macho and shit, driving around the gay club or picking up a drag queen, or going into Zarape Club, don't tell me you don't wonder.

JUAN: Not really. No.

CARLOS: Well, I do. It fascinates me. To see those men, looking so tough and so manly, and knowing they're having sex with other men, it's intriguing to me.

JUAN: Why?

CARLOS: I told you before. You know that some of those men are married and have children, but they still have sex with other men. I want to find out why they do what they do, why they don't accept who they are, and why they don't come out of the closet.

JUAN: And I told you before, I don't care.

CARLOS: I do. And I'm gonna find out.

JUAN: Fine with me. Now, can we order? I'm starving, girl.

Transition. A pool of light on DR. SANDOVAL, *smoking a cigarette and having a drink.*

DR. SANDOVAL: In my opinion. And these are not my theories because I didn't study them, but I believe in them. Tomás Almaguer has talked about them and so has Ilan Stavans. Anyway, homosexuality is . . . there's a lot . . . homosexuality is cultural. The concept of homosexuality in Western European culture is quite different from the concept of homosexuality in Mexican and most Latin American cultures.

NARRATOR 1: Dr. Trino Sandoval, Ph.D. in Mexican cinema from Arizona State University and now a distinguished college professor.

NARRATOR 2: Dr. Sandoval expressed his opinions after Carlos directly asked him what his views were concerning sexual practices between two Mexican men, and about what Dr. Sandoval thought regarding people who classified Mexican men who are having sex with other men as "gay men."

DR. SANDOVAL: I'll give you an example, and Almaguer says this. In Western European cultures homosexuality is defined by your sexual choice. If you choose to be with a man, regardless of what you do, you are a homosexual. If I'm walking in downtown Phoenix, holding hands with a guy, I'm gay. If I choose to have anal sex with another man, I'm gay. It doesn't matter what I do, just because you are with a man, you're gay. You kiss another guy, you're gay. In Mexican culture, and other Latino countries, and especially in rural areas, it's what you do in bed that determines your homosexuality. Having sex with a man doesn't make me a homosexual. What makes me a homosexual is whether I'm the one receiving the sex or not.

Transition.

NARRATOR 2: Tempe, Arizona. January 27, 2006.

ACTOR 5: There are approximately thirty-four gay bars in the city of Phoenix. Out of the thirty-four, three of them cater to the gay Latino community: El Zarape, Paco Paco, and Karamba.

CARLOS: I went to one of them but the owner did not give me permission to interview anyone.

CLUB OWNER: Sorry, I have to protect my clients' privacy and well-being.

CARLOS: I only want to ask a few questions. It's highly confidential.

CLUB OWNER: You're welcome to come in, pay your cover, and enjoy the night. But you can't ask questions.

ACTOR 4: Carlos will not make an attempt to come to that particular club until weeks later.

ACTOR 5: In the meantime, Carlos contacted friends and acquaintances who are gay but are not out of the closet.

ACTOR 4: He also contacted friends and acquaintances who know someone who is gay but still in the closet.

NARRATOR 2: Tempe, Arizona. February 5, 2006. The home of Enrique Valadez. Three-thirty p.m. A sunny but cool and comfortable afternoon.

NARRATOR 1: From Carlos's personal diary: "It was a sunny but cool and comfortable afternoon. Enrique doesn't live far from my own house, so instead of driving, I took my bike."

CARLOS: I was excited and nervous about having my first interview. Excited because I really wanted to start the project. Nervous because even though Enrique had agreed to talk to me, I wasn't sure if he was really going to do it. You see, nowadays talking about being gay is easy. But talking with a man who is Mexican, gay, and in the closet is not a conversation you easily bring out. Luckily, I have some outside help.

JUAN: (*To the audience.*) Girl, getting Enrique to talk to Carlos was easy. I mean, Enrique knows that I know that he knows, that I know, he's gay. He also knows that I know the few friends who know he's gay. So when I told him Carlos needed volunteers for his research, he had no choice. Well . . . he had a choice. And he said yes. Not right away, though.

ENRIQUE: I don't know about this, Juan.

JUAN: Come on, Enrique. How many times have I done favors and covered up for you?

ENRIQUE: Are you sure it's OK to talk to him?

JUAN: Trust me. I know Carlos; he's OK.

ENRIQUE: Are you sure?

JUAN: Hellooooo! Would I lie to you?

ENRIQUE: Yes.

JUAN: (*Melodramatic.*) Oh. I know you did not say that! (*Pause.*) Put it this way, Enrique, the interview can serve you as free therapy.

ENRIQUE: Shut up!

JUAN: I'm not kidding.

Transition. ENRIQUE crosses to CARLOS.

ENRIQUE: Hi!

CARLOS: Hey! Thanks for meeting me.

ENRIQUE: Sure. You want something to drink?

CARLOS: No, thanks. I'm OK. Why don't we start? This form is for you. It says that everything you and I talk about is confidential and that you have the right to sue me if you feel I violated such right. There's my phone number. My mentor's phone number. And other school numbers just in case you need them.

ENRIQUE: OK.

CARLOS: Ready?

ENRIQUE: Yeah.

NARRATOR 1: Every interview had the same purpose but each interview varied in length and content based on the volunteer.

NARRATOR 2: But the one thing all the interviews had in common was the first question.

CARLOS: Do you consider yourself straight, gay, or bisexual?

Each member of the company appears in a different area.

ACTOR 5: Gay.

NARRATOR 1: (*In Spanish.*) Bisexual.

ACTOR 4: Straight.

NARRATOR 2: Gay.

ACTOR 5: Free-spirited.

NARRATOR 1: (*In English.*) Bisexual.

NARRATOR 2: ¡Derecho, ése!

ACTOR 4: Gay.

NARRATOR 1: Straight.

CARLOS: (*To himself.*) "Free-spirited"? (*To the audience.*) What the hell does that mean?

ACTOR 5: Straight.

ACTOR 4: Straight.

ENRIQUE: Gay.

CARLOS: But you're not out of the closet, right?

ENRIQUE: Only a few people know.

CARLOS: Does your family know?

ENRIQUE: It's complicated. I grew up in a very homophobic environment. My dad was born in Zacatecas and . . . All his life he's been a very strict person. After all these years, he's not going to change.

CARLOS: But does he need to change for you to come out? I mean, the two of you work in the same place. How do you manage your life that way?

ENRIQUE: I'm not out at work. And it hasn't been easy. But I can handle it.

CARLOS: Do you have a boyfriend?

ENRIQUE: Yes. We've been going out for three years.

CARLOS: How do you manage the relationship?

ENRIQUE: It's hard. (*Pause.*) Just making sure I stay one step ahead of my family and everyone else is hard.

CARLOS: What do you mean?

ENRIQUE: The difficult thing is that I, ah, I have to keep my private life and my family life as separate as possible. But at the same time, both, my family and my boyfriend are part of my life. When my family asks if I have a girlfriend sometimes I tell them I don't have one and other times I tell them I do. When they ask about her, I tell them everything about him. (*Laughs.*) I play this game where I change the name of my boyfriend to a girl's name. Like, ah . . . Marcos became Marci. Then Nick became Amanda. And now I'm with Marisela, whose real name is Mauricio.

CARLOS: Isn't it confusing?

ENRIQUE: Oh, yes. Last year the whole family went to Zacatecas and I had to be with them the entire time. I kept thinking, "I have to talk to my boyfriend. I have to call Mauricio." But I couldn't say that. So I started saying that I needed to call "Marisela." That I needed to e-mail my girlfriend, that I needed to buy a present for her. After a while my mind was playing tricks with me, especially when I was very tired or, ah, drunk. I didn't even want to think about Mauricio anymore because I, ah, I, I couldn't keep the pronouns in order. Even now there are times when I just avoid talking about him because I'm afraid I'm going to slip.

CARLOS: (*To the audience.*) My gay friends and I always change our real names to female names, except that we do it for fun. It's like a game, you know? We have a friend whose name is Manuel, but we all call him "Débora" because, well, when he's making out with a guy, he's all over him. Parece que se lo está comiendo. You know, devorándolo. Devouring him. So we call him Débora. (*To* ENRIQUE.) Do your parents want to meet your girlfriend?

ENRIQUE: All the time, but I always make something up. And when my dad has business parties, I ask girlfriends to be my dates. That way I cover my bases.

CARLOS: (*To the audience.*) My interview with Enrique didn't end right there. He had so much to say that for a moment I felt like I was being his therapist.

NARRATOR 1: Carlos wrote that as a personal entry in his diary on February 5, 2006, at 11:35 p.m. The same day he had his first interview.

NARRATOR 2: He also wrote:

CARLOS: Little did I know that the more people I interviewed, the more I felt like I was their therapist. And the more interviews I conducted, the more I started thinking I needed a therapist.

FERNANDO: Hi. My name is Fernando López Ruiz. But everyone calls me Fer. I am the guy who told Carlos I'm free-spirited. I don't call myself straight, gay, or bisexual. I am a free-spirited person because to me sex is sex and well, I get it whenever, with whoever. I sleep with both men and women. And maybe for some people that makes me bisexual but I like to think of myself as free-spirited. It's no big deal. Sex is sex and no matter who the other person is, a man or a woman, you get the same result, know what I'm saying? I mean, when I go out, I don't go out looking for a man or a woman. I don't plan ahead what I am going to look for. I go out to have a good time. And if I meet someone, oh well, it happens regardless of the gender. I mean, it's all about connections. If I feel connected to someone, I go for it. And if that connection has more to offer, then maybe there's more there than sex. And it doesn't matter if that person is a man or a woman. That's why I like to call myself a "free-spirited" person, because it's all about connections.

A pool of light on DR. SANDOVAL.

DR. SANDOVAL: I have a big problem when people refer to Mexican males who are having sex with men as gay. They just generalize it by saying, "Oh, they're gay." No, "faggots." But that's not right because in Mexican culture if you choose to be with a man, it doesn't mean you're gay. It doesn't matter. As long as you are "the top." And there are men who are only tops, men who only fuck other men. Those men don't consider themselves gay. They're just fucking. To them it's just a sexual act with another guy. They are not gay.

Transition.

CARLOS: How can a man who's having sex with another man not be gay? How can a man who has sex with both men and women not be bisexual? I mean, I'm gay, so I have sex with other men. As simple as that. But with the men I'm interviewing everything becomes blurry and confusing. In my opinion, I think all these men are just afraid to truly accept who they are. They are afraid to come out, to be seen as something less than a "real man." In my opinion, they're in denial.

A phone rings.

CRISTÓBAL: Hello?

CARLOS: Hi, Cristóbal. It's Carlos.

CRISTÓBAL: Oh, hi.

CARLOS: I was wondering if I could set a time to interview you.

CRISTÓBAL: Ah . . . when?

CARLOS: When are you available?

CRISTÓBAL: How about tomorrow? Say, 10:00 a.m.?

CARLOS: Yes! That's perfect. What's your address?

Transition.

NARRATOR 1: Introducing Cristóbal Gómez. A man in his early 40s, living in Glendale, Arizona.

JUAN: But before we introduce him, we need to set the stage.

CARLOS: Juan, what are you doing?

JUAN: Hold on, Carlos. Picture the scene. A wholesome married couple, living together since before being married . . .

CARLOS: Juan . . .

JUAN: Happily raising one son. Then, suddenly and out of the blue, the shit hits the fan.

CARLOS: (*Stern.*) JUAN!

JUAN: I'm only trying to lighten things up.

Transition.

NARRATOR 1: This is Salvador. We'll call him Sal. Sal has been dating Cristóbal for about eight months now. Everything was going well until the night before.

SAL: (*Into the phone.*) I told ju, man, I don't know if . . . Honestly, I love him very much . . . Jez. Jez, and ju know that more than anyone else . . . Oh, wait. He's here. I gotta go.

CRISTÓBAL: Well, here I am.

SAL: Tanks for coming.

CRISTÓBAL: Sure.

SAL: Ju want someting to drink?

CRISTÓBAL: No.

SAL: I have jour favorite beer.

CRISTÓBAL: Don't want any, thank you.

Silence.

SAL: How is jour day so far?

CRISTÓBAL: What do you think, Sal? What do you think?

SAL: Ah . . . About last night, I'm sorry.

CRISTÓBAL: Not as sorry as I am.

SAL: I don't know what got into me.

CRISTÓBAL: I tell you what got into you: You weren't thinking, you stupid idiot.

SAL: I just wanted it to surprise ju.

CRISTÓBAL: You sure surprised me and my wife.

SAL: I don't know she was gonna be tere.

CRISTÓBAL: My birthday, Sal. What makes you think she wasn't gonna be there?

SAL: I'm sorry, OK. Shit, how many times I have to apologize?

Silence.

CRISTÓBAL: You have no idea the kind of lies I have to come up with. How to explain the flowers, the chocolates, the champagne.

SAL: They are birthday presents.

CRISTÓBAL: My wife isn't stupid, Sal. And neither are you. She recognized you right away.

SAL: She only saw me a couple of times.

CRISTÓBAL: She saw you for three days in a row.

SAL: I built your kitchen. Eight months ago.

CRISTÓBAL: You don't get it, do you? She saw you, last night, carrying flowers, chocolate, champagne. It doesn't take a genius.

SAL: I could . . . I was delivering them.

CRISTÓBAL: She knows, Sal.

SAL: Just from last night?

CRISTÓBAL: I told her. I couldn't lie to her.

SAL: Wait! Ju been fucking me for last eight months behind her back and you can't lie to her last night?

CRISTÓBAL: No. I couldn't.

SAL: So what now?

CRISTÓBAL: It's over.

SAL: Ju don't mean that.

CRISTÓBAL: Yes, I do, Sal. It's over. Whatever we have, it's over.

SAL: But I love ju.

CRISTÓBAL: Don't say that.

SAL: I do. I love ju, and ju know it.

CRISTÓBAL: And you knew that if it came to this, I would choose my family over you.

SAL: But I love ju.

CRISTÓBAL: My family comes first.

SAL: Are ju sure?

CRISTÓBAL: Definitely.

SAL: But . . .

CRISTÓBAL: Sorry, Sal. It's over.

Pool of light on CRISTÓBAL.

CRISTÓBAL: I care for Sal in a way I can't explain. I don't know what it is. But I care for him. When he came into my house to build the kitchen, there was something about him I found . . . irresistible. Yeah, that's it: irresistible. I had never felt something like that for anyone, except my wife, of course, and this kid from back in college, but I never pursued him. But with Sal, I couldn't resist. I couldn't. I couldn't resist. But Sal was careless and my wife figured it out. She wanted me to leave her, but I love her. We built our lives together, struggled together. Built a home together. Our son, well, he's growing up and he's going to need me more than ever before. High school isn't easy, I know, I was there. I couldn't leave my wife, not for Sal, especially knowing she was pregnant again. For the second time in ten years she was pregnant again. I couldn't leave her. I had to make a choice. I chose them.

Transition. A doorbell rings.

SAL: (*Offstage.*) Coming! Coming! (*Doorbell again.*) I say I'm coming. ¡Dios mío! Tis better be important 'cause I'm cooking a very special meal and I need . . .

CRISTÓBAL: Hi.

SAL: Hey . . . What, ah . . .

CRISTÓBAL: You painted the living room.

SAL: Jeah. What are ju doing here?

CRISTÓBAL: Ummm. I wanted to see you.

SAL: Why?

CRISTÓBAL: I, ah, I miss you.

SAL: A month ago ju left this place saying it was over. I missed ju a lot since then, but I knew better.

CRISTÓBAL: Many times I picked up the cell phone and wanted to call you but . . .

SAL: But . . .

CRISTÓBAL: I . . . I'm sorry.

SAL: Jeah, so am I.

CRISTÓBAL: (*Noticing the long spoon.*) You're cooking?

SAL: Jeah. I have a friend coming over.

CRISTÓBAL: A friend or a boyfriend?

SAL: I don't know jet.

Silence.

CRISTÓBAL: I miss you, Sal. I miss you a lot.

SAL: Jeah, well . . .

CRISTÓBAL: I better go. It was wrong to come.

SAL: No! I mean, ju don't have to go.

CRISTÓBAL: What about your . . . friend?

SAL: He can wait.

CRISTÓBAL: Are you sure?

SAL: The question is, can jour wife wait?

CRISTÓBAL: I'm sure she can manage without me for a while.

Pool of light on CRISTÓBAL.

CRISTÓBAL: I don't know how to explain it. I love my wife and I love my children and I'd do anything for them. But I can't stop seeing Sal. I have tried, but I can't. You asked me how I feel about this situation and all I can say is . . . is . . . I'm gonna continue living like this until life decides otherwise.

Pool of light dissolves as CRISTÓBAL transitions to a new scene.

CRISTÓBAL: I can't believe you're asking me such a thing.

SAL: It's been a jear.

CRISTÓBAL: And it has been a very good year.

SAL: Then why are ju surprised?

CRISTÓBAL: Because your request is unreasonable.

SAL: I'm tired of being jour part-time lover.

CRISTÓBAL: You knew what you were getting into from the very beginning. Don't act like you didn't know. Don't act like you have been victimized.

SAL: I am not acting like I'm victimized. I just want something better.

CRISTÓBAL: What are you saying? Are you saying you want to stop this?

SAL: Maybe.

CRISTÓBAL: Is that what you want?

SAL: Is that what ju want?

CRISTÓBAL: I don't want that, but I also cannot give you more than what I'm giving you now. My wife and my children come first.

SAL: I will never be number one, will I?

CRISTÓBAL: Sorry.

SAL: Ju better go.

CRISTÓBAL: Are you sure? Because if I walk out that door, I won't come back looking for you.

Silence.

SAL: Adiós, Cristóbal.

Transition.

NARRATOR 1: Three weeks later Sal went looking for Cristóbal.

NARRATOR 2: They talked. They argued. They fought.

NARRATOR 1: Two hours later, Cristóbal was back at Sal's house.

NARRATOR 2: Three months later Cristóbal was out of Sal's life once again.

NARRATOR 1: This "off and on again" relationship has been going on now for three and half years.

SAL: I go out with other guys all the time. But for some unknown reason, I keep going back to Cristóbal.

CRISTÓBAL: I don't know what it is, but the moment I say I won't see Sal again, I desire him more.

NARRATOR 2: Cristóbal's wife has no idea what is going on. In her mind and heart, her husband ended whatever was going on with Sal long ago. Before Carlos finished the interview, he asked Cristóbal one more question:

NARRATOR 1: Cristóbal, are you happy?

CRISTÓBAL: Happy? Am I happy? To tell you the truth, I don't know if I'm happy. But just so you know, this is the first time I've talked to someone about me and Sal . . . It feels good to tell someone.

NARRATOR 1: From Carlos's personal entries and observations on his research:

NARRATOR 2: "I do not approve of any man or woman having an affair behind their lover's back. That's just wrong, and it hurts."

CARLOS: I know how much it hurts. And to see a married man having an affair with another man it's just . . . Well, I just hope Cristóbal's wife never finds out about Sal. I wouldn't want to be in her shoes.

Transition.

NARRATOR 1: In Mexico a "chichifo" is a man who in exchange for sexual favors, receives money and/or expensive presents as gifts. By definition, he's not a prostitute or a gay man, or at least he claims not to be.

NARRATOR 2: Most of these men have girlfriends and some are even married. They usually have well-defined bodies and are attractive, handsome men.

PEDRO: The majority of these men work as private dancers and strippers. When it comes to a sexual arrangement, the chichifo is the "active partner," the "top," the "dominating person," the "man."

NARRATOR 2: Many gay men "hire" these desirable straight men to fulfill a fantasy and a need, a need that ends up costing a lot of money, and at times a broken heart.

Transition.

NARRATOR 1: Phoenix, Arizona. February 22, 2006. Downtown. A popular Mexican restaurant located just a few yards from a twenty-four-screen multiplex.

CARLOS: I don't quite understand what you're saying.

PEDRO: You want me to be explicit?

CARLOS: Sure.

PEDRO: Es fácil de entender, man. Fags worship my body; they like to look at it. They like to touch it. They like to suck me. They like it when I fuck them, so I fuck them.

CARLOS: You fuck them?

PEDRO: Why are you whispering, man? Who's gonna hear you? This place is fuckin' dead right now. And yeah, I fuck them. I'm the top. Always the top.

CARLOS: Always.

PEDRO: Yeah! Always!

CARLOS: But you also have sex with women, right?

PEDRO: Simón.

CARLOS: So you're bisexual.

PEDRO: No, man. Bisexuals fall in love with men and women. That's just weird. I don't like guys that way.

CARLOS: So to you bisexuality has to do with falling in love with men and women?

PEDRO: Yeah.

CARLOS: So you have sex with men but you don't feel anything for them?

PEDRO: Now you getting it, man.

CARLOS: Do you have a girlfriend?

PEDRO: Simón.

CARLOS: Does she know you sleep with men?

PEDRO: Fuck, no! She would get all weird and shit.

CARLOS: Do the guys you have sex with know you have a girlfriend?

PEDRO: One does.

CARLOS: Does he care?

PEDRO: Nah. I mean, look at me. Would you care if I was having sex with you and I had a girlfriend?

Silence.

CARLOS: So, how often do you get together with guys?

PEDRO: I don't know. Whenever.

CARLOS: Any guy you see regularly? For sex, I mean.

PEDRO: Not really. There's a couple of fags. They come over and we do stuff and shit.

CARLOS: The three of you?

PEDRO: No, man. ¿Cómo crees?

CARLOS: So, what do you do?

PEDRO: Whatever they want but getting fucked.

CARLOS: You mean you. Right?

PEDRO: Simón.

CARLOS: Do they pay you for it?

PEDRO: Fifty bucks or a present or something nice.

CARLOS: How do you find these guys? You go to gay clubs?

PEDRO: Actually, one of the guys is my neighbor and the other one I met at a bus stop.

CARLOS: Your neighbor?

PEDRO: Yeah. I know him since we were kids.

CARLOS: What?

PEDRO: I . . . we live in the same street since we, um, you know . . . since we were kids.

CARLOS: And you have sex with him?

PEDRO: Yeah. He comes over. We do it.

CARLOS: How about other guys? Where do you meet them?

PEDRO: Anywhere. Parks, bailes, straight bars, parties. You know, anywhere. It just happens.

CARLOS: It doesn't happen to me.

PEDRO: That's 'cause you don't look hard enough, man. They're there, man. They all want sex and they will get it when it's available.

CARLOS: So, you have sex with these guys and they pay you. Wouldn't that make you a prostitute?

PEDRO: What? Are you calling me a whore?

CARLOS: Well . . .

NARRATOR 1: Dr. Gerardo Guiza Lemus, a Mexican scholar from the Universidad Autónoma de México, described the difference between a prostitute and a chichifo as follows:

NARRATOR 2: "A prostitute is a person who charges for his services and afterwards leaves with a clean conscience while a chichifo spends his days extorting others without giving anything in return."

CARLOS: (*To the audience.*) So, according to Dr. Guiza Lemus, I was not calling Pedro a prostitute. (*To PEDRO.*) No! I didn't mean it that way.

PEDRO: Good! Because I am not a prostitute. I just have sex with men and that's all.

CARLOS: Are you safe when you do these things?

PEDRO: Of course, man. I don't wanna get SIDA and shit like that.

CARLOS: Do you get tested for STDs and HIV?

PEDRO: Sure. I'm clean.

CARLOS: Have you ever encountered a man who wanted to do you?

PEDRO: Hell, yeah! I remember one particular time. It got crazy.

Transition. A flashback.

STRANGER 1: Come on, man. It's my turn.

PEDRO: What?

STRANGER 1: You know. Do you. Let me fuck you.

PEDRO: I don't do that, man.

STRANGER 1: What do you mean, you don't do that? We all do.

PEDRO: I don't. I'll fuck you but you won't fuck me. That was the deal.

STRANGER 1: Yeah? Well, I feel like fucking you, man.

PEDRO: Sorry.

STRANGER 1: (*Angry.*) What do you mean, "sorry?"

PEDRO: Hey, take it easy, asshole.

STRANGER 1: Who you calling "asshole," faggot?

PEDRO: I don't need this shit, OK?

A fight ensues. Transition. The present.

CARLOS: Did you really beat him up?

PEDRO: You bet. He started acting all tough and shit. But look at me, man. I work out. I'm strong. I'm all muscles. I beat him up, beat him up real good. And then I came all over him.

CARLOS: What?

PEDRO: You know. (*He does the masturbation gestures with his hand.*) I came and pissed all over him, and left him there.

CARLOS: You left him there?

PEDRO: It wasn't my home.

CARLOS: Sounds . . . ah . . . kind of violent.

PEDRO: Violent? Shit! That's nothing. I bet he's into that shit, anyway. Besides, he started it. That's what he got.

CARLOS: Whoa!

Silence.

PEDRO: So . . . do you?

CARLOS: Do I what?

PEDRO: You know . . . (*Groping himself.*) You want to?

CARLOS: What? No! I don't. I mean, I can't. I can't get involved with the subjects . . . I mean volunteers . . . with the people I'm interviewing.

PEDRO: Hey, relax, man. If we hook up no one will know. Just you and me.

CARLOS: Ah. No, thanks. It's not a good idea.

PEDRO: You don't know what you missing, man. Puro chile de Chihuahua.

CARLOS: (*To the audience.*) I must confess that up to now, all the interviews have been very illuminating. I also have to confess that if I had met Pedro before our interview, I would have . . . I would have . . . I mean, look at him. He's a mount of pure muscle. He might be from Chihuahua but I'm sure he doesn't have a little Chihuahua in his pants. Oh, my God! I can't believe I just said that.

Transition. A pool of light on DR. SANDOVAL.

DR. SANDOVAL: In the United States, if you were to map the male body in a sexual act with another man it's usually the action from the "mouth to the penis." It is the most predominant one, uh, so, if men are in the street and they see another man and want to be mean to him they usually say, "Hey, cocksucker." Um, and that implies mouth to penis. Young kids when horseplaying with other young kids, they, um, grab their heads and start to push it down to the penis, saying, "Suck it." It's about sucking, cocksucking. In Mexico it isn't mouth to penis but penis to butt. So instead of grabbing your head when horseplay happens and pushing it to their penis, they grab your ass and try to hump you. In the United States it's mouth to penis, but in Mexico it's penis to butt. So, yes. Our attitudes toward homosexuality are different.

Transition. A private party. Three COMPADRES *talking to the audience as if talking to* CARLOS.

COMPADRE 1: No, no. I am married.

COMPADRE 2: Me too, just like my compadre.

COMPADRE 3: I'm the only one that's not married.

COMPADRE 2: Yeah, but your girlfriend has you whipped.

COMPADRE 1: You're a mandilón, compadre. D'eso no hay duda.

Laughter.

COMPADRE 2: I'm happily married and have four kids.

COMPADRE 1: I have three. My oldest girl is sixteen.

COMPADRE 2: And my oldest son is seventeen.

COMPADRE 3: I don't have any children. That I know of.

Laughter.

COMPADRE 3: I tell you this. I never thought of sex as a bad thing.

COMPADRE 2: And if it is, we're fucked.

COMPADRE 1: We're going to hell.

They laugh. They toast.

COMPADRE 2: To hell!

COMPADRE 3: To hell!

COMPADRE 1: ¡Salud, compadres!

ALL: ¡Salud!

They drink.

COMPADRE 3: Here's a question for the two of you. Did you ever think about what would happen if any of your children turn out to be gay?

COMPADRE 2: What?

COMPADRE 1: I do nothing. I have no sons.

COMPADRE 2: I wouldn't care.

COMPADRE 3: You wouldn't care?

COMPADRE 2: No. If he comes to me and says, "Dad, I'm gay," I wouldn't care.

COMPADRE 3: And if any of your daughters turn out a lesbian, compadre?

COMPADRE 1: I don't think I'd care, either.

COMPADRE 3: Good.

COMPADRE 2: To our children, then.

COMPADRE 1: Por los hijos.

COMPADRE 3: For the children, even though I have none. That I know of.

A pool of light on FERNANDO.

FERNANDO: I care. I don't want my son to be gay. I want him to be completely straight and get married and have kids, and . . . you know . . . do what society expects of him. I mean, I don't want him to go through the shit many of us have gone through, know what I mean? I don't want him to have the emotional problems I had . . . or have. I mean, I guess he could talk to me and I could guide him but I don't want him to be gay. I was lucky not to get involved in drugs and shit like that 'cause I know that I would have not come out of them at all. It's depressing. Gay people don't have a very happy life. So, no. I don't want my son to be gay. I want him to be a very happy straight man.

Pool of light out. Back to COMPADRES.

COMPADRE 3: No, wait, wait, wait, wait. I don't think we're doing anything wrong. Right, compadres?

COMPADRE 1: Right.

COMPADRE 3: I mean, just because they're married and I will be married and we sleep with other men doesn't mean we're doing something wrong.

COMPADRE 2: Are you judging us, Carlos?

COMPADRE 1: That's not right.

COMPADRE 3: Because we don't care that you're out and you let everyone know you're gay.

COMPADRE 1: Yeah. No nos importa.

COMPADRE 2: And I don't think there's a rule that says we need to be out or be gay in order to have sex with other men. Is there?

COMPADRE 3: No. I don't think there is.

COMPADRE 1: There's no rule anywhere about that.

COMPADRE 2: Good. I was beginning to worry.

COMPADRE 3: Really?

COMPADRE 2: No.

Laughter.

COMPADRE 1: You know, este mandilón is going to get married in a year.

COMPADRE 3: No me lo recuerde, compadre. Please.

COMPADRE 2: What? Like you don't want to? You going to get all the money and all those stores they have all over the city.

COMPADRE 1: You know "El Gallo" stores, Carlos? Well, they all belong to his girlfriend's father. And guess who gets part of the cake when he marries her?

COMPADRE 2: He does.

COMPADRE 3: Yeah, yeah. OK. Maybe I won't marry her.

COMPADRE 1: What? Are you gonna come out?

Laughter.

COMPADRE 1: Hey, I'm out of beer. Anyone want another?

COMPADRE 3: I do.

COMPADRE 2: Me too. Wait. I'll go with you. I need to take a piss.

COMPADRE 3: Hey, compadre, make sure you help him piss. He's too drunk to do it himself.

COMPADRE 3: They're right, you know. I'm, ah, I'm gonna get married soon. And no, I'm not doing it for the money. I love my fiancée. I like her parents and they like me. My fiancée loves me. She's gonna be my wife; we're gonna have children, man, and we're gonna live comfortably, you know. And, um, before you ask, I'm gonna keep doing what I'm doing whenever I can. That's why I come to these parties, you know? Ah, I want to keep the contacts. (*Long pause.*) You might think I'm cheating on her, but I don't see it that way. Don't tell me you never done something like that. Like when you lived in Mexico. Don't tell me you didn't have a girlfriend and messed around with guys at the same time. I know you did. Your eyes don't lie. And you're smiling, which means I'm right.

COMPADRE 2: Hey, I think the chicken's ready. I'm gonna get some.

COMPADRE 3: Me too. I'm hungry.

COMPADRE 2: Nice to meet you, Carlos.

COMPADRE 3: Yeah, same here. (*To* COMPADRE *1.*) Compadre, are you coming?

COMPADRE 1: Yeah. In a minute.

   COMPADRES *2 and 3 exit.*

COMPADRE 1: Hey, Carlos. I just want to say one more thing. Don't mention my name or my compadres' names to anyone. If you do, you have no idea what could happen to you. I mean, for your sake, I hope you never reveal who we are . . . Good. See ya around, then . . . Bye.

A pool of light on CARLOS.

CARLOS: My interview with the three compadres left me feeling like I was in a surreal world. Like I was . . . in a movie. It left me feeling like I was in a movie. I mean, this was unbelievable. All I wanted to do was to expose how there are men who have sex with men, even if they're married, have children, and claim they're straight. I also wanted to prove that if a man has sex with another man, he has it because he's gay. What other reason would he do it for? And here I was, in an underground sex party organized by single and married Latino "straight" men who like to have sex with other men. An underground sex party. For Latino men. In Phoenix. Wow! People really go out of the way to hide who they really are. I mean, why don't they just simply come out?

Characters appear in different areas.

ENRIQUE: I have too much to lose; my father wouldn't know how to cope with that.

FERNANDO: I just haven't found the right time for this conversation.

COMPADRE 2: There's not a rule that says we need to be out . . . Is there?

PEDRO: I'm not gay, man.

JUAN: Honey, the moment I came out of my mother's womb, I came out of the closet.

COMPADRE 3: I never said I was gay.

COMPADRE 1: I don't think I'm gay, or maybe I am, I don't know.

FERNANDO: I have a better one for you, Carlos. Why does anyone have to come out?

COMPADRE 1: I started having sex with other guys since I was a kid, you know, back in Mexico, en el rancho. But I never talk about that with anyone. I guess we all kept it secret.

ENRIQUE: I'm always questioning myself. What others think of me. What others expect of me because of my dad. What they would think if I do something that I shouldn't do.

COMPADRE 1: I don't know about my compadres but, um, I started very young. But . . . I got married and I love my wife and my children very much. But, um, I always, ah, remember the guys from el rancho and what we did in the corn fields, at the lake, by the river, or in the corrales.

ENRIQUE: And it's hard, you know. I, I, ah, shit. I, I don't come out because it's not a good thing for me to do, for my dad.

COMPADRE 1: So, when I got married I tried to change all that. I did for a while, but, um, well, here I am. Maybe if I had been born in another time, like today. Maybe things would be different for me. But I say to myself, I'm married. I have a wife. I have four kids. And I come to these parties to have a little bit of fun with some other guys. I think that's enough. ¿No crees? Why come out?

ENRIQUE: I wish I could come out, Carlos, but I can't and I won't. It's a difficult situation. You may never understand it but I have a lot to lose. Not many people know this, but I used to be a heavy drinker. And I used to get into a lot of fights with my family. I was drowning my feelings, trying to be normal. Once I even tried to end my life. I just wanted to erase the memories, end the torment. End it all. But I guess I wasn't strong enough 'cause here I am, talking to you. I did stop drinking, though. It's been more than two years since I last drank any alcohol. It's not easy; I get very depressed sometimes. I . . . I . . . I cry a lot when no one is around. And sometimes I get very angry, and, and my body shakes, and when it does, um, well, it's not . . . it's not . . . it's not . . . ah, um, it's not, um, well . . . I . . . I . . . I . . . I don't like it. I mean, my heart starts beating very fast, and, um, my hands sweat, ah, I feel very cold . . . and I just . . . I just . . . I uh . . .

CARLOS: Are you OK?

ENRIQUE: Yeah. It's hard to talk about this. God, I haven't talked about it with anyone. It's just, ah, I mean . . . I had . . .

ENRIQUE breaks down.

CARLOS: We don't have to keep talking, Enrique. We can end the interview right now.

ENRIQUE: I'm OK. Really. I actually feel good telling you all this. It is kind of like . . . um, an incredible release, you know? Like an escape, you know. Yeah, an escape. You get me?

CARLOS: Yeah. (*Pause.*) So, um, Enrique, after telling me all this, do you still plan to continue being in the closet?

ENRIQUE: I have no other choice. I mean, I'm not saying I want my father to die anytime soon but, um, I'm going to carry this with me until he dies or I die. That's the way it is and that's the way it's going to be.

CARLOS: But . . .

ENRIQUE: Do you mind if we stop now? Please?

CARLOS: Sure.

NARRATOR 1: How do you deal with such information? How do you deal with such emotions? What do you do when you learn someone is completely and utterly disturbed because of their feelings?

NARRATOR 2: How do you overcome the desire to get involved in their lives? What do you do to ignore their troubled spirits and move on now that they have confessed something so intimate, so painful, and so disturbing?

NARRATOR 1: How do you move on?

NARRATOR 2: How do you do it?

CARLOS: I wrote those entries after my interview with Enrique, who sobbed for almost an hour after we stopped talking. And all I could do was to hold his hand and feel guilty because I put him in such an emotional state.

Transition. A bus stop. From a distance, CARLOS *watches.*

STRANGER 2: Hi.

PEDRO: What's up?

STRANGER 2: It's hot, isn't it?

PEDRO: Fuckin' burning, man. And after throwing some hoops, I'm all sweaty and shit.

STRANGER 2: Oh.

PEDRO: Hey, the fifty-six hasn't come, has it?

STRANGER 2: I'm waiting for it.

PEDRO looks at STRANGER 1. *It's an uncomfortable moment.*

STRANGER 2: What?

PEDRO: You're wearing a tie and shit. Don't you have a car?

STRANGER 2: It's in the shop. Bad timing for it to break down, huh?

PEDRO: I know how to fix cars.

STRANGER 2: Yeah?

PEDRO: Yeah.

STRANGER 2: Ah, you live close?

PEDRO: Nah. I have to take two buses. Do you?

STRANGER 2: Yeah. Very.

PEDRO: Man, it's fuckin' hot.

STRANGER 2: Here comes the bus.

PEDRO: It's about fuckin' time.

STRANGER 2: Say, ah . . . if you're thirsty . . . ah . . .

PEDRO: Yeah. Sounds good.

CARLOS: And then what happened?

PEDRO: (*To* CARLOS.) I went to his place. (*To* STRANGER 2.) This is a nice place.

STRANGER 2: You think so?

PEDRO: Yeah. You must have a good job.

STRANGER 2: I do. Here is your water.

PEDRO: Thanks.

> STRANGER *2 can't stop staring.*

PEDRO: (*Groping himself.*) You want it?

> STRANGER *2 nods.*

PEDRO: It's all yours.

CARLOS: And that was it?

PEDRO: Simón. He gave me twenty bucks.

CARLOS: Are you hustling?

PEDRO: No, man. He gave me money 'cause I needed to get back on the bus.

CARLOS: How often do you see him?

PEDRO: I don't know. Once, maybe twice a month.

CARLOS: And he gives you money all the time?

PEDRO: Presents too.

CARLOS: And you have others, right?

PEDRO: Simón.

CARLOS: So from what I see, you get a lot of sex.

PEDRO: Yeah. I like it. I enjoy it. And I have a lot to give. I mean, check this out; it's hard right now.

CARLOS: So your girlfriend doesn't know about the other guys.

PEDRO: And she won't find out.

CARLOS: You sound so sure.

PEDRO: None of those fags is gonna open his mouth. I know that.

CARLOS: You know. You call these men fags because they have sex with men. But you're having sex with them too.

PEDRO: I ain't no fuckin' fag, man.

CARLOS: But you still have sex with them.

PEDRO: They get it up the ass, not me. I told ya, I don't like men that way. I like sex, man. And any mouth is good to suck me off. And if they want more, I give them more. But I ain't no fag. Get it?

CARLOS: Yeah. I guess.

PEDRO: What's this for?

CARLOS: School project.

PEDRO: Cool. (*Pause.*) So, are you sure you don't want it?

CARLOS: No, man. That's all right. I'm good.

PEDRO: Are you sure? It's hard.

CARLOS: (*Ignoring.*) Do you have any other questions regarding the interview?

PEDRO: I'm cool.

CARLOS: Good. Me too.

A pool of light on JUAN.

JUAN: Oh, my gawd! He's so fine! Why can't I be the one who gets offers like that from men like Pedro, huh? What's wrong with this world? Or at least why can't I be the guy sitting at the bus stop waiting to be picked up, huh? You tell me! (*Thinking.*) Oh, I know. I do not, and I repeat, do not do public transportation. But I always go to Paco Paco, Karamba, and El Zarape. Why don't I get picked up there? Why? (*Before anyone answers.*) Do not answer that. The question is rhetorical.

Transition. A phone rings.

GUSTAVO: Hello?

CARLOS: Hey, Gustavo, this is . . .

GUSTAVO: Gotcha! I can't answer the phone right now, but leave your digits and I'll call you back. Peace.

CARLOS: I met Gustavo at one of the gay clubs in downtown Phoenix. Paco Paco, to be exact. He was willing to talk under the condition that I wouldn't reveal anything that might identify him. His name, his age, his physical description were off limits. Everything was off limits. Everything except his story.

A pool of light on GUSTAVO.

GUSTAVO: My cousin is the first person I had sex with, and unfortunately, the first person I fell in love with. We started at a very young age. By the time we got to high school, we dated girls, but that didn't work out for me. And, um, we did it every day for a long time, even though he had a girlfriend. At first I was OK with it, but after a while I didn't like to share him with anyone else, so I took things to the next level.

NARRATOR 1: Gustavo told his cousin that he was in love with him.

NARRATOR 2: His cousin told him he also loved him, in his own special way.

GUSTAVO: He told me he's bisexual.

NARRATOR 1: Gustavo was OK with that.

GUSTAVO: I never stopped loving my cousin.

NARRATOR 1: Until one day Gustavo learned his cousin got engaged.

GUSTAVO: The news hit me like a bucket of ice-cold water. I took the news of his proposal very hard. And when he asked me to be one of his padrinos . . . I said yes. But many days before the wedding, I cried a lot. But I never told my cousin or anyone else anything about that. I just cried alone, in my room. Day and night.

NARRATOR 1: Once the wedding took place, Gustavo thought everything between them was over.

NARRATOR 2: So Gustavo made an effort to forget about him. And he almost succeeded until one day . . .

Transition.

COUSIN: Gustavo! Gustavo!

GUSTAVO: What are you doing here?

COUSIN: I came to visit, ése. (*Pause.*) What? Can't I visit my own familia?

GUSTAVO: You're drunk.

COUSIN: So what? Where's my tía? Tía?

GUSTAVO: She's watching her novela. Calm down! What's wrong with you?

COUSIN: That bitch, ése! I got in a fight with that bitch!

GUSTAVO: Calm down! You want my mom to hear you screaming like crazy?

COUSIN: I'm not going back, OK. I'm not going back to that . . . bruja, ése!

GUSTAVO: OK, OK. I'm sure you can sleep on the couch. I'll tell Mom to call your wife.

The two actors freeze.

NARRATOR 2: And so, the cousin spent the night and once everyone was asleep, Gustavo felt someone getting into his bed.

The actors unfreeze.

GUSTAVO: What are you doing?

COUSIN: Sssh! It's OK.

GUSTAVO: No. It's not OK. What are you . . .

COUSIN: I'm cold.

GUSTAVO: You're naked. Of course you're cold.

COUSIN: Gustavo, please.

GUSTAVO: What?

COUSIN: Don't you miss me?

GUSTAVO: You're drunk.

NARRATOR 1: Their love affair started when they were both very young. It went on and off for several years until it stopped once Gustavo's cousin got married.

NARRATOR 2: But a few months after the wedding, they got together once again. As of today, their affair has been going on for six years. And according to Gustavo, it will continue because . . .

GUSTAVO: Because I love him, and he tells me he loves me too. And before you start judging us, just remember this. For me, being gay has always been difficult. I live in hiding because of my family and our religion. And um, my cousin says he's bisexual and, ah, well, he wants us to be secret about our love affair. So we do. And, ah, there's something else. I'm HIV positive. And, ah, no one knows about it. And, ah, my cousin don't know about it. I figure, if he wants to keep his bisexuality and our affair a secret, it's only fair that I keep my status a secret, you know.

Transition.

JUAN: And I thought I was screwed up.

CARLOS: Juan!

JUAN: I mean, this guy really has it backwards, doesn't he?

CARLOS: Juan!

JUAN: Am I supposed to feel sorry for him just because he's in the closet and he's in love with his cousin?

CARLOS: JUAN, PLEASE!!!

JUAN: WHAT? I'm just saying. He cares more about his own personal fulfillment. What about his nephews and nieces? What if he infects them, eh? What about that, Carlos? Have you ever thought about that?

CARLOS: Yes. I thought about it, Juan. But it isn't my job to judge him or any-one else. My job is simply to present my findings.

JUAN: Is it really that simple? Well, is it?

CARLOS: No, Juan. It isn't that simple. But my job is to report. I'm not supposed to judge, or interfere, or try to solve their problems.

NARRATOR 1: The following comes from Carlos's personal entries about his interview with Gustavo:

NARRATOR 2: "I ask myself if I have some moral responsibility to say anything about what I am finding out. I mean, I can ignore everything, but what about the children? What if they turned out positive because of their father's relation with Gustavo. And doesn't Gustavo know he's putting everyone in danger? What am I supposed to do? Am I supposed to simply listen to this man's story and go on like I know nothing? Jesus! I had no idea it was gonna be this hard."

CARLOS: I need a drink.

Transition. We hear "Happy birthday, MAURICIO" in the background.

MAURICIO: When I found out I was HIV positive, I felt like my world was gonna end. I wasn't sure how to react to the news. I mean, I knew about the infection but I never thought I would get it. I mean, why? I take care of myself. I don't sleep around, at least not like other people I know. So, when I learned I was positive? I . . . I didn't accept it. And because I was in the closet, it was even easier to ignore the presence of the diseases in my body. But then I met Tony and well, I wasn't sure what to do. Things got serious between us very fast. And after a month of dating and not really going "all the way," he was ready, but I . . . I . . . well . . .

TONY: Hey, sweetie!

MAURICIO: Hey, Tony! This is a surprise.

TONY: I brought you this.

MAURICIO: What is it?

TONY: Why do you always ask that? It's a present.

MAURICIO: What's in it?

TONY: No, wait. You have to promise that if you don't like it, you'll tell me and I'll go change it for something else.

MAURICIO: I'll like it.

TONY: Promise. Please.

MAURICIO: OK. You didn't have to get me anything.

TONY: Tonight we celebrate a month. Don't tell me you forgot.

MAURICIO: Of course not.

TONY: Good. Where's mine?

MAURICIO: Where's what?

TONY: You got me a present, right?

MAURICIO: Of course.

TONY: Where is it?

MAURICIO: Later.

TONY: (*Going for a kiss.*) OK. Hey, what's wrong?

MAURICIO: Nothing.

TONY: Don't give me bull crap. What is it? (*Silence.*) Mauricio, what is it?

MAURICIO: Well . . . I know you've been waiting . . .

TONY: For this day. Yes, I have. I mean, we talked about it. And . . . don't tell me you don't want to.

MAURICIO: I do. It's just . . .

   Silence.

TONY: Look, you know I really would like to make it happen. You're the first guy I ever waited this long for.

MAURICIO: I know.

TONY: And you know why? Because I really care for you. Otherwise I would just move on.

MAURICIO: I know.

TONY: But if you don't want to, I understand. I guess I have to wait another month.

MAURICIO: (*To the audience.*) You know, I could have left things as they were: unsaid. But I knew that sooner or later I had to come clean about it. It's not that I don't want to have sex with Tony. I'm ready but . . . Oh, God! Here it goes. (*To* TONY.) The reason why I asked you to wait is because I'm HIV positive.

TONY: What?

MAURICIO: I'm HIV positive, Tony.

TONY: I heard that. I mean how?

MAURICIO: What?

TONY: Since when. I mean, since when?

MAURICIO: Before I met you.

TONY: How come you didn't tell me?

MAURICIO: I didn't know how.

TONY: How about, "Hey, Tony. Before we get into anything serious here. I'm HIV positive." How about something like that?

MAURICIO: Easy for you to say. You're not the one with the virus.

TONY: But I could be.

MAURICIO: But you're not.

TONY: Still. You could have said something.

MAURICIO: I tried. Many times. I just couldn't.

TONY: Couldn't tell me? Or didn't want to tell me?

MAURICIO: Fuck you!

TONY: No, fuck you! You could have told me from the very beginning.

MAURICIO: Why? So you could get all "high and mighty" on me, like right now?

TONY: You think I'm mad because you're HIV positive?

MAURICIO: Look at you.

TONY: I'm pissed because you waited this long to tell me.

MAURICIO: Oh, please, like you would have understood.

TONY: How do you know I wouldn't? Every day since I met you we have been sharing very personal things about each other. We have been very honest with each other, at least that's what you made me believe.

MAURICIO: I WAS HONEST! AND I'M BEING HONEST WITH YOU RIGHT NOW!

Silence.

TONY: Goddamn it, Mauricio.

MAURICIO: Go if you want.

TONY: Is that what you think I would do?

MAURICIO: I don't know. Maybe.

TONY: I thought you knew me better.

TONY tries to touch MAURICIO.

MAURICIO: Don't, please.

TONY: Do you want me to go? (*No answer.*) Well, do you? (*Again, no answer.*) Fine. I'll call you later.

MAURICIO: (*To the audience.*) He called, you know. He called about five times but I never picked up the phone. A friend told me that he ran into Tony twice after that night and he asked him how I was doing. Tony asked how I was doing. Today I'm celebrating my birthday. Tony isn't here, but he sent a present.

TONY: Have a wonderful twenty-first birthday, Mauricio. Love, me. Tony.

MAURICIO: I guess he really cared.

A pool of light on GUSTAVO.

GUSTAVO: I have been positive for many years. My family doesn't know about it. They don't even know I'm gay. I don't go out to the gay clubs, but when

I'm in LA I go to the bathhouses. You know, los baños. That's where I got it. I mean, yes, I used protection but sometimes you get so caught up in the act that you forget. And I forgot or didn't care, whatever, and now I'm HIV positive. And I don't say this so you can feel sorry for me. No. I mean, I got it and that's that. I have learned to live with it. Oh, about my cousin and his wife and their children. Well, I don't know what to do about that. I guess I could stop doing what I'm doing but . . . well, it's not easy. You may think it is but it's not, but I love him. I know some of you judge me. That's OK. You're not in my shoes, so you don't understand how I feel. Trust me, the sea looks much different if you're on the shore than if you're in the middle of it.

Transition lights.

JUAN: Oh, my gawd! From which Mexican novela did he take that cheesy line?

CARLOS: Juan! Stop it!

JUAN: Listen to him. (*Mocking* GUSTAVO.) "The sea looks much different if you're on the shore than if you're in the middle of it." (*He starts laughing.*) That's a bunch of crap.

CARLOS: I'm glad you find it amusing.

JUAN: Oh, Carlos. Relax, girl. Llévatela calmada.

CARLOS: ¿Que me la lleve calmada? ¿Calmada? How do you want me to relax when you keep making fun of people's confessions?

JUAN: Girl. First of all, I'm not making fun of people's confessions. I'm only making a few observations on their drama. And second of all, you're too tense, too stressed out, and making it very hard on yourself to enjoy the ride.

CARLOS: Juan. I have been talking to men who are married and have children, or don't have children or are not married but are in a relationship. All these men are having sex with other men. They considered themselves either gay, or straight, or bisexual, or free-spirited. That's right, you heard right, "free-spirited." They're all in the closet, telling me the reasons why they won't come out. Some of these men have cried in front of me, others have told me they feel like ending their lives, some have confessed they are HIV positive, a couple of them have offered me sex, a few have threatened to beat the shit out of me if I say anything that might identify them, and at least one of the men I interviewed is having sex with someone who is under 18. And you're telling me to relax? ¿Que me calme?

JUAN: Ay, Papi. Take it easy, please. No wonder your hair is turning white and your face is full of wrinkles.

CARLOS: And of top of that you make fun of everything.

JUAN: I'm not making fun. I'm your comic relief. That's all.

CARLOS: Whatever.

JUAN: I respect everything you're going through and I take your findings very seriously, especially when it comes to HIV and AIDS.

CARLOS: Yeah, right.

CARLOS exits.

JUAN: I do. Really I do. And I'm gonna prove it.

NARRATOR 1: The following information comes from the Department of Health and Human Services, which oversees the Centers for Disease Control and Prevention Web site.

NARRATOR 2: To be more specific, the following information comes directly from the most recent *HIV/AIDS Surveillance Report and Supplemental.*

ACTOR 4: It is estimated that more than 1 million people are currently living with HIV in the United States, with approximately 40,000 new infections occurring each year.

JUAN: Seventy percent of these infections are in men and thirty percent in women.

ACTOR 6: Half of the 40,000 new HIV infections occurring each year happen in men 25 years of age or younger.

NARRATOR 1: It is also estimated that about 7 to 10,000 of the 40,000 new infections each year happened among the Latino population.

NARRATOR 2: In each year, from the total new AIDS cases reported, about 9,000 of them are among the Latino population.

ACTOR 6: And the numbers, unfortunately, keep growing.

JUAN: Which only means one thing, honey. The Latino community isn't well informed and if they are, people are not taking care of themselves. Many are having unprotected sex and the majority have forgotten that AIDS is something that continues to kill many of us. So, please, wake up, smell the danger, and stop playing Superman. You ain't made of steel!

JUAN snaps his fingers in a "Z" formation.

DARK.
In it, a phone rings.

DANIEL: Hello?

CARLOS: Hi, Daniel. Habla Carlos.

DANIEL: Oh, hola. ¿Cómo estás?

CARLOS: I'm fine. Thanks. Hey, listen. I'm calling to see if you would like to have coffee with me sometime.

DANIEL: Mira, Carlos. I told you . . .

CARLOS: No, wait. I want to apologize. Disculparme. But I wanna do it in person. ¿Qué dices?

DANIEL: I gotta think about it, Carlos. I'll let you know. OK?

CARLOS: Ah, sure. Look, Daniel. I know that what I said, what's out of line. Y me siento mal por haberlo dicho. So, please, give me the chance to apologize. Por favor.

DANIEL: I'm a little busy right now, Carlos. And I'm going to Mexico to visit my family next week. So, how about if I call you when I get back?

CARLOS: Yeah. Sure.

DANIEL: OK. I'll call you.

CARLOS: OK, I'll wait for your . . . Hello? Hello?

A pool of light illuminates DR. SANDOVAL.

DR. SANDOVAL: By the United States definition of homosexuality, a man who engages in sexual relations with another man and a woman is labeled as a bisexual man. But by the Mexican and most Latino cultural definitions of homosexuality, he's not bisexual or gay. He's just having sex with another man. He's the top, the aggressive one in the encounter. He doesn't get penetrated by the other man. In the end, and this is very important to understand, especially when it comes to funding. Because when American institutions or government agencies give money to organizations that fight HIV and AIDS, the money that's spent on prevention programs, whatever program they have, it's based on the "American" definition of homosexuality. So they get the word out, but they are not doing it the right way, because they are not adapting the Latin American cultural definition of homosexuality. When these programs are talking about AIDS, they are not talking to the straight Mexican males, even though many of these men are having sex with men. The agencies don't think that they need to reach out to the straight Latino men because they don't understand our Latino views toward homosexual practices.

Transition. A nightclub.

VÍCTOR: I have a few stories to tell.

NARRATOR 1: May 5, 2006. CARLOS decides to go to one of the Latino gay clubs and meets VÍCTOR, a thirty-four-year-old man.

CARLOS: I'm sorry?

NARRATOR 2: Married twice. Four children. Two from the first marriage. Two from the second.

VÍCTOR: I have a few stories I can share with you.

CARLOS: Good. What's your name?

NARRATOR 1: Lives with his wife and one of his children.

VÍCTOR: Víctor Martínez. And you?

NARRATOR 2: Born and raised in Michoacán, Mexico. Immigrated to the United States in the early '90s.

CARLOS: Carlos-Manuel.

NARRATOR 1: Lived in Colorado for about a year but then moved to the Phoenix area in 2001.

Víctor: I live in South Phoenix. Near Baseline and Central.

Carlos: Tempe. I go to Arizona State. (*Pause.*) So, tell me about your stories.

Víctor: There's a few.

Carlos: Pick one.

Víctor: I was in sixth grade. I was, what, twelve? And at school there was this guy who was very . . . What's the word? Very . . . very . . .

Carlos: Flamboyant?

Víctor: I was going to say obvious, but that works too. This kid—we used to tease him all the time because of that. And we teased him so much that many times we made him cry.

Carlos: Sounds cruel.

Víctor: It was. But that's not the point. One time I got detention and as punishment, I had to pick up all the garbage on the soccer field.

Carlos: (*To the audience.*) A soccer field on the school grounds.

Transition. A flashback.

Javier: Hey!

Víctor: Hi.

Javier: I see you like picking up garbage.

Víctor: No, I don't.

Javier: It was a joke.

Víctor: Oh.

Javier: I didn't think you got detention. Ever.

Víctor: Well, I do. What did you do?

Javier: Oh, I don't get detention. I volunteer.

Víctor: Man, you really are different.

Javier: It's not the first time I've heard that.

Víctor: Hey, my bag is full. Where do we take this shit?

Javier: To the back dumpsters.

Víctor: All the way there?

Javier: Yep. Come on, I'll go with you. Come on, don't be afraid. I don't bite.

They sit on the ground, leaning against the dumpsters.

Víctor: Thanks for helping me.

Javier: No problem. Contrary to popular belief, I'm actually a nice person.

Víctor says nothing. He stares at Javier.

Javier: What?

Víctor: Nothing.

Silence. Javier now stares at Víctor.

Víctor: What?

Javier: Nothing.

Javier and Víctor stare at each other. Silence. Víctor nods his head. Slowly, Javier starts to reach for Víctor's crotch.

Víctor: Not here.

Javier: Let's go on the other side of the dumpster. No one can see us there.

Transition. The present.

Carlos: Was that your first time with him?

Víctor: It was my first time. Period.

Carlos: Did you stop teasing him after that?

Víctor: No. I continued teasing him around my friends, but he never said anything.

Carlos: Did you get together with Javier again?

Víctor: Yes.

Carlos: You wanna tell me about that?

Víctor: Let's get a drink.

A pool of light on Javier.

Javier: Back in Mexico, in the pueblo where I lived, there wasn't much to do, you know. The most exciting thing was the soccer games on Sundays. I was on a team along with other friends so I looked forward to that because I really like soccer and, um, I was able to pat my friend on the ass without them thinking anything about it. One Sunday, after one of the games, I don't remember why but I ended up being left behind and had to walk home. It was already dark and the streets were not very illuminated. Back then, the town had a lot of empty lots and it was surrounded by fields of many different types of vegetables. And, um, I was going my way when I saw him. And he said hi and I said hi and he told me he saw me playing and we talked. We were by one of those empty lots with a few houses nearby. And we were talking and he suddenly asked me if, um, if I wanted to blow him. At first I didn't pay attention, so I started walking away. He had a girlfriend so I thought he was kidding. But he asked me once again. I stopped, turned around to say no and by now he had pulled it out of his pants. I don't know what possessed me but I said to myself, "What the hell!" So I did it. And from that Sunday on he waited for me after every soccer game.

Pool of light out.

CARLOS: If you were to see Víctor you wouldn't think he's a married thirty-four-year-old man with four children. He works out, eats very healthy and keeps himself in very good shape. He looks very young. He's very charismatic and has these beautiful light brown eyes that seem to hypnotize you. We only talked once, while having drinks at the club. And not only did he tell me about his first sexual experience in the soccer field. He also told me . . .

VÍCTOR: I only find myself attracted to young guys.

CARLOS: Really? How young? (*No answer.*) College age? (*No answer.*) High school? (*No answer.*) Junior high? (*VÍCTOR smiles.*)

CARLOS: Oh.

NARRATOR 1: Carlos never saw Víctor again.

CARLOS: I couldn't. His confession about being attracted to young boys was . . . well, I couldn't stop thinking about . . . he has two boys. And suddenly I wondered if he . . . And then I thought about my nephews . . . Three of them are in high school. Three more are about to start high school. And the rest are in junior high and elementary grades. They don't live in Arizona but . . .

Transition. A phone rings.

ÓSCAR: Hi, Carlos!

CARLOS: Hey, Óscar! How are you?

ÓSCAR: Fine. What's going on?

CARLOS: I'm casting a reading of my new play, *Vaqueeros,* and wanted to know if you're available for it.

ÓSCAR: I heard about that play. When is it?

CARLOS: April, sometime.

ÓSCAR: Send me the details by e-mail and I'll let you know.

CARLOS: Cool. We'll talk later then.

ÓSCAR: You bet.

Transition.

NARRATOR 2: Bisexuality is the sexual orientation which refers to the aesthetic, romantic, or sexual desire for individuals of either gender or of either sex.

ACTOR 4: The term "bisexuality" was only coined in the nineteenth century, and has only been the subject of serious study since the second half of the twentieth century.

NARRATOR 1: Bisexual people are not necessarily attracted equally to both genders, and tend to prefer one or the other.

NARRATOR 2: It is possible for a bisexual person to be attracted to all genders but only one sex, or to all sexes but only one gender.

JUAN: Oh, my God! That's so confusing. What does it mean?

CARLOS: It means that bisexual people could be attracted to men and women because they are males or females. And not necessarily because of their genitalia. Or they are sexually attracted to them but not necessarily because they are men or women, but just because of their genitalia.

JUAN: Oh, my God! That still is confusing. I like my definition better.

CARLOS: Which is?

JUAN: Bisexual men are simply gay men who are afraid to come out of the closet.

CARLOS: What about bisexual women?

JUAN: Helloooo! It's the same thing: afraid to come out of the closet.

CARLOS: You are hopeless, you know that? You need therapy.

JUAN: I'm not confused, Carlos. I'm gay.

NARRATOR 1: Fernando López, on the subject of bisexuality.

NARRATOR 2: Or as he likes to call it, the "free-spirited" thing.

FERNANDO: It's hard. To find someone, whether it's a man or a woman, it's hard. I think it's hard for everyone. And I don't see it any easier for me. That is how things are. I'm looking for someone: man or woman. It's just how it is for me, at least. I mean I wish I had someone. It would make things a little easier. I am not confused about whether I want a man or a woman. I don't care about that. I just want someone. But it's difficult, you know. I know I have emotional problems, and for the most part it's because of this. I mean, going back and forth between men and women it's . . . I don't know. I get frustrated. I mean I wish I could tell you that it's easy but it's not. I get depressed a lot and I wish I knew how to stop that but I don't. My friends judge me. They tell me I'm all fucked up because I go back and forth. They think I'm confused or whatever. But I know I'm not. I like what I like and that's that. Sex is sex no matter with whom so I'm not confused. They just don't understand. I want to find someone I can spend my life with. I want someone in my life. And I don't care if it is a woman or a man. I just want someone who I can be happy with, someone who can be happy with me and my kid.

NARRATOR 1: February 26, 2006. Carlos has an interview with Cuauhtémoc Sánchez, better known as Temo.

A pool of light on TEMO.

TEMO: I found out I was bisexual while I was going to ASU. My roommate, who had never met anyone who spoke Spanish, was fascinated with me. He and I became good friends. What I didn't expect was for him to be gay. To make a long story short, we ended up having sex one weekend. I had been having sex with girls way before that. But the first time I did it with him, it was the most passionate sex I had ever had. From then on, I was having sex with other female students and with my roommate. I was twenty-two at the time. Our sexual affair ended when we both graduated. I moved to New York City, where I continued having sex with both men and women. Then I got married to a woman from Centroamérica. But for reasons too complicated to explain, she had to go back to her country so I enlisted in the army. And while I was training, I discovered that there were many soldiers who liked sleeping with other soldiers. And soon I discovered there was a whole network of underground sexual relations among the soldiers. Then, while I was stationed in Hawaii, I realized I was getting emotionally close to one particular soldier. And that scared me so I asked to be stationed in my wife's country. My excuse was that I wanted to be with her, but in reality, I wanted to get away from the soldier. Right before I was relocated I wrote a letter to my college friend and told him everything that had happened in the army. I also wrote a letter to my wife, letting her know I was gonna be relocated to her country. I made the mistake of putting my friend's letter in my wife's envelope. And my wife's letter in my friend's. When she showed me the letter, I had no option but to tell her the truth. I also told her she had the right to leave me, but she chose to stay with me.

Transition.

OLDER BROTHER: Finally, you're here.

TEMO: Sorry I'm late.

FATHER: We were beginning to think you were not coming.

TEMO: I had some business to take care of.

OLDER BROTHER: You want a drink?

TEMO: No, I'm OK. What's going on?

FATHER: Well, you tell us.

TEMO: I'm sorry?

OLDER BROTHER: My sister came crying to me this morning.

TEMO: What? Is she OK?

FATHER: Apparently not.

TEMO: Did something happen to her?

FATHER: My son here tells me you have some interesting . . . how should I put it . . .

OLDER BROTHER: Interesting experiences in the army.

TEMO: What?

OLDER BROTHER: Come on, Temo. You know what we're talking about. Your soldier friends, your college buddy.

TEMO: Uh . . . what . . .

FATHER: Frankly, Temo, I don't give a rat's ass if you're sleeping with half the army and the navy. That's your business. But when you get my little girl involved in this mess . . .

TEMO: Wait a minute! She isn't involved in . . .

OLDER BROTHER: Not involved? She's married to you. Of course she's involved.

TEMO: How do you know about that anyway?

OLDER BROTHER: She told me. She came crying to me this morning, not knowing what to think, what to say. And when she showed me the letter, well, I just . . .

FATHER: I want you to divorce her.

TEMO: What?

FATHER: You heard me. I want you to divorce my daughter. It's the best you can do.

TEMO: Did she tell you this? Did she say . . . ?

OLDER BROTHER: It's the best for her. For her future. For you. For us all.

TEMO: She and I talked about this last week. I don't think . . .

OLDER BROTHER: You don't think? How can you think, doing the shit you're doing?

FATHER: As I said, I don't care what you do, but it involves my daughter and I don't want that for her. The best thing is divorce.

TEMO: But . . .

OLDER BROTHER: You heard my father. We want the divorce. Let her go. It's the best for her . . . And for you if you get what I'm trying to say.

TEMO: Are you threatening me?

OLDER BROTHER: I don't think I am.

TEMO: Because it sounds like you're threatening me.

FATHER: I don't know what kind of life you really live, Temo. But I know the kind of life I want for my daughter, so please . . . listen to us.

OLDER BROTHER: Divorce is the best solution.

TEMO: Uh . . . I have to talk to her first.

OLDER BROTHER: No, I don't think . . .

FATHER: No matter what she says, you need to give her a divorce.

OLDER BROTHER: The sooner you give her the divorce, the better it's going to be for all of us.

FATHER: Come on, son. Let's get out of here.

OLDER BROTHER: One more thing. No word about this little conversation to my sister. Got it?

TEMO: (*To the audience.*) I told my wife about my conversation with her father and older brother. She didn't want a divorce. She wanted to be with me. We left her country without saying anything. We ended up here in Mesa. Then, after a few years, I couldn't go on without sexual intimacy with another man. I told my wife and we came to an agreement: I am allowed to sleep with other men under three conditions. One, I will never do it in our own house. Two, I will never spend the night over with any of them. Three, I will not get emotionally attached to any of them. And you know what? For the last ten years, it has been working out just fine.

Transition. A phone rings.

ÁNGEL: Hello?

CARLOS: Hi, Ángel. It's Carlos.

ÁNGEL: Hey, Carlos. ¿Cómo estás, cabrón?

CARLOS: I'm doing well, man. I hear you're doing another show right now.

ÁNGEL: Yeah, man. I am. You should come and see it.

CARLOS: Yeah. I'm going next week. But listen, I don't have much time so . . . I'm calling because I am casting a reading of my latest play and I need Latino actors.

ÁNGEL: Oh, cool. When is it?

CARLOS: April.

ÁNGEL: Perfecto. The show I'm in ends in two weeks so, yeah. I'll do it.

CARLOS: That's great. But listen, before anything else. I need to tell you what the show is about.

ÁNGEL: No. That's OK.

CARLOS: No. I need to tell you. It's based on a bunch of interviews I directed with Latino man who have sex with other men but are in the closet.

ÁNGEL: Oh.

CARLOS: And well, I just want to make sure that you understand the subject matter.

ÁNGEL: Is there any sex involved?

CARLOS: Ah . . . well, no, not really. I mean, characters talk about it and some kiss but it isn't really about that.

ÁNGEL: Um . . . hey, could you send me a copy of the script?

CARLOS: Sure. If you want to look it over.

ÁNGEL: Yeah. You got my e-mail, right? Just send it to me. I'll read it and let you know.

CARLOS: OK. I'll do that right now.

ÁNGEL: Cool. Then, we'll see you at my play?

CARLOS: I'll be there.

ÁNGEL: OK. Bye.

CARLOS: Bye, Ángel.

NARRATOR 1: February 12, 2006. Carlos meets Rogelio Mora at a local Starbucks.

NARRATOR 2: Their meeting took place somewhere on east Thomas Road. Between 44th and 46th, streets to be exact.

Transition.

ROGELIO: Hi, my name is Rogelio. I'm out of the closet. But there are places where I have to keep it a secret because, well, there are people who are not very accepting of us, you know. So, ah, to avoid problems, at times, I keep it a secret.

LUIS: Hey!

ROGELIO: Hey!

They look around, see no one, they embrace and kiss.

LUIS: I've been thinking.

ROGELIO: Yeah?

LUIS: I think I found a solution to our problems.

ROGELIO: Yeah?

LUIS: Sí.

ROGELIO: OK.

LUIS: You know I love you very much and I would do anything for you, but in this case I can't do much.

ROGELIO: I know, Luis. I know that. And that's OK.

LUIS: No, it's not OK, but I have a solution—marriage.

ROGELIO: We can't get married.

LUIS: Not us, silly. Your sister and I.

ROGELIO: What?

LUIS: It's perfect. I'll marry your sister and you'll marry mine.

ROGELIO: Are you crazy?

LUIS: Don't you see. That way you and her can get papers. And at the same time you and I will be together.

ROGELIO: But you'll be with my sister and I will be with yours.

LUIS: Yeah. But it will be an arrangement.

ROGELIO: A marriage of convenience.

LUIS: Exactly.

ROGELIO: I don't know. Do you think your sister will do it?

LUIS: If we tell her you're gonna pay her a few thousand dollars, she will.

ROGELIO: How much?

LUIS: I don't know. Three thousand dollars?

ROGELIO: And you will want the same for my sister's papers?

LUIS: No. I mean, I'll say that we will be charging you guys $6,000. But you will only pay $3,000 for your sister, and nothing for you.

ROGELIO: Really? You would do this for me?

LUIS: How can you ask such question? For you I'll do anything.

NARRATOR 1: Rogelio and Luis's sister got married about a month later.

NARRATOR 2: Luis and Rogelio's sister also got married the same day.

NARRATOR 1: And although the double wedding, the celebration, and the double honeymoon were very real, they all knew it was all part of a plan to fool the immigration system.

NARRATOR 2: This happened back in 1995. Seven years later both Rogelio and his sister were given permanent residency in the country.

NARRATOR 1: Everything worked out for them, at least when it came to legalization, because in terms of the relationships, things got a little out of hand.

ROGELIO: What do you mean, it's true?

LUIS: What your sister told you is true.

ROGELIO: I don't understand what you mean.

LUIS: What do you mean, you don't understand what I mean? I'm sleeping with her. We're having sex.

ROGELIO: She's my sister!

LUIS: She's my wife!

ROGELIO: I can't believe this. Why would you do something like that?

LUIS: Something like that? I love her and she loves me.

ROGELIO: Shut up.

LUIS: I mean, I know everything . . .

ROGELIO: Shut up!

LUIS: Started like an arrangement. But she's very nice and . . . and . . . well, we fell in love.

ROGELIO: SHUT UP!

Silence.

LUIS: Rogelio, try to understand.

ROGELIO: So I guess things between us are over?

LUIS: Sorry.

ROGELIO: Get out!

LUIS: Roger, please . . .

ROGELIO: Get out!

LUIS: But we need . . .

ROGELIO: GET OUT BEFORE I BEAT THE SHIT OUT OF YOU!!!!

CARLOS: Rogelio and Luis's sister never consummated their marriage. Reason number one: both knew it was all a business arrangement. Reason number two: Luis's sister turned out to be a lesbian.

NARRATOR 1: Rogelio's sister and Luis did sleep together. In fact, they have two children.

NARRATOR 2: But before the children came along, Luis and Rogelio had many encounters.

ROGELIO: Before I found out what Luis and my sister were doing, Luis and I used to get together in hotel rooms or in our own houses. And everything was OK until, ah, well, until, until, until my sister told me she had fallen in love with Luis, not knowing that Luis was my boyfriend.

CARLOS: A week before I met Rogelio for this interview, Luis and Rogelio had a conversation.

LUIS: I'm thinking of divorcing your sister.

ROGELIO: What?

LUIS: You heard me. Things between us are not working out. I want out.

ROGELIO: (*To himself.*) What a surprise. (*To LUIS.*) You know my sister is very much in love with you? And I know the news of a divorce will bring her a lot of pain. And what about your two children, man?

LUIS: Look! I'm not happy, OK?

ROGELIO: Goddamn it, Luis.

LUIS: I talked to my sister about this and . . .

ROGELIO: You talked to her?

LUIS: And she said that I should do what I think is best for me.

ROGELIO: This is gonna destroy my sister, you know.

LUIS: I'm sorry.

ROGELIO: Goddamn it!

LUIS: I'm really sorry, man.

ROGELIO: (*Frustrated.*) FUUUUUUCK!!!!

　　Silence.

LUIS: Are you OK? (*Silence.*) Roger?

ROGELIO: Well, I guess she has to deal with this. I mean, she knew the whole wedding thing was just a marriage of convenience, but she still fell for your sorry ass. (*Pause.*) But most of it is your fault because you knew it was all an arrangement and you and I were a couple and you still slept with her. I hope she gives you the divorce, man.

LUIS: What? What do you mean?

ROGELIO: No. I hope she doesn't give you anything. It will serve the two of you right for going beyond our agreement.

LUIS: But . . .

ROGELIO: Good luck, man. Good luck with that.

NARRATOR 2: Rogelio, his wife, and Luis talked about Luis's desire to divorce Rogelio's sister. At that meeting it was decided that . . .

ROGELIO: I'm going to remind my sister that our marriages were all arranged in order to get us our papers.

LUIS: I'm going to tell her that the only reason why I married her was because, at the time, I was trying to help Rogelio because, um, because . . .

ROGELIO: Because you were my boyfriend.

CARLOS: Which means that Rogelio will have to come out of the closet to his sister.

ROGELIO: And I also have to tell her that Luis, her husband, was my boyfriend for four years.

LUIS: One before we got married and three after the wedding.

JUAN: Oh, my gawd! This is just like a Mexican novela, like "Rosalinda," or "Amor sin cadenas," or "Cuna de lobos," or "Vivir un poco," or, or, or, all of them in one. I am in heaven!

CARLOS: I should interview you after you, uh, drop the bomb to your sister.

ROGELIO: We'll see, Carlos. We'll see.

NARRATOR 1: By the time this play was written, the two couples were still married.

JUAN: See what I mean? A soap opera, complete with melodramatic effects and tragic endings.

CARLOS: You are hopeless, Juan. Hopeless!

Transition. A phone rings.

CARLOS: Hello?

DANIEL: Hi, Carlos. It's Daniel.

CARLOS: Oh, hi, man! Did you change your number? Because my phone didn't . . .

DANIEL: No. I'm calling you from work.

CARLOS: Oh. Cool. How is work?

DANIEL: Fine.

CARLOS: So, are we getting together?

DANIEL: Yeah. About that. I thought about it and I think it is best if . . . ah . . . we don't talk to each other anymore.

CARLOS: What? But . . .

DANIEL: Look, Carlos. You're cool and everything but, ah, let's just leave it as is, OK? Hey, you still there?

CARLOS: Ah, yeah, yeah.

DANIEL: So, um, you get what I'm saying?

CARLOS: Yes. I guess.

DANIEL: Cool. I gotta get back to work.

CARLOS: Bye.

Transition.

JUAN: He said what?

CARLOS: You heard me. "Let's just leave it as is."

JUAN: Well, if you ask me, he's a total closet case.

CARLOS: He says he's not gay.

JUAN: Oh, please. How many times we've seen him at the bars, with his "friend." (*Pause.*) Hey! Hey! Are you OK?

CARLOS: Yeah. I'm fine.

JUAN: Look, forget about him. You have plenty of friends.

CARLOS: It's not what he said that bothers me, OK? It's . . . it's just this damn project. It has me all screwed up. Friends don't wanna talk to me anymore. I've gotten into some strange situations during the interviews. I've done more than twenty of them and my mentor still wants me to do more. Some of the volunteers have asked me to not use their stories anymore. Actors don't wanna do the reading of the play because they're afraid about the subject matter. I'm just fed up with everything.

JUAN: Hey! Relax. Take some time off. Let's go to the movies, dancing, don't work on the research any more. Do nothing. But please, relax. Cálmate.

CARLOS: I will. I just need to finish the last part of the play and find one more actor who is not afraid about portraying gay men on stage, or bisexual men, or free-spirited men, or straight men who have sex with men, or whatever the hell they believe they are.

JUAN: Wait. I thought you asked Ángel to be in your reading.

CARLOS: I did. And he said yes at first, but once I told him what the play was all about, he asked me for a copy of the play so he can "look it over."

JUAN: And?

CARLOS: It's been two weeks and nothing. He doesn't answer my emails or return my calls.

JUAN: Maybe he's busy.

CARLOS: Oh, please.

JUAN: You never know.

CARLOS: Oh, I know. He's afraid of doing the reading.

JUAN: How do you know that?

CARLOS: Because, Juan. When I asked him to be in the reading he was excited about it and said yes. But as soon as I told him the play was about Latino men having sex with other men, he changed his tune.

JUAN: Are you serious?

CARLOS: Yes. When I told him, I heard the hesitation in his voice.

JUAN: Talk about feeling insecure.

CARLOS: You're telling me.

JUAN: Still, do me a favor. Try to relax. OK?

CARLOS: I said I will relax. And I will. Now, please leave me alone.

JUAN: Are you sure you don't want to go to see a movie?

CARLOS: Juan . . .

JUAN: Or dancing? We can go dancing.

CARLOS: Juan . . .

JUAN: Or to see a play. You know I love . . .

CARLOS: JUAN!

JUAN: OK. OK, I'm leaving.

CARLOS: Thank you.

JUAN: Por eso tienes tantas canas, por enojón.

CARLOS: Get out! Get out! Before I beat you.

JUAN: You promise?

CARLOS: OUT!!!!

Transition. A phone rings.

CARLOS: Óscar! What's up, man?

ÓSCAR: Not much. I read the script. Very interesting.

CARLOS: So, can you do the reading?

ÓSCAR: You bet.

CARLOS: All right!

ÓSCAR: I got the dates and everything.

CARLOS: Cool.

ÓSCAR: Gotta run, Carlitos.

CARLOS: Sure. Hey, say hi to your wife and children for me.

ÓSCAR: I will.

CARLOS: See ya.

ÓSCAR: Bye.

A pool of light on CARLOS.

CARLOS: Dr. Sandoval told me that the one thing that bothers him the most is when his friends label Latino men, like the ones I interviewed, as gay, bisexual, confused, or afraid to come out. I didn't tell Dr. Sandoval this, but I also believed that. I believed they were afraid and in denial. As I interviewed these men, I started to see things in a different light. I started to change my narrow-minded view toward them. All the men I interviewed had some incredible things to say. I don't necessarily agree with all of them, or their practices and philosophies, but at least I understand a little more about them and where they come from. Latino men, I mean, many Latino men will have sex with other men not necessarily because we're gay, or bisexual, or straight, or free-spirited. We engage in sexual relationships because it's part of who we are, part of what we do, and part of what we like. Most people almost always want to have sex. Most people are always looking for it, and they will get it, no matter what. Men who have sex with other men hide their practices for many different personal reasons. I came out of the closet as a gay man at age twenty-two. But prior to my coming out, I was already involved in sexual relationships with other guys. If the men I interviewed chose to label or not label themselves, I guess it's OK. If they choose to come out or never reveal who they truly are, that's OK too. Like the many men I interviewed, in certain places and around certain circles, I still hide who I truly am because . . . Well, as Father John Powell, S. J., said in one of his many books . . . "I am afraid to tell you who I am, because if I tell you who I am, you may not like who I am, and it's all that I have."

DARK

End of play

BARRIO HOLLYWOOD
Additional Cast and Production Information

Barrio Hollywood had its professional world premiere at New Theatre, Coral Gables, Florida (Rafael de Acha, Artistic Director; Eileen Suárez, Managing Director) on October 14, 2004. The creative team included movement director Ricky J. Martínez, set designer Michael McKeever, lighting designer Pedro A. Remírez, sound designer Ozzie Quintana, and production stage manager Joseph M. NeSmith. Eileen Suárez provided photography. The production was directed by Rafael de Acha with the following cast:

GRACIELA MORENO	Beatriz Montañez
ALEX MORENO	Euriamis Losada
AMÁ	Marta Velasco
MICHAEL	John Baldwin

Barrio Hollywood was first produced at Borderlands Theater, Tucson, Arizona (Barclay Goldsmith, Producing Director) on March 27, 2003. The creative team included folklórico coach Karl Rodríguez, boxing coach Vicente Medina, choreographer Eva Tessler, set designer John Longhofer, lighting designer John Dahlstrand, sound designer Jim Klingenfus, costume designer Carmen Gastelum, stage manager John Sweeney, and production stage manager Glenn Stockellburg. The production was directed by Kent Nicholson with the following cast:

GRACIELA MORENO	Marissa García
ALEX MORENO	Mario Figueroa López
AMÁ	Rosanne Couston
MICHAEL	Dana Jepsen
SHADOW BOXER	Eduardo Vega

Barrio Hollywood was subsequently produced by the Miracle Theatre Group, Portland, Oregon (Olga Sánchez, Artistic Director Miracle MainStage; José Eduardo González, Founder and Executive Director; Dañel Malán, cofounder and Artistic Director Teatro Milagro), on September 26, 2003. The creative team included dance coach Sylvia Malán-González, fight coach John Armour, set designer Mark Loring, lighting designer Peter West, sound designer Gerardo Calderón, costume designer Virginia Belt, and stage manager Emily Carr. The production was directed by Olga Sánchez with the following cast:

GRACIELA MORENO .... Ina Strauss

ALEX MORENO .... Ricardo Delgado

AMÁ .... Nurys Herrera

MICHAEL .... Anders Liljeholm

SHADOW BOXER .... Tom Eveland

Barrio Hollywood was given a staged reading at San Diego Repertory Theatre under the direction of William A. Virchis with dramaturgy by Nakissa Etemad. The cast included Alida Gunn, Sol Castillo, Catalina Maynard, and James Newcomb.

WE LOST IT AT THE MOVIES
Additional Cast and Production Information

We Lost It at the Movies (with a Special Appearance by Rock Hudson) was originally presented at Arizona State University's New Works Festival in November 2005; it was directed by Erma Duricko with the following cast:

ROSALINDA	Edith Donoghue-Chávez
MEMO/NARRATOR	Aaron Wester
NORMA	María Enríquez
ARMANDO	David McCormick
VLADIMIR/ROCK HUDSON	Adam Solon
GRANDMOTHER/DOROTHEA/ENSEMBLE	Ángela Girón
HELENA/ENSEMBLE	Avery Yáñez

The play was further developed during the summer of 2007 for the Arkansas Repertory Theater's Voices at the River; also directed by Erma Duricko, it had the following cast:

ROSALINDA	Annette Cardona
MEMO/NARRATOR	Orlando Ríos
NORMA	Jessica Peterson
ARMANDO	Dominic Comperatore
VLADIMIR/ROCK HUDSON	Jim Ireland
GRANDMOTHER/DOROTHEA/ENSEMBLE	Vivian Morrison Norman
HELENA/ENSEMBLE	Marissa Duricko